LOVE BETWEEN WOMEN

By the same author

THE HUMAN HAND
A PSYCHOLOGY OF GESTURE
THE HAND IN PSYCHOLOGICAL DIAGNOSIS
ON THE WAY TO MYSELF

Dr Charlotte Wolff, a Fellow of the British Psychological Society, was born in eastern Germany (now Poland), went to school in Danzig (Gdansk) and studied medicine at several German universities. She obtained her M.D. at Berlin University. She left Germany in 1933 for Paris, where she started research on hand traits and gesture, seen in relation to temperament and mentality. She worked on this research with Professor Henri Wallon and other French psychiatrists until 1936 when Aldous Huxley and his first wife Maria were instrumental in arranging for her to live in London. She has been actively concerned with the question of lesbianism during the whole of her professional life, and has been engaged in research on the subject over a number of years.

Love
Between Women

CHARLOTTE WOLFF, M.D.

Fellow of the British Psychological Society

DUCKWORTH

Second edition 1973
First published 1971

Gerald Duckworth & Company Limited,
The Old Piano Factory,
43, Gloucester Crescent, London N.W.1.

Cloth ISBN 0 7156 0725 1
Paper ISBN 0 7156 0726 X

Printed by Bristol Typesetting Co. Ltd.,
Barton Manor, St. Philips, Bristol.

Contents

Preface to the second edition

Since this book was first published, important developments have taken place in the homophile world in general, and in the lesbian world in particular. One can speak of a new era of activity which has led to changes in old organisations and the establishment of new ones. The process has been widespread, rapid and intense, and concerns lesbians as much as homosexual men. I therefore thought it appropriate, in preparing this revised edition, to give an account of these developments in a new Appendix.

C.W. 1973.

Preface to the first edition

During the last decade the subject of homosexuality has attracted increasing interest, which has been reflected both in the popular press and in learned journals. But most of the interest has been in male homosexuality and a number of books about this have appeared in the last ten years. Lesbianism has been neglected, even in scientific inquiry, and no authoritative book wholly devoted to the subject has been published to date.

This book is intended for a general as well as a professional public. It is written in the belief that a new and candid approach is needed to a subject which affects society as a whole and women in particular. It is based on the results of a recent research study on female homosexuality, but also of course reflects my concern with the question over two decades in my practice as a psychiatrist. The co-operation of two lesbian organisations, Kenric and the Minorities Research Trust, and also of the Albany Trust, an organisation which helps people with all kinds of sexual problems, enabled me to find the subjects needed for investigation. I was lucky enough to obtain 'normal' control subjects through several public organisations. My method of research consisted in interviewing in depth everyone concerned, and in asking them to complete questionnaires. The main questionnaire contained ninety questions and was given to both lesbian and 'normal' subjects. A further questionnaire, relating solely to sexual reactions, was given only to the lesbian group.

I give here a definition of the x^2 factor used in the Tables at the back of the book. A x^2 test is used when an observed distribution of frequencies is to be compared with the expected distribution on the basis of a hypothesis. The calculated x^2 statistic has then to be compared with a given significance level found in statistical tables. For example, a significance level of 1% means that x^2 value would have been obtained less than 1 in a 100 times if the hypothesis were true.

Finally, I wish to express my gratitude to Dr Clive Spicer, Medical Statistician and Director of the Computer Centre of the Medical Research Council. He gave me invaluable help in discussing the statistics with me and in having the data processed at the Centre. He also applied the significance test to the results. I am also greatly indebted to my friend Miss Audrey Wood, O.B.E., who untiringly helped me by typing the manuscript, and in many other ways. Last but not least, I thank all those who participated in the research which made this book possible.

C.W. 1971.

PART ONE

TOWARDS A NEW THEORY

Chapter One

The Background

Certain words become in time either too light or too heavy for the load they carry, and their meaning can get so distorted as to make them practically meaningless. This has happened to the words God and Love, to mention only two striking examples. They mean different things to different people. The muddled ideas carried by the word God make its significance so indistinct that word-conscious people either avoid its use or give it an interpretation of their own. A word arises from an image or an idea. When either cannot be recognised behind the word, then it does not ring true.

The word Love has met with a fate similar to that of God. It is used today as a form of greeting by the grocer, the bus-conductor etc., as well as for sex-play. Obviously such a use has nothing to do with the original meaning. The word homosexuality belongs to this very category. It implies love for a person of the same sex, and is part and parcel of the whole concept of sensations, feelings and emotions for which the word love is the symbol.

The use of the word homosexuality has strayed so far from its true meaning that it has acquired in the western world the status of a taboo. To the man in the street, the term signifies perversion, abnormality and vice. It stands in the minds of many people for nothing else but various kinds of sex-gratification between people of the same sex.

The word itself is an unhappy choice and a misleading one. Homosexuality is, in fact, an *emotional* disposition which leads to close and intimate contact between people of the same sex, a contact which may or may not be expressed sexually. The affixation of the magical, or rather, 'black-magical', *sexual* to *homo* has overshadowed the real meaning of the word. Man has always been aware that words have a magical quality, with intense and far-reaching effects on both the one who speaks and the one who listens. The process of mental associations which all of us automatically perform, has become over-complicated and at the same time more superficial, through psychological and social pressures which lead to a mechanical use of words. Only cultured and enquiring minds resist mechanical and imitative associations, and usage of words. They go to the bottom of the well, to the image or idea from which a word comes.

The word homosexuality is, as I have said, a misconstrued symbol for a particular kind of love, and small wonder that it has led to repellent images in the minds of the majority of people on both sides of the Atlantic: it carries a connotation of perversion. Of course, there are perverted homosexuals just as there are perverted heterosexuals. It is likely that the former are more numerous in proportion, but not all homosexuals are perverted. What is perversion? I think that it is a fixation of the libido on one organic system only, which may be the sexual organs or other parts of the body. Any fixation of this kind, whether it be in homosexual or heterosexual people, is obsessional. It is a form of fetishism which leads into the blind alley of destructive habits.

Rejection stems from fear, which breeds dislike. Images of repulsion towards homosexuals arise from both collective and personal fear. The collective fear is engendered by the interests of the state, which was understandable in the past, before the danger of population explosion became apparent. The personal fear of homosexuality generally results from religious conflicts and repressed homosexual feelings and desires. The dislike of the pervert is nothing but the unconscious fear of being perverted, and reflects self-hate.

There is a direct connection between images of repulsion and their effects. In other words, images affect the minds of those

whom they concern. Undoubtedly, the homosexual has manifested and is still manifesting many of the perversions of which
he is accused. The 'magic' of images of repulsion works. This is
not the only reason for certain obsessional traits frequently found
in homosexuals. They are in a minority, and as a minority group
they develop typical characteristics of defiance and persecution
which can shape their attitudes in personal relationships. I cannot resist a comparison between homosexuals and Jews. One
finds among both groups those who resist repellent images and
those who are affected by them. The latter become self-
assertive and irritable, defensive and defiant in their behaviour,
to mention only some of the emotional consequences of rejection.
This comparison is particularly apt if one remembers the treatment which was meted out to homosexuals in Germany under
the Nazis. They, like the Jews, were dumped into concentration
camps and classed as outcasts.

How these fears and dislikes accumulated into wholesale condemnation of homosexuality can only be understood through
certain ideas and ideals about the male and the female, which
were the natural outcome of a man-made society where the male
is the master and the female subservient to him. The ostracism of
homosexuality is directed more against men, while homosexual
women have, as a rule, been less exposed to it. This attitude
resulted from the inferior place of women in society. The fact
that, in the main, it was men who were dragged before the
Courts of Justice for homosexual offences is proof in itself that
their behaviour was always considered of prime importance to
the state. The female sex was and still is regarded as of minor
importance; it is indeed the 'second sex'. The idea of male
superiority does not allow men and man-ruled society to accept
homosexuality among women as either a serious threat to their
sexual needs or to the interests of the state. Lesbianism is
regarded by many men as a joke, or perhaps a playful diversion,
where in cases of sexual competition the male would always
emerge as victor. It is the arrogance of the male which has
protected homosexual women from suffering the same degree
of persecution as homosexual men. There is no law against
lesbianism in the whole of Europe, except in Austria and Spain.
Both these countries still cling to the Carolingian law, introduced
in 1532, although it is, in fact, no longer applied. It is worth

mentioning that Georg Groddek accounts for the greater hostility towards male homosexuality on the grounds of a possible confusion in the translation of 'homo' and 'homos'. 'Homo' means 'man' in Latin, and 'homos' means 'same' in Greek.

The term lesbian is more frequently applied to women than the word homosexual. However, the few English research workers who have written on this subject generally use the term female homosexuality. The word homophile is widely adopted in the United States. As long ago as 1917, the German-speaking Hungarian psycho-analyst, Ferenczi, coined the word *homo-erotisch* (homoerotic) as Freud reports in his *Three Essays on the Theory of Sexuality*. The word has a different meaning in German and English. It is well chosen in the German tongue, but it leaves a doubtful aftertaste in English. *Erotisch* means that which is attributed to Eros, the God of Love. It expresses the sensuous and emotional side of love, though perhaps not its complete meaning and nature. Ferenczi differentiated between a subjective and an objective homoerotic man, leaving woman out of the picture. The subjective homoerotic is the 'feminine' type, the objective one is indistinguishable in physical features and expressive behaviour from the so-called 'normal' male. Ferenczi rightly pointed out more than fifty years ago that, if ever any treatment were attempted to change the libido of a homoerotic man, it was only the objective type who could be changed, if not 'cured'. The word homoerotic is unsatisfactory because of its linguistic limitations, while homophile is an adequate term in every European language, certainly in English, German and French. But when one speaks of homophile women or men one seems to water down the nature of the relationship. While the word is too indefinite to be applicable in a fully explanatory way, it might improve the mental images associated with homosexuality. This is a point in its favour, although the effect would probably be noticeable only after a period of time. Indeed, it takes many years for new concepts and words to penetrate the collective imagination. It took psycho-analytical thought about fifty years to sink into the public mind, but today even conservative and old-fashioned people are willy-nilly using psycho-analytical terms in their vocabulary. In fact, once new and meaningful thought-systems affect the masses, they are anchored for long periods, provided there is no other ideology

more convincing to substitute for them. By now Freudian thought
is as firmly established as Darwin's theory of evolution. Behaviourism with its various forms of psychotherapy is much prop-
agated today as a possible successor to psycho-analysis. It will,
in my view, have a long way to go before it can claim to be of
an all-embracing significance. While I doubt whether it will ever
be a substitute for Freudian ideology, it is invaluable in conjunction with it.

Behaviourists have given us blatant examples of the im-
pressionability of the mind, which is indeed a frightening
prospect. It supports the assumption that words of an emotional
flavour and impact affect the mind intensely, especially when
they are uttered by people in authority. They can produce semi-
hypnotic or even hypnotic effects. Changes which human beings
can produce in the minds of other human beings through words
and their suggestive power are a form of brain-washing. And the
process of 'learning' entails, by its very nature, both brain-
feeding and brain-washing.

Behaviourists make us aware, among many other things,
of the weighty responsibility we have in using words, particularly
those applied to emotion-laden subjects. Words like lesbian and
lesbianism are now frequently used by everyman in a derisive
way, debasing their original meaning. Groddek applies the
denomination sapphic to feminine homosexuality. In some ways
the word is well chosen because it is untarnished and specific.
It refers in fact to the first time when love between women, which
is the main theme of Sappho's poetry, was recorded.

Sappho lived about 2600 years ago on the island of Lesbos.
She has become a legendary figure through the beauty and
originality of her verse. She and her contemporary, Alcaeus, who
venerated her, were supreme among the Greek lyric poets. Her
name and her incredible reputation have survived in spite of the
fact that only a few fragmentary poems, in addition to one
completely preserved, are left to us. Sappho was married, apparently happily, and she had a daughter, but her homosexual tendencies dominated her life. Her poetry reflects her bisexual
nature, but it is her poems to women that give touching
expression to her feelings and reveal the power of her art. Even
the fragments that have survived are overwhelming in their
suggestive force. They reveal great depth of feeling, ranging

from nostalgia to ecstasy. A sensitive reader could not fail to be moved by the inspiration of her poetry. Beram Saklatvala has attempted to restore a number of her poems in his recent *Sappho of Lesbos, her Works Restored*. Though his presentation and recreation of her poetry is inevitably incomplete, he quotes one poem *To the Girl Brachea*, which has survived in its original complete form. Here it is, in Saklatvala's translation.

Ah, in my mind he shares the high gods' fortune,
And is their equal who may come beside you,
And sit with you and to your voice so lovely
        Attend and listen.
And he may hear your laughter, love-awaking,
Which makes my heart beat swiftly in my bosom.
But when I see you, Brachea, O my voice
        Fails me and falters.
And my tongue stumbles even when I glimpse at you
Through all my flesh the fire swiftly running;
My eyes see nothing, and my ears hear only
        My own pulse beating.
O then the sweat streams down me and I tremble
In all my body. Pale as the grass I grow.
And Death itself, my strength and power fading,
        Seems to approach me.
So like a poor man I must be contented
To worship from afar your golden beauty,
To hear you laugh, and speak of all your loving
        Only to others.

This poem is one of many typical examples which express Sappho's feelings for women. It shows a sensuous and emotional abandon in spite of painful frustration and deprivation. She considers herself to be at a disadvantage, as men come between her and her beloved ones, but as far as we know she did not express resentment and jealousy towards men. In some poems, however, Sappho has shown herself to be vicious towards the faithlessness of her women friends who left her for other women. Hers is a sophisticated love, a love of beauty, grace and charm. The emphasis of her poetry is on the sensuous power of aesthetic love. The lesbians of her circle who probably belonged, as she did, to the aristocratic class, were artists of love, if not poets like herself. Saklatvala, in a brief account of the known facts of her life, speaks of her five great sorrows: her father's death when she was a child, her widowhood, her exile from Lesbos to Sicily, probably for political reasons, her brother's shameful marriage to an Egyptian prostitute, and last but not least, that sorrow which overshadowed all others, her wonderful but heartbreaking love of women.

Sadness is part of ecstasy, and both belong to the original image of sapphic or lesbian love. There was another aspect of Sappho's involvement with women, namely the love of the teacher for a pupil. Maximus of Tyre, according to Saklatvala, wrote that her love had strong similarities to the affection Socrates had for his young companions and pupils. Both were drawn to many, and all their loves were persons of beauty. Sappho's love for women was criticised by some historians and writers of ancient Rome, and though her fame as a poet has never been less than that of one of the greatest in human history, her homosexuality has, as a rule, since her death been condemned, played down, or flatly denied.

I have spoken at length about Sappho in order to explain the real image of sapphic love. To start with, it shows that no valid comparison can be made between male and female homosexuality. I shall explain more fully later why this is so. Most writers on the subject have not seen the real differences, but have only emphasised superficial similarities in male and female homosexuality. Lesbian women possess a more global, all-embracing love-potential than their male counterparts. It was Sigmund Freud who emphasised that all human beings are bisexual by nature. Could it be that women, and lesbians in particular, remain closer to this natural condition than men, when they are not suppressing their homosexual side? The statistical results of my research on lesbianism provide evidence for this assertion. Most of the homosexual women I interviewed had sexual contacts with men, and the majority were not repelled by them. A considerable number of my interviewees were married or had been married. It is a fact that there are homosexual men who marry, but the difference in their attitude to the opposite sex lies in their fear of the female sex organs, a fear which goes with a feeling of repugnance. There are, of course, also lesbians who are repelled by men, and who only love women physically and emotionally.

Lesbian feelings have two distinct features :
a) their highly aesthetic quality and reverence for beauty,
b) their intense emotionality.
It is in the latter quality that female homosexuality stands apart from any other form of love, and this has not changed in 2600 years. It is amply verified by the results of my research. The teacher-pupil relationship which can be part of lesbian love is akin to, if not identical with, maternal feelings—the need of mothering and also the wish to be mothered. An element of unavoidable frustration, greater than in male homosexuality, gives lesbianism a tinge of tragedy. It results from the impossibility of complete sexual fulfilment, and particularly from childlessness.

Nostalgia grows on the soil of frustration and thrives on the desire for the unobtainable, which is inseparable from lesbian love. Of course, all love goes with longing and suffering, but with lesbian women, nostalgia is based on a physical void set by nature. People who cannot find fulfilment are inclined to restlessness and instability. Sappho herself was not without the artfulness of the fickle lover, and she was deceitful as well as deceived. Instability has always been part of the image of homosexual relationships, and this image corresponds to reality. One must not confuse the behaviour of homosexuals in general, and lesbians in particular, with the essence of their kind of love. It was Sappho who expressed the original image of lesbianism in her poems. They show that popular ideas on the subject are miles apart from, and indeed irreconcilable with, the original. The word lesbian has become the symbol for undesirable and shameful feelings in most people's minds. Only the few, the minority of broadminded people, whether or not professional psychiatrists, understand sapphic love.

Of the 108 homosexual women whom I interviewed, only a few were independent of public opinion about lesbianism. I had considerable difficulty in obtaining enough subjects for my investigation because many lesbians were afraid of a possible leak of the information they might impart to me. This attitude surprised me because assurances of absolute discretion were given in the appeals made for my research by several lesbian organisations. The fact that as a physician I am bound to professional secrecy should have been sufficient in itself to dispel any fear. The lesbian organisation, Kenric, publishes a newsletter every month. No surname of any of the members is given, and Christian names together with telephone numbers are the only indications as to where and when certain social or other events are taking place. This measure shows great fear of public opinion. A similarly furtive attitude was also recognisable during the interviews. I often had to assure my subjects of complete secrecy before they would give an account of their emotional autobiography. Almost all of them spoke to me of their terror of being recognised as lesbians, and of the subterfuges they had to take in order to hide the fact.

Plays, films and books about male homosexuality and lesbianism are now quite in vogue, but so far they have not, in spite of their mostly sympathetic character, noticeably changed the collective image. Homosexual women are haunted by the dread of losing their social status, should their lesbianism become known. Some of them even go so far as to associate with men and pretend to be 'normal'. Civil servants, teachers and nurses are particularly fearful, but women in industry and business are also apprehensive that they may lose their jobs if their homosexual inclination is revealed. Many of them were sensitive to the social stigma in itself, even when they were self-employed and financially independent.

All the subjects I saw were anxious to play their full part in society, but were convinced that they could only do so through mimicry. A handful of professional women among them, such as physicians, architects, chartered surveyors, etc. showed considerably more independence of public opinion than the rest. They felt more secure because they were not easily replaceable. The effect of a negative public image is a psychological trauma, varying in intensity. Though certain individuals may appear to be comparatively free from obvious effects, the shadow of something 'disturbing' undoubtedly falls even on them. One must remember that exaggerated psychological reactions, be they neurotic or not, result from the injuries of the past. I think this holds good in the case of certain fears of homosexuals.

I have reason to believe that the public image of the lesbian is slowly changing. I shall enlarge on this point further on, but the effects of such a change will only be felt in another generation. One can, however, assume that in many cases the feelings of isolation and rejection which homosexual women experience do not quite reflect the real situation. I am of the opinion that many employers are aware of the 'secret' of their employees, but that they do not mind. They are concerned with the efficiency of their staff rather than with their 'normality'.

The gods of ancient Greece had nothing against love for one's own sex, and Sappho herself evidently never suffered any humiliation because of her love for women. Judaism and Christianity made homosexuality a sin and a deadly one. This persecution in thought and through the law has done much to create hypocrisy and subterfuge in human society up to the present day. This is a heavy psychological load for every homosexual, woman and man alike, which affects her or his reactions and behaviour. One may well wonder what lesbians themselves think about sapphic love, how they see themselves, and how they feel about their inclination. The answers to these questions may be a surprise to many people. I can summarise them like this: the original flavour of sapphic love still permeates the imagination of almost all homosexual women with whom I have come into contact. There is a common denominator in the conception and ideal of their love, which to a great extent tallies with the emotions and feelings Sappho expresses in her poems. It is obvious that expressions of love differ widely in different people. Education and sophistication enrich and refine ways and means of expressing thoughts, feelings and emotions. But I recognised in all the subjects under investigation the same intrinsic quality of their love. There was no difference in this respect between the old and the young, the well-educated and those who had left school at fifteen. The image of love is an ideal, and I need hardly emphasise that ideals cannot be translated into practice without compromise because of the unavoidable shortcomings of human nature.

One may wonder whether all human beings, be they heterosexual or homosexual, do not carry in their minds an ideal of love which has not undergone much change over the centuries? This is probably so. Lesbian love, however, has a definite profile which is quite different from that of heterosexual love. Its 'radioactive' core lies in emotion and romanticism, while physical contact is a by-product only, and neither a goal nor a necessary outlet. There have been and there are many lesbians, particularly in the older age-groups, who have lived happily with their beloved friends over the years without any sexual acts.

A certain feeling of resignation and sadness which I have already mentioned as being intrinsic to female homosexuality, came to light in my research in either an outspoken or a hidden form. It was the same sadness to which Sappho gives voice in the poem I have quoted. As a matter of fact, some of my interviewees did not admit this, simply because they wanted their relationship to be and to look a perfect thing. Their strong verbal protestations when I mentioned this point, and even more their defensive postures and gestures, proved that all was not as well as they wanted it to be.

Emotion is the life centre of lesbian love. It often leads to emotionalism because of certain sexual frustrations. As all of the interviewees saw emotion as the very essence of their attachments and relationships, I coined the word 'homoemotional' to replace the terms lesbian and homosexual. However, as a new word like 'homoemotional' needs time to become accepted and incorporated into the vocabulary, I have mainly used the customary terms, homosexual and lesbian, in this book.

Chapter Two

Some Psychological Theories of Homosexuality

One of the oldest theories of homosexuality is a legend. It is related in Plato's *Symposium*. Before I speak about this myth, I must clarify the word 'theory', which, like so many other words, has become a vague term, mechanically used by many. The word is derived from the Greek *theoria* which means view or sight. A theoretician is therefore a person with a view, or, as I want to suggest, a person with a vision. What kind of vision is it that makes a theory distinct from other visions? It is a vision which comprises a whole range of events and data under one large umbrella, and brings into focus what has been strewn around or hidden out of sight. It creates, so to speak, a mosaic out of many small, differently shaped stones, which would have remained unrelated little bits of material without a theory to give them structure.

The word vision is more readily applied to a poet or artist than to a research worker. But there is not much difference, in fact, between the poet or artist and the creative thinker. The first theory of homosexuality is indeed a vision of great poetry.

In Plato's *Symposium* Aristophanes reminds his companions of the old myth which relates that in the beginning of man's existence there lived three hermaphroditic human types: one was a man-man, the second a woman-woman, and the third a man-woman being. These first human creatures committed acts which were offensive to Zeus, the ruler of Olympus, and he separated each double person into two people. Since those legendary times, it is only love that can unite again what has been split asunder. Every human being searches for his or her original counterpart. Thus it came about that men who formerly were man-woman creatures search out and love women, while all men who formerly were man-man beings can only love another man. The latter aspire to all that is masculine, not only in the person they love but in their own behaviour. They are the best among the young because they are the most masculine. They are destined to become leaders in the state and in the army. It follows that those who once had been woman-woman beings look for and can only love another woman, though this situation was not directly stated in Plato's *Symposium*.

In his *Die Homosexualität* (1963) Dr Rudolf Klimmer, an East German psychiatrist quotes the Greek philosopher Parmenides (515-460 B.C.) as one of the first theoreticians of homosexuality. In Parmenides' view this disposition is innate, hereditary and natural. Klimmer also mentions Aristotle as upholding the naturalness of homosexuality.

It is a long jump in time from the philosophers of ancient Greece to the enlightened physicians of the nineteenth century in Central Europe. But there had not been either an enlightened or even a rational attitude towards homosexuality in the centuries between. The subject had eluded investigation altogether. Religion and law dealt with homosexuals in the most cruel and brutal fashion through the middle ages right into the age of reason. The first attempt at a scientific theory came from the medical profession. The pioneer in this field was a Dr Casper (1796-1864), a German who, like many others before Freud, was convinced that the causes of homosexuality were innate and due to constitutional tendencies.

Modern research workers, as a rule, take the view that both constitutional and accidental factors play their part in deciding a person's sexual preferences and fixation.

The first comprehensive theory of homosexuality is found in Freud's *Three Essays on the Theory of Sexuality*. It is a classic which, in many ways, has not been surpassed by any other, and

I am therefore giving a particular place to the Freudian viewpoint. His theory of sexuality is based on the fact that all human beings are bisexual by nature, in accordance with their phylogenetic and ontogenetic history. Freud, however, was not the first to point this out. He took the idea from two earlier investigators, Gley (1884) and Chevalier (1893), both of whom he mentions in his book quoted above. Man's natural bisexuality is part of the psycho-analytic theory of homosexuality. Embryology has taught us that men and women start the journey into life as sexually undifferentiated beings. In other words, in early foetal life human beings are potentially double-sexed creatures, and they retain rudiments of the opposite sex. One cannot overlook this fact, which points to the naturalness of bisexuality and thus of homosexuality. Freud quotes the following sentence (p. 8):

> The theory of bisexuality has been expressed in its crudest form by a spokesman of the male inverts: 'a feminine brain in a masculine body'.

The author is not named, but he anticipated results of present-day research into the genetic and hormonal influences on a possible feminisation of the brain in the male and masculinisation of the brain in a female.

Bisexuality, the heritage of every human being, is most easily recognisable in the child. It goes with a lability of object-choice, which in itself opens the way to homosexuality. There are other causes too, which are no less important. Freud referred to these in his writings on infantile sexuality and its repercussions in adult life. It was he who gave us a new concept of 'sex' by taking it out of its limited context. He explained how infantile sexuality is established in conjunction with the development of erotogenic zones. They are, according to him, directly linked to primary functions of the body, and centre round the mouth, urethra, anus and genitals. Other areas of the skin, for example the palms of the hands, the neck, the back of the ears, and many more, belong to the same category. In fact, the whole of the skin can be sensually responsive to touch. The sex organs themselves are, of course, the erotogenic area *par excellence*. The sources of pleasurable excitement in the child are manifold and diffuse, and show considerable independence of the sexual organs. This leads to an autonomy of pleasure via the sense of touch. It is only in the 'phallic' phase (Freud) that the different components of the sexual instinct are welded into a unified whole, directed towards a love object. But even in adult life the infantile haunts of pleasure are never given up, and the erotogenic zones are as important for a happy sex life in adulthood for both hetero-sexual and homosexual people. They are as a rule more acutely sensitised in the latter where they can replace sex-acts altogether.

According to Freud, there is no clear dividing line between the hetero- and homosexual person. He even expresses suspicion about the emotional health of anybody who is, or thinks he is, completely heterosexual. I quote from a footnote in *Three Essays on the Theory of Sexuality*, p. 11 footnote (added in 1915):

> Psycho-analytical research is most decidedly opposed to any attempt at separating off homosexuals from the rest of man-kind as a group of special character.

and further on in the same footnote:

> On the contrary, psycho-analysis considers that the choice of an object independently of his sex – freedom to range equally over male and female objects – as it is found in childhood, in primitive states of society and early periods of history, is the original basis from which, as a result of restriction in one direction or the other, both the normal and the invert types develop.
>
> Thus from the point of view of psycho-analysis the exclusive interest felt by men for women is a problem that needs elucidation and is not a self-evident fact based upon an attraction that is ultimately of a *chemical nature*.

It is interesting to note that Freud only speaks of men's exclusive love for women, and does not mention that the same applies to the female sex. In the past, research workers have paid more attention to male than to female homosexuality, although Freud almost reversed this position in his later writings. He and other psycho-analysts used the term 'invert' for homosexual, a term which has remained idiosyncratic. The word is rather an unfortunate choice in the English language as it has a ready association with 'introvert'.

It is general knowledge that the Oedipus complex, a term coined by Freud, is linked with homosexuality, and that it is as important for its understanding as the knowledge of bisexuality. The concept of the Oedipus complex is often misunderstood, and I shall try here to explain its meaning. Its name is taken from Sophocles' play *Oedipus Rex*. According to the legend which is the theme of the play, Oedipus killed his father accidentally, and unknowingly married his mother. When he realised the truth of the situation, he blinded himself, driven by guilt and grief. This terrifying legend concerns the lives of all of us. From the age of about three, a boy unconsciously desires his mother, and feels rivalry, resentment and jealousy towards his father. Parents of boys will readily testify to the truth of this. The Oedipus situation changes when the boy reaches the age of about five. At that time, repression of his libidinous wishes leads to the next phase in his development. This is the latency period which lasts until puberty.

What I have said so far sounds straightforward and simple, but the concept under discussion is far from either. The description I have given refers to a situation which is already the product of a number of developmental processes. The child experiences two phases of pre-oedipal attachment. The first one, called the oral phase, is related to breast-feeding. The pleasure of sucking the mother's breast supersedes all else. The second is the anal phase, when hate and resentment interfere with the bliss of inner peace. The Oedipus complex proper is only established with the phallic phase, the time when genital drives become unified and prominent. One cannot separate the Oedipus concept from that of constitutional bisexuality, and both the pre-oedipal and oedipal situation must be understood in conjunction with it. The Oedipus complex arouses twofold desires and loyalties which fight one another. Love for the mother is ambivalent, and turns at times into resentment and hate. Rivalry towards the father exists side by side with affectionate admiration for him. Bisexuality does not allow for a unilateral Oedipus complex. The boy's feminine side turns to his father as a love object, and resents his mother as a rival. However, in the case of normal development, the Oedipus complex is finally resolved with the adoption of the 'female' (mother) as love object, and ambivalent feelings towards the father. This situation represents, according to psycho-analysis, the positive Oedipus complex of the boy. A *negative* Oedipus complex exists when a 'normal' choice of the love object has not been attained. Under such circumstances, the boy identifies with the mother and wants to be loved by the father. Nobody ever sheds the negative Oedipus complex altogether, but homosexual people remain fixated on it for good. In 'normal' persons the love for the same sex is generally sublimated into friendship etc., if it is not altogether suppressed. The double orientation of love in the oedipal phase arouses inner conflicts of considerable magnitude. The fear of castration represents the dread of punishment the son feels for having betrayed his father. The anxiety resulting from the castration complex not only affects a man's sex life, but permeates wide areas of his psyche.

I have so far only mentioned the boy's pre-oedipal and oedipal development. The girl has been left out of the picture. Why? First, it appears that the psycho-sexual development of the boy could be more readily understood. This is, however, not the only reason for the neglect of the girl. The historical and social preference for the boy child makes him the obvious first choice for psychological investigation. The girl has always been regarded as a 'background-figure', more an 'appendix' than an entity in herself. Her place as a dependent person is reflected in the convention of language. One speaks of man and woman, boy and girl, he and she. Freud was aware of this situation when he mentioned in *Some Psychological Consequences of the Anatomical Distinction between the Sexes* that it has always been the custom to turn to the boy child as psychological subject. He admits in his paper *Female Sexuality* that *he* had particular difficulty in finding out about the girl's psycho-sexual development because of the fact that his female patients had a father transference on him. His first ideas about the girl's oedipal and pre-oedipal position ran on parallel lines to that of the boy. While the boy chooses his mother as primary love object, the girl bestows all her loving emotions on her father in the first place. Freud's first concept of the girl's psycho-sexual development appeared to be right in theory, but it turned out to be wrong in reality. It took him over thirty years to reach a more final insight into female sexuality and feminine homosexuality.

Freud was much preoccupied with the problem of homosexuality; he was one of the first investigators to give it a new, psychological slant. The research of every pioneer must proceed by trial and error. He has to grope towards understanding before the cloud of unknowing lifts. And progress runs in a zig-zag line. Freud mentioned in his *Three Essays on the Theory of Sexuality* (footnote p. 10, written in 1910), that psycho-analysis has not yet produced a complete explanation of the origin of homosexuality. But it has discovered the psychical mechanism of its development. At a later date, in 1920, he becomes far more cautious in his claim when he points out in *The Psychogenesis of a Case of Homosexuality in a Woman* (p. 230), that psycho-analysis cannot solve the problem of homosexuality. It must be content with tracing the psychical mechanism that results in object choice.

Freud was the explorer of a terra incognita more elusive than any other, because the mind is fluid and resists being mapped out. The moment one hopes to discover a fixed point, it is swept away by a wave. The many footnotes of corrections in the *Three Essays on the Theory of Sexuality* symbolise the odyssey with its detours of Freud's journey into the interior.

Although I am much influenced by psycho-analysis, I am not one of its practitioners, and I differ also in my theoretical thinking in many ways from Freud and his successors. But Freud was the first to create a model for the interpretation of homosexuality. Apart from this unequalled merit, I found that some of the basic ideas on female homosexuality, as expressed in his later writings, corresponded to my own findings. This is one of the reasons why I devote so much of this chapter to him. There are other considerations also. As far as I know, he was the first to treat two cases of homosexuality in women. The second case deserves particular attention, as the 'patient' had no other 'abnormality' than lesbianism. I shall refer to both case histories presently. Before I do so, I want to mention that, in my view, a *general* lesson can be learnt by tracing Freud's steps in conducting the research on this difficult problem. This lesson is mainly due to his uncompromising integrity and courage in face of great doubts, setbacks and failures. He constantly learned through his mistakes and never hesitated to correct himself, to abandon results he had taken years to reach. He made psycho-analysis a living thing. It has remained an open, fluid system ever since, largely, I think, because of his example. He was the eternal student *par excellence*, as every research worker should be.

I am stressing here Freud's personal attitudes, but I consider them important enough for an extended exposition of his thoughts in relation to my subject. I also think it necessary for the understanding of the psycho-analytic viewpoint on girls' psycho-sexual development to show the changes in Freud's conception of it. Certain inconsistencies and even contradictions can only be clarified by giving the full story. Let me start with the beginning of his ideas about female sexuality, which date back to 1900, to the publication of *The Interpretation of Dreams*.

His ideas about female homosexuality can only be fully understood in relation to those on normal sexuality. He says on p. 251 of that book:

For analysis tells us that sexual wishes of the child – in so far as they deserve this designation in their nascent state – awaken at a very early age, and that the earliest affection of the girl child is lavished on the father, while the earliest infantile desires of the boy are directed upon the mother. For the boy the father and for the girl the mother, becomes an obnoxious rival.

Freud had a long way to go before he could free his research from the idea of male superiority. A definite step in this direction appears in his *Analysis of a Case of Hysteria*, published in 1905, and generally known as the Dora Case. Here is a very brief summary of the case:

Dora, a girl of 18, was apparently normal. She had a tender attachment to her father, amounting to an Oedipus complex, while her elder brother was similarly attached to her mother. She had been a victim of severe psychosomatic symptoms from the early age of 8. She had suffered first from attacks of dyspnoea. Later on she developed attacks of migraine, nervous coughing and aphonia. At about 17 she became depressed and threatened suicide. Her more serious symptoms developed after the age of 14, when a Mr K. had suddenly kissed her. Dora had been in love with him, so it was thought. His wife nursed her father on many occasions during Dora's formative years. One day (this was at the age of 16) she was asked to stay with the K's. She vehemently refused, giving as her reason indecent sexual approaches by Mr K. These were false accusations unconsciously designed to hide the truth. The same holds good for another indictment of hers, namely that her father had a love-affair with Mrs K. Her jealousy was, to all appearances, directed towards her father whom she loved, and whom another woman had taken away from her. The analysis revealed that, in fact, she was even more jealous of Mrs K. whom she loved, and who she imagined had betrayed her with a man who happened to be her father. This disappointed love, betrayed for a number of other reasons also, was the true cause of her illness. Mrs K. had given away confidences about Dora to her husband, and Dora's 'infatuation' with him was mainly an act of revenge. Freud explains this situation like this:

When in a hysterical woman or girl the sexual libido which is directed towards men has been energetically suppressed, it will regularly be found that the libido which is directed towards women has been vicariously reinforced.

Freud of course, goes deeper in his interpretation of Dora's homosexuality than this quotation implies. He traces it back to a fixation on the oral erotogenic zone, which attaches a special significance to the act of kissing. This particular fixation found expression in Dora's early childhood when she was indulging in thumb-sucking, while at the same time tugging at the lobe of her brother's ear. The desire for sucking was later on transferred to the male organ. Freud mentions that this 'exceedingly repulsive and perverted fantasy' of 'sucking at a penis' has the most innocent origin. He maintains that it is nothing other than a very early memory of the mother's breast. We see here the germ of Freud's later concept of female homo-sexuality and sexuality, but at this stage he has not yet formulated it in any decisive way. His lack of clarity about it may be due to his early ideas about a girl's primary love-object, the father.

In the same year, 1905, Freud published his *Three Essays on the Theory of Sexuality*. The parts which deal with inversion are almost entirely concerned with male homosexuality. His only reference to lesbianism is in an aside, when he says nothing more than the following :

> The position in the case of women is less ambiguous [than that of men]. For among them, the active inverts exhibit masculine characteristics both physical and mental with peculiar frequency, and look for femininity in their sexual objects – though here again, a closer knowledge of the facts might reveal greater variety.

Can one find a more obvious proof of Freud's vagueness and lack of real knowledge of the problem of lesbian love? It is only much later that he develops a new and completely different insight into both female sexuality and homosexuality. His new ideas become apparent from about 1919 onwards, and begin to be *firmly* expressed first in his paper *Some Psychological Consequences of the Anatomical Distinction between the Sexes* (1925), and most clearly in *Female Sexuality*, published in 1931.

A sign-post of his *developing* insight into female homosexuality is his paper *The Psychogenesis of a Case of Homosexuality in a Woman* (1920). He starts it with the following words :

> Homosexuality in women, which is certainly not less common than in men, although much less glaring, has not only been ignored by the law, but has also been neglected by psychoanalytical research.

Freud was inaccurate about the neglect of the law in regard to lesbianism, as legislation still exists today in Austria and Spain and many states of America. He was quite right when he stated that research on homosexual women was neglected : indeed, he was prophetic about it, as even today there is only scant literature on the subject.

This paper is of particular importance as it deals with homosexuality in an otherwise normal girl. One must not forget that Freud, as a psychiatrist, dealt with and saw sexual abnormalities related, as a rule, to neurosis and mental illnesses. Here is a very brief summary of the case.

Freud's patient was a beautiful and very intelligent girl of

eighteen. She had a rather masculine bearing, masculine interests, and altogether took after her father, an intelligent and highly
civilised man. Her mother was a dull, stupid woman, whom the
daughter despised. The girl had been attached to an elder
brother, with whom she had much in common. At 18 she had
fallen passionately in love with a woman much older than herself,
who was considered to be a *cocotte*. At the time, this lady was
having an affair with another woman, and there could be no
doubt about her homosexual inclinations. However, she never
encouraged the girl in her passion; on the contrary, she tried
to keep her away. She had allowed her no other contact than a
hand-kiss. The hand-kiss is a form of greeting in Austria, used
by men when they meet a lady. This convention is now mainly
symbolic and the words 'Kuess die Hand' generally replace the
act. The young girl behaved like a cavalier, like a well brought
up young man whose love is adoring and romantic. She seemed
happy enough in this relationship, which was of her own
imagination, and she remained unshakable in her resolve to go
on with it in spite of fierce opposition from her father. He seems
to have been aware of his daughter's homosexual tendencies, and
had severely reprimanded her about them long before this
romantic attachment. In other words, he took his daughter's
inclination very seriously indeed. His opposition made her
passion grow stronger, as was to be expected. When one day the
father saw the girl with the lady in question in the street, he
glared furiously at her. A crisis blew up in consequence. The
lady had been aware of the silent scene between father and
daughter, and had been alarmed. She forbade the girl even to
come near her again—and that had to be the end of it. After
this event the girl tried to commit suicide, and this prompted
her father to seek psycho-analytic treatment for her. The treatment remained incomplete because of the patient's strong
resistance to a male analyst.

In her early years, the girl had a strong father attachment,
that is, a feminine Oedipus complex. She also felt slightly
attracted to her older brother. However, the comparison between
his genitals and her own was a shock experience contributing to
her subsequent homosexuality. (Penis envy, according to Freud.)
At about 13, she bestowed great affection on a small boy, hardly
3 years of age, and became friends with his parents. Freud inter-

prets the situation as the wish for a child, and a boy child at that, which means the revival of her feminine Oedipus complex. She soon grew indifferent to the boy, and at the same time started to love mature women. All of them had children and were between 20 and 30 years old. In other words, she loved mother substitutes.

When she was 16, her own mother became pregnant, and from this time onwards her tastes changed. She fell for a non-maternal woman with homosexual tendencies and androgynous appearance. Her mother's pregnancy had definitely turned the scale from an original feminine Oedipus complex into an inverted or negative one. She had by now given up motherhood as a condition of love, and searched for a type opposite to the maternal. There are other factors which I cannot touch upon here, which put the seal on her homosexual orientation.

This paper stands midway between Freud's earlier and later ideas on female homosexuality, when he makes it clear that not every girl disappointed with her father must perforce become homosexual. More profound conditions lie at the origin of homo-sexuality. From infancy onwards her libido had been bisexual. The homosexual one was a direct and unchanged continuation of her inverted or negative Oedipus complex. This girl appears at first sight to be a case of acquired homosexuality, as she started off with a feminine or positive Oedipus complex. But a deeper insight into her condition revealed that her lesbianism was innate and had become fixed at puberty. She had a strong mother fixation which had remained unconscious. Freud draws our attention to the difficulty of differentiating between constitutional and acquired factors in homosexuality. He concludes that one always finds a blending of both. In the last resort, he considers three factors to be essential in producing homosexual orientation in both men and women. Firstly, physical sexual characteristics, (physical hermaphroditism), secondly, mental sexual character-istics, and thirdly, the kind of object choice.

We find in Freud's later writings a complete reversal of his concept of female sexuality. The latter is, as I already men-tioned, basic for an understanding of his ideas on female homo-sexuality. His two papers, *Some Psychological Consequences of the Anatomical Difference between the Sexes*, 1925, and *Female Sexuality*, 1931, reveal this new view. They can be seen in conjunction with each other, as the second paper is the continuation, and in some parts, a repetition, of the first, which Freud starts with a kind of apology. It is an apology for the neglect of psycho-analysis in not investigating the girl child's psycho-sexual development. By this time he realised that the boy's oedipal development is far simpler than that of the girl, while only some years before he had been of the opposite opinion.

The male does not change his love object during his life-time. He remains bound to a woman, first the mother, then another female who takes her place. He pursues one love object, while the girl is destined (if she develops normally) to have two. And the crossing from one to the other, from mother to father, presents a bewildering as well as a hazardous task. The mother is the original love object for girl and boy alike. The attachment is equally strong in both, but if anything, that of the girl may be more intense. Her negative Oedipus complex lasts longer than the complex of the boy. Freud uses the adjectives *negative* or *inverted* in attachments of the child to the parent of its own sex. He is convinced that the girl has the same *sexual* desires for her mother as the boy, and he goes so far as to include part of her exclusive attachment to her in what he calls the positive Oedipus complex, the one that is directed towards the parent of the opposite sex.

Freud, in fact, regards a little girl as a masculine creature since her early psycho-sexual life is governed by clitoral excite-ment and masturbation. He claims that she passes through the phallic phase like a boy. The girl is 'male' as long as she is governed by her clitoris, the rudiment of the penis, and she only changes into a female when the father has become her love object. This strange transformation is supposed to take place when her sexual reactions, which have so far been active, become passive. It is at such a time that she moves into the feminine Oedipus complex. Her vaginal reactions are now awakened, signalling the change in her libidinous orientation. The age when the change-over takes place varies from the third to the fifth year. In the latter case, the Oedipus complex binding her to her mother lasts longer than that of the boy. I need hardly emphasise that a girl's negative oedipal situation can be the starting point from which female homosexuality develops.

Freud equates active and passive with masculine and feminine, as was customary in his time. He explains the termination of the girl's negative or inverted oedipal situation through a change from active into passive reactions. But how does such a transformation come about? Freud's explanation appears to be a very simple one. When the girl discovers the male organ of the father, a brother, or any other male, she goes through a decisive shock-experience. She grasps in a flash that she is a mutilated, deprived creature, castrated from the start. She now regards herself as something rather contemptible, and the male as something to be envied—a superior being. She is seized by *penis envy*. She loses ground with her mother whom she despises for not having provided her with a penis and for not having a male organ herself, as she had believed in infancy. This depressing and totally negative situation, so Freud assumes, leads the girl into normality. She turns to her father, the male, and wants to have his children. As she cannot possess a penis, she must at least get it in another way. The total identification with her mother has been achieved, an identification which is accompanied by rivalry, envy and contempt. The girl has been ushered into the positive Oedipus complex through her castration complex. Freud emphasises that the boy's situation is the very opposite to that of the girl. He terminates his Oedipus complex through his fear of castration. Both sexes must perforce go through a period of narcissism in their psycho-sexual development, and this phase plays a particular role in homosexuality.

Freud remarks in a paper *On Narcissism*, 1914, rather ominously, that perverts and homosexuals take their own selves as love objects. He refers to the male in this context. He does the same in a more explicit form, in a footnote to the *Three Essays on The Theory of Sexuality*, on p. 11, when he says:

> Inverts proceed from a narcissistic basis and look for a young man who resembles themselves, and whom they may love as their mother loved *them*.

Homosexual boys glorify their sexual organ for good. Girls, according to Freud, focus their narcissism on their own, mutilated organ, the clitoris. They indulge in an illusion, and their rude awakening after they have seen the 'real thing', represents a decisive turning point in their lives.

The girl has, so Freud tells us, three ways out of the dilemma of realising that she is only a girl:

1. She can turn her back on sex altogether.

2. She maintains that the whole situation cannot be true, and clings to her masculinity. If she does so, she may make a homosexual object choice.

3. She manages to achieve a positive Oedipus complex, and from then on her father becomes her love object. Freud observed that the strength of a girl's attachment to her father was proportionate to her former love for her mother. She has in fact, so he says, not really changed her love object, only transferred her affections from one to the other. His final conclusion is that a woman always remains more mother-bound than a man.

I think it possible that Freud overbalanced the position he finally took on female sexual development by completely reversing his ideas about it. I am reminded of a delightful remark of his, recorded by W. H. Auden in an interview in *The Observer* of 21st June, 1970. Freud one day turned to an old colleague of his and asked her: 'Marie, can you tell me what women really want?'.

Melanie Klein, who developed her own psycho-analytic school, gave a new slant to the 'normal' and inverted Oedipus situation of girls. Her ideas, strange as they may be, were conceived through her psycho-analysis of children. The most striking result of her observations is the fantastic mythology about sex in earliest infancy. Babies, from six months onwards, perceive both parents as one rather monstrous hermaphroditic unit. The mother is furnished with a penis, and the father with a breast. According to her, the child separates the parents into two figures only when it has entered the oedipal phase, which begins much earlier than Freud maintained. In the pre-oedipal period, the libido goes towards both parents, and, even later, vacillates between them. When in her second year, the little girl already experiences a feminine Oedipus complex, and turns her love more towards her father. She experiences, so we are told, unconscious vaginal reactions. But fixations remain fluid. At about 18 months or so, the girl turns back to her mother, and enters or re-enters an inverted Oedipus complex.

At first, libidinous desires are interwoven with oral, anal and urethral sensations and fantasies, and are accompanied by aggression. Melanie Klein puts the whole emphasis of the girl's fixation from early infancy on the breast, or, to be more precise, on the nipple, from where she transfers her libidinous interest to the father's penis. When that happens she has already identified with her mother. At the same time she also has sexual feelings for her mother. Under their influence, the girl desires to take the father's place, and these masculine reactions may lead her into homosexuality. But there is always rivalry connected with any desire in the child, and both love and hate are carried over into her relationships with brothers and sisters. Melanie Klein writes in *Love, Hate and Reparation*, p. 64:

> The desires and fantasies in connection with mother and sisters are the basis for direct homosexual relationships in later life.

Melanie Klein differs from Freud in her ideas about a long exclusive mother attachment. According to her, the girl desires both parents equally in her early pyscho-sexual development. She is also critical of Freud's view regarding the girl's fantasy that her mother possesses a penis. She maintains that the girl has an unconscious knowledge of the real sexual situation. She whole-heartedly agrees with Freud on the importance of the girl's castration complex and penis envy, and their repercussions on female homosexuality.

I end my survey of psycho-analytical theories of homosexuality with the fascinating views of Georg Groddek. He was an eccentric psycho-analyst. He discovered Freud's teaching when he had already advanced his own ideas, which went in the same direction. Groddek (1886-1934), a German physician and psychiatrist, was looked upon by his patients as a healer. A man of vision and remarkable culture, he had the courage to break through almost every convention of medical and psychological thinking of his time.

Groddek was an episodic and intuitive writer, and his powers of persuasion lie in these very qualities. He expresses the gist of his concept of homosexuality in the following passage, taken from *The Book of the It*:

> Yes, I hold the view that all people are homosexual, hold it so firmly that it is difficult for me to realise how anyone can

think differently. Man loves himself first and foremost with every sort of passionate emotion and seeks to procure for himself every conceivable pleasure, and since he himself must be either male or female, is subject from the beginning to a passion for his own sex.

Groddek goes so far as to question how man can come to love the opposite sex. He turns the question of homosexuality into a question of heterosexuality. Groddek relates the ignorance about lesbianism to prudery and repression.

The subject of homosexuality was pointedly acute in Germany before the First World War. Legislators suggested at that time that the famous paragraph 175 of the German Law which made male homosexuality punishable should be extended to lesbianism. Groddek tells of the courage (because courage it was at that time) of a well-known and highly respected woman who publicly gave voice to her objections to this proposal, which she considered to be most dangerous. She expressed the view that it would be disastrous to prohibit female homosexuality because Germany's cultural development largely depended on homosexual women. It 'would shake the foundation of society', she wrote, 'as several millions of able German women would have to go to prison if such a law were introduced'. Groddek himself was convinced that 'the whole world rests on the love between mother and daughter and father and son.'

Although his ideas on homosexuality must be taken with a grain of salt, they deserve attention because they touch the field of cultural evolution.

Adherents of *behaviourism* show striking differences from psycho-analysts in their view on homosexuality. Behaviourism emerged from observation of and experiments on animals, and is intrinsically linked with genetics, zoology and anthropology. The frontier between innate and adaptive behaviour is not clearly defined, because the latter can take the place of the former. According to this school, sexual behaviour in animals and man is expressed by signals which are dictated either by the genetic code or by outer stimuli. The latter may alter the innate pattern of behaviour.

Desmond Morris has made this process poignantly clear in

The Naked Ape, where he explains homosexuality as a behaviour pattern under stress, which is reversible in animals but rarely so in man. We know from his studies and those of Konrad Lorenz, Ford and Beach and others that both male and female homosexuality is practised right through the animal kingdom from the guinea pig to man. It is particularly frequent among anthropoid apes.

Desmond Morris paints the picture of homosexuality in black and white because, for him, it is a malfunction, a second-best activity which ceases when 'normal' conditions re-occur.

Ford and Beach in their book *Patterns of Sexual Behaviour* give a different picture of homosexuality. Theirs is a detailed anthropological and psychological study which confirms what has been known for a long time, that homosexuality in animal and man is based on innate bisexuality. They mention for example, that young male chimpanzees prefer sexual intercourse with members of their own sex. All these investigators are unanimous in their conclusion that sexual submission is used by animals as a weapon against danger from a highly aggressive member of their group. This holds good for both male and female. In making themselves sexual objects, they ensure their safety. In other words, sex is used to please the powerful in order to get his or her protection.

The psycho-analytical theory of sexuality assumes that a fixed link exists between libido and sexual activity. Behaviourism claims that sexuality is an amorphous force which can be used in many ways according to circumstances. It is within the sphere of everyone's observation that many human beings are driven by motives other than libido in their love life. The fact that animals apply sexual submission to ward off danger to life and limb makes one more understanding of a somewhat similar attitude in man.

Sexuality is a complex force with a touch of mimicry, and in the Ark of survival, both man and beast use sexual submission as a means to prevent drowning.

I have discussed those psychological theories which, in my opinion, are among the most significant contributions of this kind to the subject of homosexuality. Probably none of them holds the master-key, but each enlarges our understanding of what is rather inadequately covered by the word homosexuality.

Chapter Three

A Theory of Lesbianism

No theory has so far been evolved which deals exclusively with lesbianism. The homosexual woman has been treated by research workers as women are generally treated, namely as the second sex. Certain writers such as Cory and Magee have stressed the fact that fundamental differences exist between the male and female homosexual. They arrived at this conclusion through sensitive understanding and careful observation, but they were not equipped to embark on a scientific study of lesbianism and to formulate a theory. Kinsey, in his mammoth work on *Sexual Behaviour in the Human Female*, hinted at considerable differences in the nature of male and female homosexuality. However, he neither made an exclusive study of lesbianism, nor ventured on a theory about it. His work is descriptive and statistical, and as such, a masterpiece of its kind, but it does not directly contribute to the theme of this chapter.

The first step towards finding a theory is an intuitive process. A theory is sensed intuitively before it can be formulated, its *gestalt* is subconsciously known before it can be expressed in words.

When I was a student of medicine in the Berlin of the twenties, Magnus Hirschfeld's *Institut für Sexualwissenschaften* was the centre of research on homosexuality, and I can trace my first attempts to understand lesbianism back to those early days.

Hirschfeld, his assistants and other research workers of the period were convinced that homosexuals are born not made. At the same time Steinach pioneered the transplant of sex glands in various animals, and was able to show that a male could be made to behave like a female and vice versa. His experiments boosted biological research on homosexuality in spite of the fact that his method had failed where human beings were concerned. He had however demonstrated that a link exists between endocrine function and contrary sexual behaviour.

The pioneer work of Hirschfeld and Steinach gave a strange glamour to the study of sexual deviation which was not only of absorbing interest to the medical student but to many young people in different walks of life. I was fascinated by the new views on the subject provided by the budding science of endocrinology. The books by Krafft-Ebing, Havelock Ellis and others, well known to the general public, also pointed to a physiological cause of homosexuality.

Then, at a time when a biological explanation seemed to be close at hand, came the great change of ideas brought about by psycho-analysis which, by then, had come into its own. Freud's theory of homosexuality delivered a heavy blow to the purely biological approach of research, and relegated it to second place.

I must have already understood in those early days that many lesbians did not fit into the biological concept of Hirschfeld and others, who identified the intersexes with homosexuals. Intersexual people are hermaphroditic in the widest sense of the word, with secondary characteristics of the opposite sex. They may or may not be homosexual as well. The majority of lesbians are obviously of 'normal' feminine appearance, and this fact had probably made me aware that psychological factors play a great part in homosexual orientation.

Medicine and psychology undergo the whims of fashion as do many other human activities and pursuits. And fashions have revivals. The social climate of the sixties shows certain similarities to that of the twenties. In both periods permissiveness and a sense of daring are the outstanding characteristics of the time.

Although psychological theories of homosexuality have not lost their impetus and persuasive power, biological research has taken a big leap forward today. As in the twenties, an answer to the problem of homosexuality is looked for in man's biological

make-up. The most recent physiological investigations favour
the dysfunction of the endocrine glands during foetal life as the
responsible agent for male and female homosexuality. Discoveries are often made simultaneously by several people in different
countries, and this happened to the extraordinary finding that
homosexuality is determined in foetal life through either the
feminisation or masculinisation of brain reactions. This means,
in simple terms, that a male develops a feminine brain and a
female a masculine one. Discoveries of this kind were made in
America, England, Germany and Sweden. But in my view, the
most far-reaching and detailed investigation of the phenomenon
has been undertaken by Professor Guenther Doerner, Director of
the Institute for Endocrinology at the Humbold University of
East Berlin. He describes his method of research and its results
in a paper in *Die Medizinische Wochenschrift* of 21st February,
1969. According to Doerner there can be no doubt about the
fact that a disorder in the development of the sex glands in foetal
life alters permanently an erotisising zone, seated in the hyp-
thalamus, which is a part of the mid-brain mainly responsible
for man's emotional responses. This disorder produces male
responses in a female and the opposite in a male individual. The
same occurs when women receive a certain hormonal treatment
during pregnancy. If they have been given male hormones,
particularly in the first five or six months of childbearing, the
erotisising zone in the mid-brain of a female foetus is impregnated
with maleness, creating a masculine type of lesbian – an
emotional male in a female body.

Anthropometric studies of lesbians and research into the
finer deviations of their chromosomes are in progress in Great
Britain. The former investigations are related to endocrine
function, and link up with research which started over 50 years
ago. The latter are comparatively new and may, in time, through
technical advance, yield new information about the genetic factor
in female homosexuality.

The constitutional concept has a strong appeal for those
research workers who are not psychologically minded. But the
psychiatrist has also become biased in favour of a biological
explanation of the causes of mental and emotional events and
disturbances, because of the advance in the treatment of mental
illness through drugs.

Perhaps we have come full circle from the twenties to the sixties. The questions were the same then as now, but the answers, incomplete in those early days, are now far more convincing. Nevertheless, some crucial queries still remain. They are these :

Are the results of the investigations by Professor Doerner and others the last word on the problem of homosexuality in general and lesbianism in particular? Can biological research ever be sufficient to give us the key to it?

On the other hand, does the psychological approach, be it psycho-analytic, existentialist or behaviourist, provide significant explanations as to the causes of lesbianism?

Is there perhaps a need for a new definition of the terms feminine and masculine?

What has been the impact of anthropological and social history on the development of woman, the lesbian in particular?

I shall try to answer these questions in the course of this chapter.

I myself have been vacillating in my ideas about the possible causes of lesbianism since my student days. My own preference for the constitutional approach became reinforced through my studies of hand traits and gesture, which I pursued over a period of nearly 20 years, from the thirties into the fifties. I always realised, of course, the importance of environmental influences, but believed that the basic structure of the individual could only be understood through biological functions, particularly those of the endocrine glands, and through genetics. But the biological concept alone seemed to be inadequate, the more I understood how well psycho-analysis explained the inexplicable in human behaviour and misbehaviour. It is today unthinkable to concentrate only on one type of research. Biological and psychological functions form an unbreakable unit, and nobody really knows where the frontier lies between the two. And this no man's land is the most stimulating and exciting challenge to inquiry and experiments. I remember Dr Humphrey Osmond telling me that Carl Jung, when already nearing the end of his life, expressed to him the conviction that schizophrenia was a mental illness of biological origin. What an astounding feat, I thought, that Jung could adopt so late in life a revolutionary approach to the causation of this psychotic condition! Freud, who had perhaps the most profound and far-reaching insight of all innovators in the knowledge of man, and who explained homosexuality through bio-psychological events, never lost sight of the importance of purely biological research. He believed that, in time, physiology would assist in solving the problem of deviation together with many other psychological problems.

A theory of lesbianism is a new venture, and I have embarked on it with caution and hesitation, weighing over and over again the importance of existing knowledge against my own ideas. I was able to formulate these after I had completed my research, the results of which substantiated many of my earlier observations, and also provided new and unexpected information. During the course of my life I have known a considerable number of homosexual women, in my practice as a psychiatrist and in personal contacts. But I experienced the real impact of the make-up of a lesbian through my research and my visits to group meetings of Kenric, the organisation which so greatly contributed to this book.

I arrived at a mosaic theory of lesbianism where every single item had to be studied separately as well as in relationship to the whole.

It is obvious that women who love members of their own sex are likely to have a different image of themselves from those whose emotional and sexual feelings are mainly directed towards men. This difference in self image reflects on gender identity. We have recently heard a great deal about gender identity, a term which is applied in the research into and treatment of transsexualism. I must explain the concept and meaning of these two words.

Firstly, what is gender identity? It is concerned with qualities usually associated with either sex. It refers to what is popularly called masculine or feminine. A woman who feels masculine has a male image of herself which changes her gender identity. The same naturally holds good for a man who feels like a woman.

What is transsexualism? It not only refers to contrary gender identity, but manifests a syndrome of its own, the main characteristics of which are the following:

1. The desire to be a member of the opposite sex, both in physical characteristics and in official status. This wish is more often than not compulsive to the point of seeking sex change through operation and hormonal treatment.
2. A considerable number of transsexual people belong to the intersexes, and in their case sexual identity is affected as much as gender identity, so that they feel utterly uncomfortable in their personal and gender status. It is with these people that operations and endocrine treatment can be most successful, because of an underlying hermaphroditic or pseudo-hermaphroditic condition.
3. Transsexual individuals are often but not always homosexual. Some are particularly enamoured with the other sex, probably because of severe psychological difficulties.
4. Transsexualism is frequently found in psychotic conditions, and it is essential to be aware of this before any operation or endocrine treatment is attempted. In every case of suspected mental illness, the psychiatrist should have the last word.

Gender identity has, in our time, undergone such extensive changes, that even the vox populi now speaks of a unisex, at least in the world of fashion. Transsexualism, which has been studied for about twenty years, is not only far more widespread now than ever before, but it has also been made respectable through the important work of psychiatrists, endocrinologists and gynaecologists, particularly here and in the States. A symposium on transsexualism was recently held in London, sponsored by the Ericson Foundation of New York and the Albany Trust of Great Britain.

The problem of sex and gender identity is one of revolutionary dimensions in the field of psychology and ethics. It is because of a new concept of the human being, to whom certain verbal symbols regarding sex have always been automatically attached, that I have put the question of gender identity first in my theory of lesbianism.

GENDER IDENTITY AND LESBIANISM

A fixed gender identity is an illusion. Embryology and psychology have revealed that every human being has a bisexual foundation. In the very beginning of foetal life no differentiation of the sexes exists, and it is likely that memory traces of our early hermaphroditic structure never die. We certainly are bisexual creatures, and this innate disposition is reinforced by the indelible memory of childhood attachments, which know no limitation of sex. Both the physiological and the psychological bisexuality of the human being make the concept of a definite gender identity look absurd. We acquire this so-called identity through the brain-washing process of education. Our elders hammer into us: 'You must behave like this or like that, because you are a little boy or a little girl'. In spite of this wrong teaching, gender identity is at its most labile in childhood. Games and play are outlets for all possible roles a human being can adopt by being either male or female.

Gender identity does not originate from the facts of our physique, but from the facts of our imagination. I have already mentioned that it is linked with the image of oneself, and where else can an image come from but its matrix, the imagination. The capacity to feel oneself alternately to be masculine or feminine adds richness to every aspect of living. It broadens the understanding of everything human, and lends the colour of change and playfulness to relationships. This is most happily so in love relationships. The art of love needs imagination to give it variety and the windfalls of surprises. It is in the unexpected that love constantly regenerates itself. Eros loves to laugh and to play as well as to play-act. The imaginative world of the child is the best playground for the god of love. Norman Brown pointed out in his book *Life against Death* that we need more Eros and less Thanatos in human relationships. He praises, rightly, the playfulness and fluidity of imaginative games in children's eroticism. And I can only wish with him that the charades of childhood may never leave us.

Lesbians possess, through their very nature, a labile gender identity which might be interpreted as a sign of immaturity or arrested development. I do not share this view – quite the opposite. *The retention of the capacity to change feminine into masculine feelings and attitudes, and vice versa, is one of the assets of female homosexuality, because it makes for variety and richness in personal relationships.*

Masculine and feminine gender identity are subjective con-notations. Convention has given them a special flavour accord-ing to the ideas and fashions existing in different countries and at different periods of time. What is masculine in the western world, may be considered feminine in other continents. For example, the men of the Tuareg tribe in Africa, wear veils, stay at home, do so-called feminine tasks, and are asked in marriage by women. The latter do what is considered in our world to be a man's work. Tuareg women are the bread-winners who work in the fields and control governmental affairs. Clearly we have a quite different conception of the terms masculine and feminine from that of the Tuaregs.

This is only one striking example of the subjective concept of gender identity, which unfortunately carries strong emotional undertones. It must be said, however, that the old-fashioned ideas of what is masculine and feminine have started to become blurred with members of the young generation in our society. Some modern men automatically help their women with the housework etc. and do not regard themselves as effeminate because of it. Therefore gender identity, in the traditional sense, has received a sharp knock, and is evolving towards a new and broader image, in which it is accepted that men and women can interchange roles without losing prestige. The manliness of earlier times is now thought of by many young people as false pride or silly, and the femininity of those days is regarded as outdated as the crinoline. The eccentrics among the young demonstrate most vividly in their clothes and behaviour that the old ideas of gender identity are dying out.

SEX IDENTITY AND LESBIANISM

Even modern young people might find it difficult to understand that one could doubt one's physical sex. Cases of a contrary feeling of sex identity are rare, but they exist, and they are, in a marginal way, relevant to my theory of lesbianism. There are homosexual women and men who suffer from psychosis, and with them contrary sex identity is not uncommon. The illusion of being a member of the opposite sex occurs more frequently in the lesbian than in the male homosexual.

Although this condition is not directly relevant to the research on which this book is based, and has no general application to lesbianism per se, it nevertheless throws some light on certain lesbian predicaments. We learn about extraordinary behaviour through extreme cases, and mental illness is therefore a valuable teacher in our understanding of the unusual. I vividly remember two patients of mine who believed themselves to be male. Both were homosexual; one told me that she was able to 'penetrate' her girl friend, and the other assured me that she had frequent ejaculations of semen. Both were schizophrenics.

The possibility of an illusion like this testifies to the fact that sex identity is not an absolute certainty. There are several periods in life when a person feels uncertain about identity in general, and this is particularly so in puberty. Adolescent homosexual girls can, because of this predisposition, experience an uncertainty of their sex identity, even if they are otherwise mentally sound. There is an anatomical reason for this which clearly divides the female from the male homosexual. It is this:

A woman's sexual organs retain a masculine part, the clitoris. The whole scale of her sexual pleasure from mild stimulation to orgasm is bound up with this male rudiment. This condition can, under certain circumstances, alter a woman's image of herself, with a special reflection on her sex identity. *The disposition to bisexuality and therefore to homosexuality is built into every woman by nature.*

The psycho-analyst Marie Bonaparte and also Professor Brüll have emphasised the same point, and both consider female homosexuality to be a natural phenomenon. There are, however, other consequences of this anatomical condition which, according to my knowledge, have not been described before. The clitoris is more developed in some women than in others, and it changes its size considerably under the influence of sexual excitement. This is a normal process in all women. Lesbians are particularly responsive to clitoral stimuli, and with them one finds not infrequently a habitually enlarged clitoris. If this condition is extreme, the clitoris looks like a small penis, and signals an endocrine syndrome: pseudo-hermaphroditism. It has no parallel in the male. Adrenal and pituitary dysfunction may be responsible for this. It may also be due to the masculinisation of the female foetus through hormonal treatment of the mother, or to another developmental disturbance during the early weeks of embryonic life.

Women of such a make-up are most often, but not always, homosexual. Whatever their sexual preference may be, they are highly aggressive. In the case of lesbian tendencies, a masculinised girl can easily experience doubt about her sex identity without suffering from mental illness. She is not likely to imagine that she is a full-blown man, but she may think of herself as a hermaphrodite with male preponderances, when in fact she is a woman of the pseudo-hermaphroditic type.

When an adolescent girl of this description falls in love with a member of her own sex, she can enjoy a highly satisfying sexual contact, but, at the same time, is likely to experience a sense of frustration and distress. She is close to the complete sexual satisfaction of the male, but unable to achieve the last step. She may thus consider herself to be a mutilated man. *Female pseudo-hermaphroditism has no parallel in the male, and is one of many essential differences between homosexual women and men.*

The masculine lesbian is conspicuous, although less so today than in previous generations; but one can identify her for what she is. In the days before and after the First World War, it was this type of homosexual woman who was assumed to be the lesbian. This is, as we now know, a fallacy. The majority of lesbians are indistinguishable in appearance from women who are by conventional standards considered to be 'normal'. In any case, through the evolution towards a unisex, the *masculine* lesbian has acquired a cloak, and is much less easily recognisable than in earlier days. It needs a fine perception and attentive eye to single her out through her expressive behaviour. It is her unconscious gestures that give her away, and in this she resembles the feminine type of the male homosexual.

But how can one diagnose the feminine lesbian if she is indistinguishable from 'normal' women? Certain endocrine dispositions can produce the *feminine* type of lesbian. The very tall eunuchoid woman, who does not menstruate until the age of 17 or later, is a case in point. She is usually undersexed and perhaps because of this, her sexual ambivalence is accentuated and her natural homosexuality reinforced. Infantilism of the uterus and the vagina also predispose a girl to homosexuality because of the difficulty she experiences in normal sexual intercourse. However, both types are ambivalent in their psycho-sexual disposition, and those who are lesbians cannot be diagnosed at a glance. They are in disguise, but a physician's trained eye may divine their libidinous orientation.

As I have already mentioned, women are *physically* "double-sexed", and therefore homosexual by nature. Much of the understanding of lesbianism depends on this fact, but it could never completely explain it. The causes of female homosexuality are both biological and psychological. Psychology, existentialism, sociology, anthropology – all these branches of knowledge must be consulted in the search for a theory of lesbianism which leaves no loopholes.

A PSYCHOLOGICAL VIEWPOINT

Before I explain my own psychological viewpoint, I must comment on the theories outlined in the previous chapter. I have given prominence to the psycho-analytical concept of homosexuality, that of Freud in particular. I must describe how far his and other psycho-analytical concepts are acceptable to me, and where I diverge from them. Certain psycho-analytical ideas on my subject are indisputably true, but I do by no means accept all of them, and even doubt some of their premises.

I have no quarrel with the outsider, Groddek, who treats this serious subject with a remarkable lightness of touch, although he does not go into the heart of the matter. He clarifies, however, the important connection between female homosexuality and cultural evolution. Indeed, the social reformer and the artist are unthinkable without marked homosexual tendencies. How could a woman artist, for example, create anything worth while without knowing the other half, the male side in herself? If it were otherwise, every work of art, be it a painting, a sculpture or a book, which is a world in itself, would be lop-sided. The same applies, of course, to the male artist.

Groddek sees the essence of homosexuality in narcissism. This is a half-truth, as narcissism is never lived down by either homo- or heterosexual people. It remains with all of us throughout life in different degrees of intensity.

The overwhelming evidence of the naturalness of homosexuality in women comes from Freud. He made an essential contribution to the general understanding of homosexuality through pointing out its correlation with the erotogenic zones, and man's bisexual nature. But his specific knowledge of female sexuality and homosexuality took three decades to mature.

I wish to mention first those Freudian ideas which I fully accept:

1. The equally strong love of the girl and boy child towards their mother.
2. The fact that the mother is an all-dominant, God-like figure to the child, and plays an even more important part in the girl's psycho-sexual development than in that of the boy.
3. The importance of the oral fixation on the mother's breast. I must however mention at once that I attach a much more symbolic meaning to this fixation than Freud does.
4. Homosexuality in women (and men) is brought about through constitutional and acquired factors.
5. The psychological importance of the *anatomical* bisexuality of women.

My disagreement starts with Freud's concept of the Oedipus complex.

1. The Oedipus complex is the backbone of Freudian libidinous theory in regard to both homosexuality and heterosexuality. While I believe in the closest attachment of the child, girl or boy, to a parent, I cannot convince myself that this comes about through libido in the first place. Freud and his followers have made sex the nucleus of emotional, and to a certain extent, mental development. This is too stereotyped an attitude. First of all, the fundamental need of every living being is for shelter and food, which means that the drive to keep alive has preference over everything else. And libido may be used to achieve this end. The Oedipus complex exists, but it must be interpreted on different lines from those of psycho-analysis. Already at an early age, the child senses that an adult has the power to decide over its safety, and it uses love to ensure its security. The first attachment is accompanied by fear, which leads to unconscious ingratiation. The child is supported in its need for safety through the maternal instinct of its mother or her substitute.

2. I cannot agree with Freud's concept of the girl's castration complex and penis envy. Almost all homosexual women whom I interviewed wanted to be boys, but did not wish to be male when they were grown up. Why did they want to be boys? It was not because they envied the male organ in itself, but because to them it symbolised freedom, and the power to put them into second place in the affections of their mother.

3. I also disagree with the length of the girl's exclusive mother-attachment which Freud claims.

4. Freud thinks the following conditions are essential for the development of homosexuality:

        a) physical hermaphroditism,

        b) mental sexual characteristics,

        c) kind of object choice.

The third condition is unquestionably true, but physical hermaphroditism is not necessarily correlated with female homosexuality. The idea of mental sexual characteristics is outworn, as they are, in fact, indefinable.

Melanie Klein naturally adheres to the libido theory. I find her concepts of sexual reactions and bonds in earliest infancy fascinating but doubtful. Although she maintains that she deduced them from her analyses of children, I ask myself how much is real, and how much is subjective interpretation. In spite of my criticism of the primacy of sexual libido in infancy, I think her ideas about the early attachments of the child are more realistic than those of Freud. She believes that the child loves and hates both parents equally in infancy. After it sees the parents as separate people, the emphasis of its love alternates from one to the other at different times. Ambivalence in emotional relationships, which is particularly evident in childhood, is a well-known fact. I disagree with Melanie Klein about the castration complex and penis envy in girls, a concept she has taken over from Freud.

I need not comment on the behaviourists' interpretation of homosexuality, as my own views are implied in my brief summary of it.

I can now go into an essential point, my understanding of a girl child's dilemma. The mother is the girl's first and greatest love. The father may be her first flirtation, but he can only be her second love. What about the mother's attitude to the girl child?

A normal woman will, as a rule, prefer a male child. This is due not only to some chemical magnetism, but also to the much greater appreciation a boy enjoys in our man-made society. A girl instinctively knows from an early age that her chances of getting her mother's attention and love are less than those of a brother or of her father. She realises that the male is the winner, and that she is relegated to second place in her mother's affections. There are of course women who prefer their daughter to their son, and have a complete relationship with the former. This is the exception rather than the rule.

When a relationship is labile, incomplete and difficult, emotions of nostalgia and frustration are aroused. Nostalgia can fill a gap in a love relationship, and it surely increases its intensity. Frustration, on the other hand, means distress and more often than not evokes rebellion. Emotions feed on difficulties, and emotional love always has strong ingredients of both nostalgia and frustration. A girl's love for her mother must be looked at from this angle. It is a tragic twist of fate that, in childhood, when a girl most needs her mother's love, she generally gets it in half-measure only, whereas when she is grown up and her mother has reached middle age, the tables are turned. The middle-aged woman desires a complete relationship with her daughter with whom, by then, she identifies. It may however be too late for the daughter to respond to her mother's feelings, and the two pass each other by through the wrong timing of their love for one another. I asked a number of heterosexual women who had sons and daughters about their attitude to them. With two exceptions, they all said they felt emotionally more involved with their daughters after they had reached middle age.

All human beings are throughout life governed by an emotional matriarchate. As neither hetero- nor homosexual people can ever really cut an emotional umbilical cord, the feelings of the deviant personality should be understandable to all because of this common bond. Girls and women are regarded by family and society as the second sex, and this can create another point of contact between the hetero- and homosexual woman. The stigma and degradation of coming second hurts any female particularly badly, because of her mother's attitude to her own sex. One must not forget that the mother is unconsciously regarded by the child as a goddess, and her preference for the male is of equal concern to all females, 'normal' or homosexual. In spite of the fact that the inequality of the sexes is on the way out, albeit rather slowly, the girl still cannot free herself from the fetters of her fundamental insecurity with her mother. This problem persists and will persist because of the natural difficulties in the mother-daughter relationship, a bond which is beset with conflicts.

A girl's psychological destiny starts with doubts and uncertainty. The effects of a feeling of insecurity have to be combated, otherwise life would be a most depressing affair for her. Perhaps the most valuable weapon the girl can use is the will to please and to ingratiate herself, in an attempt to reconcile an enemy. And behind many enemies lurks the image of the mother. The good and clever little girl is a case in point. She attempts to win over the beloved enemy, who would have preferred her to be a boy, through virtue and ambition. Other girls identify with the male and acquire muscle. It is a well-known fact that many girls prefer climbing trees, or any outdoor game for that matter, to playing with dolls and imitating their mother. But little tomboys are in the minority.

Most girls take the opposite role, the imitation of mother, and become women long before the time is ripe. Everything the mother uses to underline her femininity, is applied by the girl, who is inclined to overdo the proceedings. This unconscious defence mechanism serves two purposes, namely, to please the male and to outdo the mother. In this way the girl revenges herself for the loss of what she believes to be her birthright, that is, to come first in her mother's affections. The feminine little girl who plays with her dolls etc. is the *femme à homme* in the making. She rarely becomes a lesbian. These children perpetuate an old-fashioned femininity, not only as a means of escape from their sense of insecurity, but also because of narcissism. They love the admiration of their father and any other male, and blossom out in the realisation that they are more attractive than their male siblings. In short, they get their own back by being wanted and loved, achieving a feeling of security into the bargain. One can assume that complete identification with the old-fashioned female role leads a girl, in the majority of cases, towards 'normality' when grown up. But any girl can develop passionate feelings for another during adolescence. This is part of her normal development, whether or not it leads to sexual contact. Homosexuality in the adolescent girl or boy is part of the normal process of learning to love. At the same period of life, girls experience heterosexual attractions because of the endocrine stimulation attached to the process of growing up. And lesbians, as a rule, are no exception. We must not forget that a woman's anatomical and physiological make-up is *bisexual*, and this manifests itself most strongly in adolescence.

It is not only common- but psychological sense to assume that the feminine little girl has done another job, apart from revenging herself on her mother and satisfying her need to be wanted. She has formed a pathway towards a 'normal' psycho-sexual future by turning her predominant interest to the male. She did not do this, in my view, from a primary sexual interest while playing the little woman as a child, but from puberty onwards, the easy contact with men and a natural attraction put her well on the way which society and family want her to go – the way of marriage and childbearing.

It would be erroneous to assume that the *femme à homme* is *eo ipso* a highly sexed woman. This may or may not be so. Her main interest is to secure a life modelled on the example of her mother and of present-day society, and to feel that she is protected and accepted. She therefore complies with the rules. Convention is a formidable force, and it pays well to obey it.

The marrying type of girl is frequently sexually inadequate or even frigid, while one who is homosexual has a better chance of being sexually alive. It is interesting to note that almost all homosexual women whom I interviewed were tomboys as children. This holds good for the more masculine as well as the more feminine lesbian. Both types, if one can differentiate them at all, showed sexual *virility*. Before they realised their true libidinous preference, they had, with few exceptions, sexual contact with men. Although many found heterosexual intercourse less enjoyable than homosexual love-making, they were, as my statistics show, living out their bisexual nature. Many of them were married, and a number of these realised their homosexuality only after years of marriage.

I have no doubt that lesbianism makes a woman virile and open to *any* sexual stimulation, and that she is more often than not a more adequate and lively partner in bed than a 'normal' woman. It is her virility and aggressiveness that enable her to subject herself to heterosexual intercourse without feeling humiliated. I shall treat this important point later on in this chapter.

Before I do so, I must return to an experience a girl is likely to go through in childhood. A child who is put second by its mother becomes not only insecure but lonely. The loneliness of the girl remains with her throughout life, and it makes a woman a more lonely person than a man. As a girl she combats this feeling of isolation through a herd-like community life. Girls come together in a sort of pseudo-intimacy. They sleep in the same bed in order not to be alone, but without any thought of intimacy. They exchange confidences easily, and walk hand in hand as if they were lovers, adopting such gestures and behaviour as a defence mechanism against loneliness. But in spite of this, it does not disappear. In the end, a girl can develop, through the trauma of her youth, into a woman of real humanity, understanding the needs of others and having genuine sympathy with them, qualities which women so particularly need in their relationships with men, who *emotionally* are the second sex.

Before a girl can reach the stage of sublimating traumatic experiences into constructive attitudes, she has to overcome many difficulties, and sometimes serious emotional disturbances. Anxiety states, phobias, depression, destructive or delinquent behaviour result from bad family conditions in general, but mainly from difficulty in the mother-girl relationship. They refer, in most cases, to the need for love and attention from the mother. They are the pathetic means of forcing her to give to the child what she is withholding – complete attention.

While all women are disposed to loneliness, the emotional disturbances described are found significantly more often in girls who are potential lesbians than in those who are not. In childhood, the capacity for repression is very strong, and in many people neurotic illnesses only become apparent in adult life. The incidence of neurosis and psychosis is significantly higher in homosexual than in heterosexual women. Apart from the innate difficulty of the mother-girl relationship, there is another explanation which may help in the understanding of this situation. While the so-called 'normal' girl forms an early bond with her father and the male in general, the potential lesbian has difficulty in doing so, and a disturbed relationship with father and brothers accentuates her precarious position.

But what about the only child? She has the advantage not to be in competition with a brother, and may be the only focus of interest and emotion for both mother and father. She may grow up under the terrifying umbrella of over-protection and constant parental anxiety for her welfare. If her mother's overpowering presence creates a predominantly 'feminine' world around such a child, she becomes frightened of the male, and she may, because of this fear, develop into a homosexual, feeling safe and cosy only with women. Over-protection has an effect similar to that of lack of protection. It turns people into clingers and hermits. They will search throughout their lives for the female world and the protection of a mother. As a rule they remain infantile in their emotions.

Several of the subjects of my investigation were born during the second world war, and the return home of their father was a shock to them. They regarded him as an interfering and unwelcome stranger, and wanted to get rid of him to be alone again with mother. A traumatic experience such as this is likely to reinforce lesbian tendencies. Dr Eva Bene, in her paper *Female Homosexuality*, deems an unsatisfactory relationship between father and daughter to be a highly significant factor in the origin of lesbianism. She raises a relevant point, but over-stresses its importance by singling it out as a major cause of the condition, which it is not.

The essence of the father-daughter relationship lies, in my view, in the fact that he is an *alien* to the girl. He belongs to a category of beings utterly different from herself and her mother. This alien man arouses curiosity, just as any foreign object arouses curiosity in a child. The girl is compelled to find out about the strange object, and to make herself familiar with it.

The fact that she is the *same* as her mother allows for a natural contact without barriers, except for those which are created by the preference of the mother for the male. A girl's position with her father is in complete contrast to this. Here she is confronted with the unfamiliar. Her approach towards him is impeded by all sorts of signposts indicating difficulties and dangers. In other words, the barriers are up. How can they be surmounted? The alien, as a rule, demonstrates pleasure in the company of his little daughter, and gives her preference over her brothers. This makes her voyage of discovery easier. However, the discomfort of a feeling of strangeness remains, and has to be dealt with step by step.

Curiosity is the root of the tree of knowledge. It is part of the innate equipment of animal and man, designed to control environment. Control is gained through experience and learning, which lead to knowledge. This process can be impeded through frustration and anxiety, resulting from a brain-washing education by parents and teachers. Although brothers are a help to the girl in learning about the male, they are not identified in her mind with the all-powerful father. The problem of getting close to him still remains the same. The fact that he is a god-like person to the child can completely repress her *sexual* curiosity about him. This puts the process of getting to know him into a category of its own. While brothers are, as a rule, only rivals, the father is expected to be both protector and comforter. The girl has to make sure that he fulfils both roles. Flirtation is one way of gaining some control, or even power, over him. She knows that she can win his favours by being feminine, but an independent girl will resent this. To play her role as a woman would add to the inferior status allotted to her by family and society. She must therefore aim to be equal with or superior to the male. She must get her father (and all other male figures for that matter) under her thumb, in order to secure a feeling of safety and self-esteem. She tries, through her relationship with her father, to find a secure place in her environment, and to integrate the alien male into her mental and emotional processes.

Sameness and harmony are the staple of love, while conquest and a sense of power are inimical to it. The alien object may arouse admiration, excitement, and even adoration, but it cannot inspire love. The girl who succeeds in getting the better of her father (and the male in general) without recourse to feminine tricks, may be full of satisfaction and triumph, but she will have learned little about the realities of love in the process. Excitement and adoration are basically narcissistic expressions, and neither can be equated with love.

Sexual curiosity can lead to sexual excitement and satisfaction, but the cycle of sensations stops there. Love is the endless peace of being enveloped by something stronger, fuller, and greater than oneself; it can be compared with the Nirvanah of the Buddhist: the real unalterable bliss. This bliss can only come from the mother and her feminine world.

I have described the structure of the typical father-daughter relationship. The lesbian girl is the one who, by all means at her disposal, will try to find a place of safety inside and outside the family, through her fight for equality with the male. She will not, like other women, play up to him: indeed she despises the very idea of it.

Before I outline a father's possible influence on his daughter's lesbian tendencies, I must discuss the old notion of incest. Sexual excitement, which can be a by-product of learning about the male, is not, as a rule, aroused by the father, but by a brother. The father has an incest problem with his growing daughter which is not reciprocated by her. She uses his sensuous interest in order to dominate him, and to gain confidence in her own powers as a woman. A sexual incest problem exists between sister and brother, but not between daughter and father.

While the mother represents the source of life and love for the child, the father represents the protective wall against the outside world, and, to the girl, the school of knowledge about the male world. The emphasis is on the word male, and not the word masculine, qualities generally attributed to the male. The father may have a more feminine personality than the mother.

Any lesbian girl has the ambition to be worth a man, even if she is what one calls the feminine type. Father and brothers are rivals in her desire for mother's love, far more so than is the case with the 'normal' girl. Even if the lesbian has a positive relationship with her father, he is never her desired object. She may come into very close contact with him because she must know him in order to beat him vis-à-vis her mother. On the basis of rivalry, this relationship can lead to an ambivalent friendship and to admiration. It is built on identification and resentment, and jealousy grows only too well on this ground. The lesbian girl rejects her father even under the best of circumstances. But she may look for friendship and companionship to him and the male, because, for obvious reasons, she prefers the male world to the female one. The main cause of this preference is her persistent feeling of inferiority in regard to her mother's affections.

The girl whose libido develops in a heterosexual direction, has, in some ways, a more difficult life to face than the homosexual woman. She may be stuck in the infantile position of little girl trying to please father, and go on pleasing lover and husband. She is destined to be an even more lonely person than a lesbian. The love a man can give her is bound to fall short in essentials, which only a mother can provide. It is she herself who has to supply these. She has to become what she could not possess – the mother – in her relationship with the male. This transformation is the basis of her relationship with lover or husband. The reward for her maturity lies in a 'normal' family life and children.

The term maturity needs examination. Maturity, so far as it exists at all, is patchy, as everybody is immature in some ways. The heterosexual woman remains immature because of her way of playing up to men, but she becomes mature in her capacity to deal with her problem of loneliness. The homosexual woman is mature in her pursuit of independence from male superiority. It need hardly be mentioned that many heterosexual women strive for the same goal, but with the homosexual woman the fight for independence has more teeth, and is decisive in her human relationships. A lesbian may be considered immature because of her desire to re-establish a lost paradise – the union with her mother. She is unable to transform herself into the genuinely maternal female, and to become what she was unable to possess. While her 'normal' sisters have an incest problem of a predominantly sexual nature with their brothers, she has an incest problem of a predominantly emotional nature with her mother. *Emotional incest with the mother is indeed the very essence of lesbianism.*

It governs the whole range of emotional reactions of all homosexual women, be they the masculine or the feminine type, or, more accurately, the more or less *virile* lesbian. Homosexual women possess a considerable flexibility in their emotional attitudes, and can adopt the role of mother or child, of aggressiveness or surrender with equal ease.

One cannot underline too strongly that masculine and feminine qualities are independent of sex. However, a father whose behaviour and outlook on life are feminine is unlikely to give a feeling of stability to his family. A weak father is unable to implant in his daughter the conviction that he is a protector and a strength. If his conduct and beliefs lack ethical values, the girl is bound to feel completely let down, especially if she is put into the background by her mother's preference for a male. The influence of a weak and bad father undermines the sense of security in any child. The effect of a family situation without paternal love and authority is even worse for a girl with lesbian orientation. A negative father-image certainly reinforces homosexual tendencies to the point of exclusive lesbian fixation.

Parental neglect is a frequent cause of neurotic illnesses, but lesbians are more likely than 'normal' women to suffer from these conditions, because of their feeling of isolation and the social pressures to which they are subjected.

Psycho-analysis, like other branches of psychology, could not escape the erosion of its teaching by time. Certain psycho-analytic concepts, for example the notions of masculine and feminine and of the sanctity of the family, are cases in point. They have lost their authoritative relevance. The era of high capitalism stood at the cradle of psycho-analysis, and the shadow it cast over it has never vanished, in spite of the considerable transformation which Freudian thinking has undergone.

AN EXISTENTIALIST VIEW

The existentialist who has contributed most to the understanding of lesbianism is not a psychologist or psychiatrist, but the writer Simone de Beauvoir. The chapter *The Lesbian* in her book *The Second Sex*, contains the most enlightened view on the subject which I have come across so far. She also touches in other chapters of her book on lesbian love. Here are a few quotations from Chapter IV (*The Lesbian*):

> Whether a matter of infantile fixation or of masculine protest, homosexuality is thus regarded as arrest of development. But as a matter of fact, the lesbian is no more an 'undeveloped' woman than a 'superior' one. The history of an individual is not a fatalistically determined progression: at each moment the past is reappraised, so to speak, through a new choice, and the 'normality' of the choice gives it no preferred value – it must be evaluated according to its authenticity.

And:

The great mistake of the psycho-analysts is, through moralistic conformity, to regard it (homosexuality) as never other than an inauthentic attitude.
Further :
And if nature is to be invoked, one can say that all women are naturally homosexual.
And :
As I have already pointed out, when men set themselves up as subjects, they also set themselves apart : when they regard the other as a thing to be taken, they make a deadly attack upon the virile ideal in the other, and likewise in themselves.

In the last paragraph of Chapter IV one finds the following :

The truth is that homosexuality (lesbianism) is no more perversion deliberately indulged in than it is a curse of fate. *It is an attitude chosen in a certain situation* – that is at once motivated and freely adopted.

The passages quoted reveal the gist of existentialist thought, and they had a considerable influence on my theory of lesbianism. I have fully adopted some of Simone de Beauvoir's statements, others with a certain criticism. I am in complete agreement with her when she confirms that all women are by nature homosexual. I find it equally convincing when she says that man looks at, and treats, woman like an object, and sets himself up as a subject. This sentence, by the way, contains the most relevant insight into the situation of woman as it has been for some thousand years and still is today. I am critical of Simone de Beauvoir's assumption that psycho-analysts consider homosexuality to be an arrest of development and an inauthentic attitude.

Freud makes it perfectly clear in his *Three Essays of the Theory of Sexuality* that homosexuality is a normal condition and not a neurosis, and he stresses the point that homosexuals should not be set apart from the rest of the community. It follows from this that homosexuality represents the same authentic attitude as heterosexuality in psycho-analytic thought.

It seems strange, but is nevertheless a fact, that different schools of psychology look at each other from behind a wall of mistrust and hostility. Existentialists have entrenched themselves against psycho-analysis, although Simone de Beauvoir does give it some credit for its merits.

Be that as it may, nobody can deny that existentialism has revolutionised modern thinking. I had the good fortune to be taught in my youth by the fathers of existentialism, the phenomenologists Professor Husserl and the then Dr Heidegger. An early training in a new doctrine leaves an indelible mark on one's mind, especially when one's teachers are of a brilliant and creative cast of mind. My penchant for existentialist thought and attitudes goes back to my first year at the University of Freiburg im Breisgau, where I read philosophy apart from studying medicine.

Existentialists proclaim that an individual can at any given moment alter his attitudes, and thus change the course of his life. The freedom to reappraise one's situation at any time, and to take decisive action about it, gives dignity to man without the crutches of morals. Existentialism is a philosophy of liberation, which looks at the original nature and meaning of man and objects. Its human importance lies in the attempt to make people think for themselves, and discard second-hand thoughts and attitudes. Such an ideal is well worth aiming at even if only those who are creative can achieve it. Existentialism is really both a philosophy and a creed, because it stresses the absolute necessity for authenticity in all and everything, and insists that every human being must take full responsibility for his behaviour and actions under all circumstances. Neurosis, for example, is no excuse for failing to do so.

If one keeps this in mind, one can understand Simone de Beauvoir's assertion that lesbianism is an attitude of choice, a way of life preferred to any other. The implication that human beings are in control of their destiny through the power of consciousness over unconscious drives is, however, a doubtful assumption. It contradicts the Freudian and other psychological schools. This is of course no argument against it. My personal doubt about the validity of this point of view comes from my experience as a psychiatrist, as an observer of human behaviour, and last but not least from statements made by lesbians themselves. I asked a number of my interviewees why they chose to

live their lives in the way they did. They all stared at me in
astonishment, if not with disapproval. Their unanimous answer
was: 'I had no choice; it happened that way'. The educational
and intellectual level of the person concerned made no difference to her reply. The most brilliant ones were as sure about the
inevitability of their way of life as those who had a mediocre
I.Q. Although the said existentialist assertion is contradicted by
the actual situation, it can nevertheless hold its own on another
account. It is a postulate for the psychical evolution of man
through consciousness – a goal towards which all of us must
strive. If we do not accept this challenge, we are bound to perish
as individuals and as people. Ideas can be right and wrong at
the same time, and their relevance depends on the context in
which they are tested.

It is a fact that the emotional element is far more decisive for
a lesbian ménage than for a heterosexual one. Whether she is
married or not, a woman who chooses a man may be ruled by
her head rather than by her heart. A heterosexual marriage, in
the conventional sense, makes its début as a social contract as
well as a personal one. The approval of society eases the pressure
of emotional issues. It is, in other words, much easier for a
heterosexual woman than for a homosexual one to make a
conscious choice of her partner. Many other forces, apart from
their emotions, cause lesbians to combine their lives on an
explosive ground, which is a danger to themselves and their
relationships. One cannot say that they are less mature than
'normal' women, as their pronounced emotiveness is the result
of their situation rather than the state of their psychical development. The challenge to make a conscious choice can be answered
successfully only by very few and very independent lesbians. I
know only one woman who consciously entered a partnership
with another because it gave her greater scope for development
as an artist and a personality. The stability of partnership
between lesbians is endangered through their high degree of
emotionalism. But true *emotion* is the key to their attachments
and their search for fulfilment. It overrides reason and often
plays havoc with their professional application and achievement. *Thus emotion is both the rapture and the danger of the
lesbian's personal and collective life.*

When Simone de Beauvoir says that 'man sets himself up as

a subject and treats woman as a thing to be taken', she touches on the most sensitive spot of a woman's predicament. The male commits emotional violence on the female by reducing her to the status of an object. This crime of trespassing on another person's right to be herself also damages him, since it must, at some time or other, lead to alienation between the sexes. So far man has been victorious in implanting a feeling of inferiority into most women. The female psyche has for centuries absorbed the idea that woman is reactive and placid, and her emotional responses are tuned accordingly. Although this male imposition must be regarded as an influence outside herself, a woman's acceptance of it as an inevitable necessity has become a leading motif in her emotional repertoire. How is one to sever an outer pressure which produces a special brand of emotion from natural emotion itself? Both are welded together so as to be indistinguishable from one another.

Behaviourists could explain this state of affairs through wrong learning. Brainwashing over the centuries has certainly been responsible for the female position. A change towards a greater equality of the sexes is now almost in sight, if women want it or are able to want it. Habits of several thousand years are difficult to break, and too many women are afraid of freedom.

How odd that young men of today refer to girls as 'birds' and 'chicks'! Girls do not, as far as I know, return such back-handed compliments. They allow themselves to be put into the same category as pets. To treat another person as an object shows a condescending attitude, and condescension is alienation. Women who do not rebel against the status of object have declared themselves defeated as persons in their own right. They have become inauthentic by accepting the role of puppets on a string performing movements directed by the hand of man. It is difficult to understand why present-day young men depreciatingly refer to women by the names of animals, because the gap between the sexes has never been as narrow as it is now. I suspect that the flippancy and condescension expressed in words is only a pose, and not a genuine attitude. Or is it simply the last reflex of a dying male arrogance in the face of a new appraisal of woman by herself, an appraisal which is shared by many men in progressive quarters of society? The 'baby', the 'chick', and the 'bird' may still make a show in the street, but it is difficult

c

to find this type of woman in the centres of learning, the professions, the civil service, the police.

The lesbian has never accepted the status of an object. It is in this rejection of female inferiority and masquerade that she steps outside the 'eternal' habits of her sex. Although the Suffragettes gave invaluable service to the social liberation of women, real emancipation starts with the realisation that they are entities in themselves, persons who are both connected with and separate from other people, regardless of their sex. In other words, their inner liberation begins when they rebel against being an object. Only those who can live alone in the widest sense can successfully live with others.

The lesbian was and is unquestionably in the avant-garde of the fight for equality of the sexes, and for the psychical liberation of woman. She has the makings of the best soldier in the battle for a woman's right to independence. Whatever their physical type, educational level, temperament or mentality, all homosexual women are *one* in their rejection of bondage to the male. They refuse to be the second sex. Already as children, they loathe girlish giggles and behaviour, and resent having to do the household chores from which their brothers are exempt. It is deadening for a homosexual woman to be regarded by a man as a thing, as a background for or an instrument of enjoyment. The lesbian's nostalgia for a homosexual world and her compulsive wish for a woman's love make it easy for her to opt out of conventional society. She has far less to lose than a heterosexual woman, and this fact diminishes her merit somewhat. She follows the command of her emotional needs in giving a lead in the liberation of woman from man and from an outdated image of herself.

A 'normal' woman, conscious of herself, needs a far more complex mechanism to reconcile her wish to be a self-contained, independent person. On the one hand she must allow herself to be an object in order to get a man, on the other she will look down on herself for doing so. Unless she takes a cynical view of the use of her femininity, she is bound to suffer from a sense of inferiority. Perhaps the division between femininity and self creates the famous mystique of woman! She suffers from conflicting loyalties, one to herself, the other to her heterosexual instincts. Remarkable women and staunch feminists frequently suffer from masochistic tendencies, and are constantly afraid of being unattractive to men. Theirs is a difficult lot, as they are inclined to get fixated on a sadistic male.

The best way out of the woman's dilemma appears to be a change of roles : she taking that of the subject, and making *him* the object. Indeed, one finds this very attitude among many aggressive women, with strong lesbian tendencies more or less successfully suppressed. Many lesbians themselves are married with families, and though they prefer women to men, they remain in the stream of ordinary life and convention. They do not have the courage to show their true colours, and they deny that they are homosexual and unable to fall in love with men. They also suffer from divided loyalties : one to their real nature, the other to their responsibilities towards their families.

The one and only way to achieve equality and progress in human as well as love relationships lies in the expression of the whole bisexual nature of every man and woman. Are we on the way to it? It looks like it, although social rules of past centuries still exist side by side with modern conventions and a new outlook on the future. In a society where bisexuality could be fully expressed and accepted, the family as we know it would be broken up. Such a situation, should it come to pass, could alter the problems of lesbianism, but it is my task to explain the latter as it is seen under present circumstances.

Women who consider themselves integral persons, and independent of male dictation in their personal and professional life, are called feminists. The term suggests both a somewhat eccentric and a partisan attitude, which could be interpreted as an affront to men, but in fact it is not so. The word feminist does not express the meaning of what it tries to convey. A better description would be the term equalist, since all feminists, be they homo- or heterosexual women or men, have the same objective, namely the equality of the sexes in every sphere of life.

The lesbian's refusal to be an inferior to man is absolute, while with 'normal' women the rejection of man's superiority remains relative. Married lesbians often conform automatically to conventions, and are not always conscious of themselves as integral entities. My survey showed that a number of them only discovered their homosexuality after years of marriage, but when that happened, they changed in their attitude to their husband

and—far more important—to themselves. They discovered their *selves*, and with it, their *absolute* rejection of being an object. They realised then that they had never felt their position as wives as genuine, but had played a part which education and convention prescribed for them. The unease they had always felt was only brought home to them when they experienced the spontaneity of homosexual society.

The majority of my subjects were unmarried professional women, and with them the subject-object relationship to men could be seen in its fundamental state. None of them had any doubt about their early realisation that they could not bear to be looked at by a boy as a desirable female. One can easily explain this symptom of rejection in the masculine lesbian with hormonal abnormality, but it was by no means confined to her. The existentialist and the psycho-analytic interpretations of the lesbian's attitude are, in this particular instance, so closely connected that they can hardly be separated from each other.

The lesbian's yearning for her mother's love is always put in jeopardy through the existence of a male. Even as an only child, the girl cannot get over the suspicion that her mother would be more profoundly loving towards her if she were a boy. Competition with the male is one of the principal causes of her rejection of him. By resenting the male as a rival, either in reality or in imagination, she identifies with him and tries to outdo him, just as a naturalised citizen overdoes his patriotism in order to be equal to those who are natives of the country. She wants to be the one who chooses, and cannot accept that he wants to make her feel a chosen object. The core of an independent personality finds a good opportunity for growth in this atmosphere of self-assertion and aggression.

The girl with exclusive lesbian tendencies, whose rejection of the male sex is absolute, has to find some way of living in the society of men, whom, after all, she cannot avoid in her professional and social contacts. She often seeks the friendship of homosexual men, although the latter frequently exhibit prejudice and dislike of lesbians. Comradeship with 'normal' men is another way out, and is successful in many cases. Indeed, the exclusively homosexual woman may prefer friendship with ordinary men to friendship with either homosexual men or women. The lesbian of outstanding intellect and gifts may find friendship with men not only a way out of a dilemma but a necessity. Her love for women is whole-hearted, but may not supply all her needs. Even if she finds a partner of equality, she needs approval of her work in her profession from a man, if she is to feel on safe ground. Gertrude Stein is said to have lived according to this pattern. She somehow looked down on women as intellects, and at her celebrated gatherings, she concentrated on her men friends, who were the most creative and famous people of her time. This happened some 40 years ago, and the social situation has changed meanwhile. I heard, however, of a similar attitude from a number of my interviewees, who preferred men to women as friends, simply because they felt better adjusted to their surroundings in being accepted by men. Although they were among the most intelligent and gifted of my subjects, they could not claim to be particularly brilliant.

The issue of being either the subject or the object in a relationship is not confined to the relationship between a man and a woman. It has far wider repercussions. It dominates, by all appearances, homosexual bonds, and indeed most human relationships. A lesbian who wants another woman treats her as an object, and the one who makes herself attractive to a partner treats herself as an object. What then is the difference, if it exists, between them and heterosexual people, since their behaviour seems to be alike? The answer is this:

To be the object of another woman's love is the primary aim of all lesbians, who (unconsciously) seek nothing else but emotional incest with their mother. This, however, does not mean that they all wish to be objects, only wanting to be the child and on the receiving end. Although the full development of maternal feelings is outside the reach of most lesbians, they adopt different roles at different times, and often in quick succession. In fact they change from the lover to the beloved as children do in their games. Far from labelling this as arrested development, which implies moral judgement, I consider their flexibility in changing roles to be an asset. Lesbians show enough individual differences in their virility and imagination to create the tensions which are necessary for any emotional relationship. With them the role of subject or object is a matter of emphasis, an emphasis which is handed over from one partner to the other with ease. Homosexual women are therefore both subject and object to each other at the same time. Herein lies the fundamental difference between homosexual and heterosexual relationships. Women who love their own sex love the sameness in the other. It could be argued that 'normal' people in love are also both subject and object to each other, and sophisticated heterosexual partners often change from the male to the female role and vice versa, and include a lesbian repertoire in their love-making. One must not, however, be deceived by a superficial similarity. When a heterosexual woman loves a man she is confronted with otherness, and so is a man who loves a woman. Otherness implies something completely different from oneself, something one has to learn to understand and to live with. Otherness is therefore the key to our understanding of the real difference between lesbian and 'normal' love. The similarity of behaviour is only spurious, as it does not reveal the model on which heterosexual love is built. At one time or another, the 'normal' woman will always be put back into the place of being an object.

The crux of the matter is the lesbian's emotional negation of the male, which goes with her refusal to be his object. Her *sexual* rejection of men is not absolute. The question of heterosexual intercourse is taken rather lightly by many homosexual women because, for them, it has nothing to do with love and therefore does not touch the heart of the matter – their emotional fixation on women. Many lesbians have affairs with men, especially in the experimental period of their life. Physical contact with the opposite sex is easier for them than for the homosexual man, because of their anatomical bisexuality. But an emotional love-relationship with a man is unthinkable for a lesbian, as it would annihilate her in the quick of her being. The necessity of emotional independence from the male puts the lesbian's attitude to men in its proper perspective. *It is not homosexuality but homoemotionality which is the centre and the very essence of women's love for each other.*

Sexual expression between them is far more emotional in character than it is with heterosexual couples. It is not that the sexual act remains unsatisfactory for them. They experience, in many cases, great satisfaction because of the complete knowledge of their mutual reactions in both their primitive and subtle varieties. The sex act is, however, always secondary with them. It is only a manifestation of their emotional love, but for this very reason they attach so much importance to it. Sexual embraces symbolise for lesbians a kind of oath, a commitment to one another. Perhaps this could explain much of the well-known violence of their feelings of jealousy. Theirs is a different kind of commitment and jealousy from that of heterosexual couples. With normal people the range of physical contacts as well as responsibilities and commitments is wider, which allows for a firmer basis of relationship and a better balanced emotional climate.

REACTIONS TO SOCIAL PRESSURES

Apart from the times of enlightened paganism in ancient Greece and Rome, homosexuality has been severely punished since biblical times. The Old and New Testaments considered sexual intercourse between man and man, and woman and woman as a deadly sin, to be punishable by death. It is generally known that male homosexuals were in greater peril than women during most periods of history. Nevertheless female homosexuality, although it has remained more protected from the vengeance of the law, was always regarded as an unspeakable vice. The deadly witch hunt of homosexuals went on until the nineteenth century, in any case where men were concerned, and the death penalty for them was still in force in England until 1861.

During the middle ages the persecution became fanatic, and the Carolingian Law prescribed the death penalty also for women who committed sexual offences with women. In Article 116 of this infamous law of the year 1532, one finds the following passage, which I quote in German from Dr Klimmer's book *Die Homosexualität*, and in the English translation:

So Mann mit Mann, Weib mit Weib, Mensch mit Vieh Unkeuschheit treibed, die haben auch das Leben verwirket.
(If man and man, woman and woman, people and animals, are found to have sexual intercourse, they will be punished by death.)

This law is officially still in existence in Austria and Spain, though it is of course never applied.

The eighteenth century saw the first opposition to this inhuman persecution. Voltaire, for example, pointed out that homosexuality is no crime if it does not harm other people, and is not practised for ulterior motives. (This is mentioned by Dr Klimmer in his book cited above.)

This very brief summary of a history of persecution makes certain emotional reactions of present-day homosexual women and men understandable, since no minority escapes the shadow of its past. The effect of a threat to life and limb lingers in the ancient part of the brain of those who belonged to persecuted units. They are marked people. Even if the sign that distinguishes them from others has become more or less invisible, it lives on as a residue in their minds. The hand of the law is retracted, but moral condemnation persists, and homosexuals are treated as outcasts and driven into hiding places. In the year 1971, lesbians are still in hiding. They dare not show their inclinations openly either inside or outside their family. Many do not let their heterosexual friends know that they are homosexual, such is the persisting fear of rejection. They are absolutely secretive about their orientation in social contacts, and most of all in their professional milieu. Only very few, who are militant either because of conviction or because of their own character, never deny what they are and how they feel. Some do so from bravado and exhibitionism. Others never raise the question whether to hide or not to hide, but show themselves in their true colours without making anything of it. They can be found among artists, writers, and professional women. The outside world does not bother about their private life when their merits are outstanding. Gertrude Stein, Natalie Barney and Renée Vivienne are examples of an authentic attitude towards themselves and society. Their emotional orientation certainly made no difference to their impact on literature and the milieu in which they lived. They must have given strength and pride to many lesbians who knew them either personally or through their work. The women named are now dead; they belonged to the first half of the century, but they are succeeded in their attitude by lesbians of today, whose names, for obvious reasons, cannot be mentioned.

Although the three great women quoted were quite exceptional people, their influence on the morale of ordinary lesbians must not be underestimated. Renée Vivienne's poems are now read at literary evenings arranged by lesbian societies in London, and books by Gertrude Stein and Natalie Barney are in all the reputable libraries here and in America.

While the lesbian of today holds her head high when she is among her own kind, she is still the 'odd woman out' in the outside world. Every lesbian is heir to the fate of her predecessors. Their past is a mental burden which singles her out as a person who has to live down a destiny fraught with tragedy. It is a destiny which has much in common with that of the Jews. The very image of the wandering Jew who cannot settle down anywhere, who is nowhere really at home, illustrates the fate of most homosexual women. The Jews have now found a country of their own, and the existence of Israel has already altered many of their self-protective and defensive characteristics. Perhaps, in the not too distant future, a greater tolerance and understanding by society will produce the same result in homosexual women. The fact that the destiny of a lesbian is fundamentally tragic in both her own eyes and those of outsiders underlines the inevitability of being a lesbian. Hers is not a life chosen, but a destiny beyond choice. Homosexual women are more violently overcome by their emotions than heterosexual women. They are, indeed, cornered through their emotionalism in every aspect of their relationships. Psychological interpretations of their deviation cannot explain their situation and their dilemma without taking into account the social factor past and present.

Many lesbians whom I interviewed would have preferred to be men, particularly in their youth, not because they wished to have male sexual organs, but because of the social and professional advantages accorded to men in our society. They did not wish to be 'normal', and thought that being a lesbian was the next best thing to being a man. This attitude applied to all of them, irrespective of their more masculine or feminine dispositions. It was not that man's supremacy in our society had made them lesbians, but it had strengthened their natural inclination and nourished their sense of identity and personal freedom. The majority of my sample belonged to the middle and lower middle classes. Most of them were secretaries, typists, bank clerks, nurses and teachers. They are, like most of us, cogs in the wheel. At work, where they are dependent on superiors on the one hand and colleagues on the other, their deviation, if it were known, could be considered an outrage against decency. Lesbians who want to safeguard their jobs and enjoy the security of an ordered life are therefore forced to become hypocrites. Even if they were not dismissed from employment, the strain of enduring a possible ridicule and rejection, should they dare to show their true colours, would make their life hell. Inevitably, the conflict between integrity and adaptation to circumstances casts a persistent shadow over their collective existence. Some lesbians try to overcome this difficulty by keeping away as much as possible from their comrades; they stay aloof through adopting what one may call neutrality of behaviour and appearances. They settle for a compromise, which allows them to remain themselves up to a point, by making as few concessions to convention as possible. In other words, they refuse to play-act at being normal, neither admitting nor camouflaging their homosexuality. I know of a few lesbians who actually did let their employers know of their emotional orientation, yet suffered no setbacks in their jobs; but they were exceptional people, who held key appointments in industry. The majority of the homosexuals in my study were in rather menial jobs, and might have had good reason to fear dismissal if they gave themselves away.

Some lesbians make stupendous efforts to hide their deviation. They behave like chameleons, and take on the colours of their milieu in every way, even over-emphasising their femininity by using extra make-up and wearing extra feminine clothes. They chat with other girls about the other sex and accept dates with men. They pay a heavy price for their pretence, because of the nervous strain and anxiety involved in dissimulation. In spite of subterfuges, they live in constant fear of being found out, as if they were delinquents in hiding from the police. The effects of either continuous restraint or play-acting and hypocrisy are obvious. They narrow down, for example, the scale of any real feeling towards heterosexual men and women, and put a stop to spontaneity in any other milieu than their own. Herein lies a tragedy : lesbians truly want to be good and law-abiding citizens, and to contribute their bit to the community as people accepted on their merits. They contribute, in fact, just as well and as much as normal people, but their credit might be immediately minimised if their deviation were known. Most lesbians bring the cargo of goods they have to give to society into port under a neutral flag, a flag which denies their true identity. The majority of my interviewees insisted that they managed to integrate themselves into their working milieu very well, but I had the impression that this was wishful thinking. And if they do manage to feel safe in their jobs, they must unconsciously be haunted by the knowledge that they always have to deny what they are. Their wish to be 'normal' citizens overrides the realisation that they have to over-stretch themselves emotionally to appear so. It is mainly in the estimate of their collective cohesion with society that they deceive themselves. They are fully conscious of their own problems, and of the difficulties of the lesbian situation in general. They know that they have to be secretive, even furtive, and also that the fear of being outcasts makes them actively or defensively aggressive.

Extreme social pressures must lead to emotional defects. Two of the most regrettable are the lesbian's unreliability in personal relationships, and her emotional instability. Both traits affect her personal life rather than her profession, where she shows, as a rule, consistent and conscientious behaviour, probably more through fear than virtue. As in all general conclusions, there are a good many exceptions to the rule, but the trend towards these defects is unquestionable.

Lesbians live their lives underground, and wear a mask in their contacts with the outside world. Different psychological schools claim that paranoid traits are part of the homosexual syndrome. It is true that a feeling of persecution follows the lesbian throughout her life, a reaction which, however, is not due to her particular emotional difficulties but is induced by society. A heightened apprehension, ideas of reference etc., must therefore be regarded as a defence mechanism, which has been evolved through both the historical and actual situation in which lesbians found and find themselves. This reaction type shows again a transmission of mental traits which is bound not to chromosomes and genes, but to a spiritual link between generations. According to Teilhard de Chardin, in his *The Phenomenon of Man*, consciousness of the past exists in the present and goes on existing and evolving in the future. He has coined the term 'Noosphere' to describe this process, which does not only work constructively, but also destructively. For generations, lesbians have been actively or passively persecuted, and this has forced upon them a constant sense of danger, accompanied by a heightened fear and awareness of hostility. *Paranoid tendencies are endemic in lesbianism.* They cannot be considered a symptom of psychosis, because they are, in the first instance, induced by an outside source, society. However, this defence mechanism represents a potential danger to the mental equilibrium of many lesbians. It can only be changed and perhaps cured through a changed attitude of society.

How then does society in England and America look at lesbians, and how can one find this out apart from studying the reactions of homosexuals themselves? I saw an article on homosexuality in the periodical *Time*, of October 24th 1969, which reports on a poll taken for CBS television. The following is a quotation from this article : 'It (the poll) revealed that two out of three Americans look on homosexuals with disgust, discomfort or fear, and one in ten regards them with outright hatred'. The article mentions that 12 million American men and women are homosexuals. In a recent survey of the attitude of young people in England to homosexuals, a similar verdict was returned. The quoted sentence gives an idea of the collective judgment in both countries, but the aim of the article is to report on a survey on homosexuality by a research team sponsored by the Federal Government's National Institute of Mental Health. The psychologist, Evelyn Hooker, principal of the team, prepared the report, which shows that popular prejudice is unfounded. The report recommends a complete change of attitude to homosexual men and women, by employers and by society as a whole. Misinformed, prejudiced opinions persist among the public in many other countries, apart from America and England. This seems strange after seventy years of psychological teaching on the subject by Hirschfeld, Havelock Ellis, Freud and others. At the present time newspapers, the theatre and the cinema give male and female homosexuality a sympathetic hearing and viewing. The mass media are promoting better conditions for both male and female homosexuality. Two years ago, Bryan Magee showed a good and entirely sympathetic film about lesbians on television. A play, *The Killing of Sister George*, subsequently made into a film, aroused some public sympathy, even if it did not present an entirely attractive picture of lesbianism. Serious newspapers like the London *Times* and the German *Die Zeit* are alert for news of scientific publications about lesbianism from Great

Britain, America and other countries. Aston University, Birmingham, has organised several symposia on homosexuality at which lectures on lesbianism have been given. A founder member of Kenric also lectured at the University of Loughborough on the same theme, and her talks were reported in *The Daily Telegraph*. Undoubtedly, public opinion has changed, for otherwise newspapers would not be interested in giving up space to information on this taboo subject. As far as one can judge, no change in the attitude of the average person has yet occurred, and the lesbian population does not feel any more secure through the attention given to it and the publicity made in its interest. Is this publicity in the true interest of lesbians? Everybody knows that neither show business nor newspapers can avoid giving a somewhat sensational slant to lesbianism because this is in their business interest. It is questionable whether it is to the advantage of the people concerned, although it is healthier to have the subject aired than suppressed. One may ask what the words 'society' and 'public opinion' really mean. Are these terms vague generalisations, words reduced to indistinct shadows of a meaning because of the mechanical and unthinking use made of them? I think that this is the case. It is more useful to speak of *groups* of individuals reacting similarly to ideas, problems and people. Groups with an international and broadminded outlook, for example, will probably be glad to see strangers in their midst; other groups not endowed with the same spirit will hate outsiders. Broadminded and intelligent people are, as a rule, prepared to accept what may be personally alien to them. 'Public opinion' is therefore non-existent as a united or unifying voice. One can only speak of group opinions inside a population.

We live now in the second age of reason, an age which is geared to dispel superstition and prejudice. In spite of this, most groups inside Great Britain and the United States retain their idiosyncrasies and reject homosexuals. Why? Lesbianism is too near the bone for many women, and too disorientating to the arrogance of most men. In the sphere of primitive emotions, rationality cannot overcome prejudice. I suspect that one would find also in the broadminded groups some men and women who cannot accept the lesbian in their midst. Most heterosexual people assume that their emotional and sexual territory is threatened by these 'abnormal' individuals. Only when it is recognised that the territories of hetero- and homosexuals do, in fact, overlap can a new era of tolerance begin. The time will come when the fact that every human being is bisexual is understood and accepted. It will come when the present permissive and obsessive society is transformed into a relaxed, understanding, and knowledgable one. There is no sign of it so far. Lesbians who have to earn their living are still frightened of coming out into the open. Those who belong to the upper classes do not reveal that they are homosexual for another reason. They are apprehensive about their status in society, and it is this that compels them to conceal their emotional orientation. In most instances they only succeed in deceiving themselves, but not their friends and acquaintances. They may, however, manage to silence evil tongues because nothing can be proved.

The beginning of a more self-assertive attitude can, however, be observed among members of the middle classes. The fact that several organisations such as Kenric, the Albany Trust and the Minorities Research Trust have come into existence during the last seven years signals constructive resistance against persecution, and the establishment of a new collective background – a homeland for the like-minded. Journals such as *The Ladder* in America, *Arena Three* in Great Britain, and the newsletters of Kenric give expression to lesbian views and provide a means of communication between them. The newsletter sent out every month by Kenric, which at present has a membership of about five hundred, never publishes a member's surname. Meetings held in private houses are advertised by telephone numbers only. Fear of discovery was also apparent when a number of my interviewees expressed the wish not to give me their surnames and addresses. It came to my knowledge that several lesbians did not participate in my research because they were afraid that some information about them might leak out, in spite of the fact that they knew that as a physician I was bound to professional secrecy, as had been made clear in all my appeals.

Woman as we know her today is essentially an artifice, except in those areas of the world where civilisation has hardly scratched the surface of life. The sense of property, culminating in capitalism, shaped both the appearance and the behaviour of women in the western world. The male also underwent a shaping and mis-shaping process through the pressures of civilisation. He has however been less affected by it than the female, who became what he wanted her to be. Although the proclamation of women's rights gave them a certain freedom, particularly in the professional sphere, the old custom of subjugation to the demands of man dies hard. The lesbian has not escaped the inevitable change through social evolution either. But has she perhaps remained closer to the authentic woman than the 'normal' female? She has been far less gripped and affected by male demands which determined character traits and emotional reactions in other women, and she insisted on the equality of the sexes long before women's rights were declared. Nevertheless social pressures took their toll of her too, and brought about the characteristic mental and emotional features I mentioned earlier in this chapter. It is because of their influence on the character and personality of homosexual women that responses to social pressures form an essential aspect of lesbianism.

EARLY HISTORY AND THE LESBIAN

The question whether the lesbian is at least as authentic a woman, if not more so, than the 'normal' female, may possibly be answered by anthropologists. Eva L. R. Meyerowitz made a special study of the Akan peoples of Ghana, who have a matrilineally organised society in its most developed form. It is the only one which has survived into the twentieth century. Eva Meyerowitz maintains that its earliest stage was the matriarchate which is believed to have come into being in the fertile regions of the Near East at the time when the growing of foodstuffs was discovered. From the fourth millennium onwards, the matriarchate was diffused by emigrants into Africa. There were four phases in all, the latter two developed by the ancient Egyptians, and each a further step towards patrilinearity.

Characteristic features of the first phase, the matriarchate, are the following:

The matriarch was thought of as a divine woman, for she personified the great Mother Goddess on earth, and ruled a clan or confederation of clans. The women of that era were busy tilling the fields while the men were away hunting. The women were consequently bound to the soil, and became the rulers of the community. To start with, they became rulers of villages, then of towns, which were finally organised into a confederation of several cities. Women therefore created the first state.

In contrast, the patrilineally organised peoples were nomadic, and lived in tribal groupings. They invaded the Near East, fused with the matriarchal peoples, and joined them in the government of the community. From that time on (about 4000 B.C.) the city states were no longer exclusively ruled by the divine matriarch, for her son ruled at her side as the divine king and governor of men. According to Meyerowitz, we know through the history of the Akan that the matriarch or 'female king', (queen mother is the European term) continued to rule the women folk. She presided over a council of women, had her own government officials, treasurers, judges, etc., who had the same rank and title as the ministers of the king, and she had the last word in state affairs. She also had a bodyguard whose members, women beyond the menopause, were active soldiers. They fought in the front line to encourage the men, and when killed in battle, were buried with military honours. They are in direct line of descent from the Amazons of Asia Minor in antiquity.

The great Mother Goddess of the matriarchal peoples was worshipped as the creator of the universe, and she was accredited with both female and male powers. Long after the matriarchate had come to an end, she was still worshipped in Mesopotamia as the 'Bearded Ishtar', and in Syria and Phoenicia as the 'Bearded Ashtart'. Eva L. Meyerowitz reports that the matrilineal type of society still persists in Ashanti, Ghana, where women were in the front line of battle right to the end of the nineteenth century, just before the country was colonised by Britain. Even to this day remnants of female power make themselves felt in Ashanti, where a female child is more welcome to both parents than a male.

Claude Lévi-Strauss gives a different picture from that of Eva Meyerowitz, a picture adopted by Simone de Beauvoir in *The Second Sex*. Matriarchal rule and matrilineal society do not, in Lévi-Strauss's view, prove that woman was superior to man at any time in history. Marriages were made by the family in matrilineal and patrilineal societies, and a woman's position was simply that of a bartered bride. In fact, marriages took place between men and men. However, there must have been some doubt in Lévi-Strauss's mind about this clear-cut view, as he also mentions a predominant influence of the mother in the arrangement of her daughter's marriage when he says in *Elementary Structures of Kinship* (p. 305): 'The Kolhen go even further, [in paying tribute to the female side of marriage partners] since the bride price is paid exclusively to the mother, the brothers and the maternal uncle', and he quotes another author, Sternberg, as saying: 'Can it be a survival of the mother-right?' The following sentence reveals a similar tentative attitude, (p. 118):

> The reign of women is remembered only in mythology, an age, perhaps more simply, when men had not yet resolved the antinomy which is always likely to appear between their roles as takers of wives and givers of sisters, and making them both the authors and victims of their exchanges.

The concept of the matriarchate is essentially a religious one, because it is built on the worship of the Mother Goddess. It is therefore appropriate to mention the views of one of the foremost authorities on comparative religion, Mircea Eliade. He has no doubt that matriarchy existed, but he is not sure about the extent of its influence and power. He says in *Myths, Dreams and Mysteries*, p. 179:

> We do not know whether the matriarchate ever existed as an independent cycle of culture – in other words, whether a certain stage in the history of mankind was ever characterised by the absolute ascendancy of woman and by an exclusively feminine religion. It is more prudent to say that matriarchal *tendencies* or *predispositions* are manifest in certain religious and social customs. It is true that certain social structures – for example, uterine descent, matrilocalism, the avunculate and gynocracy – show the social, juridical and religious importance of woman. But *importance* does not mean absolute *predominance*'.

Eliade's concept of matriarchy is closer to that of Eva L. Meyerowitz than to that of Lévi-Strauss, but Meyerowitz alone gives a definite picture of woman in early history, whose gender identity must have been masculine by our standards. Her activities were equal to those executed by men before patrilineal society was firmly established. Indeed, her mental prowess must have been superior to that of man, as it was due to her talents that the first cohesive communities and cities were founded, and *she* was the ruler over both men and women for a long time.

A similarity between her virility and freedom from the fetters of being an object of the male makes the homosexual woman resemble the image of woman in matriarchal times. This similarity applies particularly to the more masculine type of lesbian. The wide range of activities, the undoubted capacity to manage her life without dependence on men, is the ideal of the homosexual woman. Female homosexuality is inseparable from the very qualities which were the prerogative of women in early history. It is of no consequence to these conclusions whether the matriarchate existed as a definite period of history, which I believe it did, or in mythology only. Mythology *is* history, transcending concrete data and revealing their true meaning.

THE LESBIAN'S EMOTIONAL BIAS

Emotion is both incentive and reward in animal and man. It plays an omnipotent role in human life from its very beginning. The first expression of a newborn baby is emotional – a cry. Present-day psychologists question concepts which have hitherto been taken for granted. The concepts of instinct and emotion are cases in point. They are now thought of as being of one and the same nature, and the dividing line between them is considered to be either blurred or non-existent. I myself incline to this view, because both instinct and emotion are signs of *being moved*. Emotion appears to be a step forward from instinct, an ascendance which is obviously related to brain development. In man its range and complexity extends from the primitive to the intrinsically differentiated and eccentric. Emotion has, however, one hallmark entirely its own : it increases in intensity through expression. We are all, seen from this perspective, conditioned by the power and complexity of our emotions. While human beings grow and mature, rationality and objectivity grow also, and up to a point, take the wind out of the sails of emotion. These 'superior' functions are meant to balance and to check the emotional force. Circumstances of personal and interpersonal relationships demand emotional inhibitions. In the constant fight with the *Umwelt*, powers other than that of emotion are necessary, if we want to avoid defeat through competitiveness and a perpetual onslaught on individual freedom. The task of developing an adequate inhibitory mechanism, which controls but does not squash emotions, is more than difficult, particularly in present-day society. In many people, emotional difficulties in childhood, together with other factors, inhibit the process of growing up, and in them 'emotional brakes' work either wrongly or in a contrary fashion. Misapplication of the inhibitory mechanism impedes or prevents growth into the right kind of maturity, which should enable us to see ourselves and our surroundings in proper perspective.

We know that normal people exist in theory only, and the number of those who suffer from psychical malfunction of one kind or another increases with the way our society is advancing. Life situations may therefore arise which are too difficult to cope with for certain categories of persons, namely those who are either personally or socially ill-equipped. The latter are the minority groups to which the lesbian population belongs.

With lesbians, emotion is bound to play a special, if not an all-important part, in the way they look at others and arrange their lives. I know of nobody who has so profoundly penetrated the essential nature and meaning of emotion as Jean-Paul Sartre. He testifies to the omnipotence of emotion in the Introduction to his *Sketch for a Theory of the Emotions*, when he says:

Thus the phenomenologist will interrogate emotion about *consciousness about man*, he will enquire not only what it is, but what it has to tell us about a being, one of whose characteristics is just this, that it is capable of being moved.

And Sartre gives a definition of emotion which is directly relevant to my theory of lesbianism, when he says:

We can now conceive what an emotion is. It is a transformation of the world. When the paths before us become too difficult, or when we cannot see our way, we can no longer put up with such an exacting and difficult world. All ways are barred, but nevertheless we must act. So then we try to change the world; that is to live as though the relations between things and their potentialities were not governed by deterministic processes, but by *magic* (italics mine). But, be it well understood, this is no playful matter: we are concerned and we fling ourselves into the attitude with all the force at our command.

These sentences have a direct application to the lesbian situation. The emotional world of the homosexual woman is of particularly high intensity for many reasons, an outstanding one being the fact that she is an outsider, and by old-fashioned, but not yet dead standards, an outcast. Her position in the world presents the circumstances which Sartre describes. Hostile humanity (or rather inhumanity) around her would make her life unbearable, if she had no refuge to some kind of transformation of her situation, by means of which she can blunt its impact. She circumvents a provocative or unbearable situation instead of facing it. She adopts an emotional attitude to her surroundings by playing hide and seek with them. The lesbian cannot afford a direct challenge to her emotional orientation, and this fact alone colours her whole world, from peripheral to intimate contacts, from professional relationships to her attempts at social integration.

Let me take the last point first. Most of my interviewees assured me that they were ordinary citizens, who did not feel outside, but definitely inside their professional and social milieu. These statements appear to contradict my assumption. This is, however, not the case. Lesbians show a typical flight into wishful thinking, because they want to be accepted by the community at large, want to be of high repute and to possess those attributes which give people a sense of social security. Alas, their self-deception came only too clearly to light when they admitted that they had, of course, to hide their homosexuality from anybody outside. They just shut their eyes to their situation. Undoubtedly, homosexual women are, as a rule, most conscientious in any task they undertake, whatever their profession may be. Many indeed excel in their work, by giving that extra effort to it, which is so characteristic of the over-anxious person.

It is understandable that lesbians want to hide from themselves the fact that they are alienated from the milieu in which their life and work places them. They can never be themselves with their heterosexual colleagues, let alone their superiors. Should they dare to admit their emotional disposition, people might look on them as freaks, and worse than that, they might lose their employment. For them, honesty could lead to losses of many kinds, and in particular, it could result in their being completely stranded in a hostile world.

There are exceptions to the rule. The artist, the talented technician, and last but not least, independent professional women can, in most instances, dare to show their face to the milieu in which they live and work. They are accepted by virtue of their being exceptional or particularly useful. But the majority of homosexual women have the dire need to find a way out of their dilemma, which puts them at odds with the community.

As Sartre categorically pronounced, the way out of an unbearable conflict with the *Umwelt* can only be found through the emotional approach, which transforms reality as if by magic. The magical picture of the *Umwelt* endows reality with attributes, qualities and relationships which in fact do not exist. Anybody who is capable of transforming reality into a kind of 'dream world' or 'make-believe' must be blessed with a lively imagination, an easily accessible subconscious, and a sense of the dramatic. Sartre rightly names this process *magical*. The emotion involved in this manoeuvre represents, according to him, an inferior form of consciousness. Why should it be inferior, I ask myself? True, the 'magical' glance at things, the emotional involvement in everything, can arise from failure of some kind or other. It may come from fear of incompetence, from fear of loss, but most of all it arises from fear of the *other* – of others. The last is the most dreaded fear because it entails personal and collective alienation. The dread of isolation hangs like the sword of Damocles over the heads of many lesbians. Isolation is indeed the key word for the position of the homosexual woman (and man) in patrilineal societies. And apart from some enlightened periods in history, the lesbian has been suffering from it over the centuries. Although a social upheaval with changes in sexual attitudes is taking place in our time, the bulk of the population still cannot accept the homosexual in its midst. Consequently, homosexual women (and homosexual men for that matter) consider themselves to be minority groups. In the last six years or so, lesbians in Great Britain and the United States have organised themselves into groups, which fulfil the function of intimate communities, where members can shed the mask they have to wear in the world outside, and can be themselves. These communities issue monthly publications, such as *The Ladder*, published by the Daughters of Bilitis in America, and *Arena Three*, published in Britain and much read there and abroad. Newsletters are regularly given out to members by Kenric and the Albany Trust. The latter also publishes a periodical of high standing, *Man and Society*. Kenric is a particularly lively and well-run lesbian society. Its newsletters announce meetings for discussions and social gatherings. They make appeals for the furtherance of knowledge about homosexuality, and encourage their members to participate in research. *Arena Three* and the Albany Trust follow the same course. In the exclusively lesbian publications, Kenric newsletters and *Arena Three*, one also finds a personal column, which provides for pen-friends and meetings of like-minded members, who have no opportunity to make friends with other lesbians in their own milieu. I know that these organisations have made and are making a considerable difference to the problem of lesbian isolation. They try to dispel and overcome it in the best possible way. We must not forget, however, that homosexual women, more than others, need emotional outlets and fulfilment through emotional and sensuous intimacy. To most of them, emotional intimacy means all and everything. With an emotional disposition inclined to intensity and drama, homosexual women resemble hunters in constant pursuit of 'magical' love.

An aspect of magic must be mentioned here which is not covered by Sartre's definition. This aspect concerns romanticism. Homosexual women who live in emotions and imagination more intensely than others yearn for romantic love more than most people. Romanticism gives light and fire to the imagination and the emotions. Romanticism possesses the magical power to project one's emotional needs on the image of another person, giving her qualities and attributes which are not necessarily in line with reality. The magic of romanticism can either creatively transform reality, or it can lead to complete illusion. In the first instance it is the power of the imagination which has a magical touch; in the second instance it is chaotic fantasy which produces nothing but the bubbles of day-dreaming. Whatever kind of magic is at work, the image of the loved person never fails to be a romantic ideal. Romance is the core of love in all human beings, but again, it means far more to homosexual than to heterosexual women, because of their restriction in sexual intimacy, and in many cases, the lack of a family. Those lesbians who possess imagination cannot fail to experience the wonders of elation and intimacy, even when the person they love corresponds little to their image of her. Those who are driven by fantasy and indulge in illusion are bound to experience disappointments or disaster in their relationships. They may fly from one person to another, like moths to the light, always hoping the next woman will be the right one. Even with the unhappy lesbian who hunts in vain, the romantic ideal directs her emotions into preoccupations other than those which strive for material and animal satisfaction only. Although friendship plays its part in the life of homosexual women as it does with heterosexual people, their hunger for emotional love endangers calmer relationships, or makes them appear to be of minor importance. Nostalgia never ceases to gnaw at their feelings and thoughts, because of the frustrations which are unavoidable in their situation. This is probably the reason why lesbian women find it so difficult to establish a settled existence, even when they have children either in or out of wedlock. Nostalgia is like a drug: it can provide the wonder of a magical inner world, but it can also deplete vitality and lead to apathy and depression.

What is the motivation behind this haunting drive towards romantic love, which has the qualities of an obsession? Lesbians expect from one another nothing less than the wish-fulfilment of an incestuous mother-daughter relationship. It has to be an all-enveloping union, from which the male is absolutely excluded. Their desire and their search reach out for a goal which is entirely their own. It is essentially different from the longings of heterosexual people and homosexual men. One may ask, why is their love essentially different from any other kind of love? Because the sameness of their psycho-physical reactions entails the possibility of an understanding on every level so complete as to be incomparable to any other form of love. There is no need to grope for the right response; it is given per se. Thus lesbian love can, at its best, fulfil the impossible : the intertwining of the most exciting emotional ecstasy with the greatest sensuous intimacy. The anatomical bisexuality of woman allows for a considerable variety in love-play, when the masculine partner of one day becomes the feminine one on another occasion.

All human beings endow the object of their love with ideal traits through the magic of emotional transformation. Again, the lesbian takes pride of place in her capacity and need for make-believe. As Sartre rightly points out, the make-believe of emotion is deadly serious. It is also authentic and therefore sincere. Emotional expression is in fact the only *direct* communication between people, and its directness is both a blessing and a wonder on one hand and a curse on the other. The violence of negative emotional expressions may deal annihilating blows to both partners of a relationship.

A number of women who call themselves homosexual do not belong to the lesbian minority. They join lesbian groups for sensational or mercenary reasons, but they do not concern the heart of the matter, and must be discounted. The same holds good for the so-called professional lesbian, who for reasons of extreme narcissism and sense of power counts the heads of the victims she has seduced. It is in these two small groups that one comes across perversion, which is the unauthentic imitation of an authentic and natural emotional orientation.

It is no chance phenomenon that lesbians tend to seek jobs which promise security of a particular kind. They prefer the aura of respectability to the more adventurous types of occupation. Government employment, the police, the teaching and nursing professions are favourite choices. They have to be doubly careful to have the highest reputation in such occupations because of the exemplary standards expected of them. Many lesbians join the ranks of the army, navy and air force with equal enthusiasm in peace and in war. A uniform is not only a mask, it also appears to certify service to the state, and personal integrity. And a uniform obscures individual differences and idiosyncrasies.

The lesbian exists between the magical make-believe of romantic love in her private life, and the nervous strain of constant play-acting in her official life. This is a precarious existence, and it is no wonder that many lesbians are demoralised by it. They have no hope of a change in their situation until society is ready to put the image of lesbianism into its proper perspective. Although a change in the attitude of 'normal' people to lesbianism could not alter its basic structure, it would reduce the negative repercussions resulting from prejudice.

PART TWO

THE RESEARCH

Chapter Four

The Method of Investigation

The revival of interest in homosexuality in the sixties links that decade with the thirties in this respect as in many others. There is of course, one essential difference: the advance in our knowledge of genetics and psychology during the last twenty years, which has changed our understanding of the causes of emotional reactions and of behaviour. For reasons which I mentioned earlier in this book, lesbianism was a neglected subject until quite recently. Projects on the study of female homosexuality are now under way in America, Great Britain, Denmark and other countries, but so far publications are scant and short. No methodical, statistical study has yet been published in book form.

American publications are mainly concerned with unusual cases of lesbianism. Some deal with one individual case only. Dr Socarides of the Albert Einstein College of Medicine, maintains in his paper *The Desire for Sexual Transformation*, that transsexual people, be they male or female, are homosexuals who cannot cope with guilt feelings about their deviation. Dr Newman and Dr Stoller present the history of one lesbian with pseudo-hermaphroditism. Dr Simon of the Jackson Memorial Hospital describes in detail one case of female homosexuality with transsexualism. A paper on adolescent lesbians by Dr

Malvina Kremer and Dr Rifkin, presents a statistical study. Twenty-five adolescent lesbians are compared with normal subjects. The results are interesting, although the number invest-igated is too small to be reliable. I was especially interested in a paper by Grundlach and Riess on the position of lesbians in regard to birth order and sex of siblings. Among the scant liter-ature on lesbianism published in Great Britain, I want to mention four papers. Two surveys came from women psychologists, Dr Eva Bene and Mrs Hopkins, and two from the psychiatrist Dr F. Kenyon. The number of subjects studied by the two psychol-ogists is small, although the research itself goes into depth. Dr Kenyon's investigation extended over a larger number of individuals, and he looked at many aspects of female homo-sexuality.

Dr Bene and Mrs Hopkins interviewed their subjects person-ally, and gave them some psychological tests. Dr Kenyon sent a questionnaire by post and analysed the answers received. I should also like to refer, in this context, to a paper by Dr Eliot Slater, which is a study of the maternal age at the birth of homosexuals, both male and female.

The great majority of the lesbians who participated in my research were working, and they mostly came from families generally described as belonging to the middle classes. I found it desirable to choose controls who would match the subjects as to their family background, and their professional as well as social situation. The latter in particular plays a part in certain aspects of lesbianism. I thought it necessary, for this reason alone, that social homogeneity should exist between the two groups compared. Every research worker knows how difficult it is to match two groups completely. I did the best I could.

The lesbians investigated, and also the controls, belonged, in the main, to the same professional classes, namely II and III. There was a comparatively small group in classes I and IV. I must explain that the population in Great Britain is divided into five social groups, according to the General Register Office classification of occupations. To put people into a social class according to the work they perform is a crude method of desig-nation, and one which has lost some of its meaning as to social implications. Many members of the working classes have reached the status of the middle class and vice versa. In spite of this, I used this classification because of its simplicity. A few examples may make it clear.

Professional people belong to Class I. Among them are, for example, judges, lawyers, solicitors, doctors, dentists, university professors, pharmacists, executives in industry and banking. To quote from the Classification of Occupations published by the General Register Office in 1966 :

> To provide more homogeneous groups, and as a useful altern-ative axis for classification, Social Classes II, III, and IV have been divided into manual, non-manual and agricultural sub-groups. Within this framework, Class I is wholly non-manual and Class V wholly manual.

I have combined Classes II and III in my survey for the follow-ing reason. Class II includes, for example, nurses, secretaries, civil servants without university education, writers, artists; Class III includes typists, some of whom are attached to the head of the firm, and might describe themselves as secretaries. Clerks in a government office belong to Class III, but might call themselves civil servants, as indeed they did in my survey. In fact, it is too difficult to differentiate between the two Classes. Class IV com-prises, in the main, the skilled worker in all branches of industry, and covers most of the working class. Class V encompasses the unskilled manual worker.

I divided subjects and controls into six age groups from twenty to sixty and over. Although there were more lesbians among the younger ones, the average age of the two groups taken as a whole corresponded very closely, and so did the number of married women.

My aim was to get a general picture of female homosexuality. I decided, therefore, on a number of different assessments. I asked the subjects to write their emotional autobiographies, without any conditions as to length or content, and with as explicit and complete information as possible about homosexual feelings and experiences. After receipt of the documents, I asked the writers to come and see me for an interview. This was con-ducted at length and in depth, and at the end of it the inter-viewee answered my questionnaires.

Two lesbian organisations and the Albany Trust helped me

to find a significant number of subjects. Several appeals announcing the project of my research appeared in *Arena Three*, with the help of the Minorities Research Trust, and in the newsletters of Kenric and the Albany Trust. I wanted ordinary lesbians, not those one comes across in Institutes of Sexology or the consulting rooms of psychiatrists. *Arena Three*, as well as the Kenric newsletter, put this point over very neatly with the words: 'Dr Wolff wants people, not patients'. Fear of being recognised as a lesbian, furtiveness, and a general tendency to withdraw into their own private world made the task of finding enough people difficult. In order to get more lesbians into the fold of my research, the then secretary of Kenric suggested that I should give a talk at one of their discussion groups. And one day in September, 1967, I spoke at the Caxton Hall to members of Kenric about my research on the psychology of gesture. This had some effect, because a number of those present made some kind of contact with me. At least I became a person to them, which eased the way towards active interest in my investigation. Those who had been to see me for an interview drew attention to the project, and together with canvassing by some Kenric members, enough participants were eventually produced. But in the end, I had to abandon my request for written emotional autobiographies, because I learnt that the idea of written reports discouraged many lesbians who would otherwise have come forward. I had, however, collected 43 written documents, among them some of great length. Several people even sent me postscripts almost equally extensive. Apart from the 43 'ideal' cases, another 65 subjects came forward bringing the total to 108. With the latter, I had to rely for my information entirely on the interview and questionnaires. The interview was extended to about two hours or more with this group. I took less time in many (but not all) cases with the people who had sent their written histories, but with them the situation was different. The moment one has a starting point already prepared, one can go ahead without certain preliminaries. A special contact immediately developed when they came into my consulting room. Apart from facilitating contact and knowledge of the person, the documents were of absorbing interest to me. Many were written by hand and difficult to decipher. These were among the most moving and revealing; they were also by far the longest ones. The flavour of drama and, with some, of dramatisation came through the badly written pages. Those women had blossomed out through writing about themselves, and had obviously had some kind of catharsis in doing so. A streak of exhibitionism and self-pity was more frequent in the written than in the spoken words. The interview appeared to have both an inhibitory and a soothing effect.

A considerable number of personal histories followed a different pattern. They were, as a rule, beautifully typed, and they were short. Information was clear and objective. These scripts stuck to facts, reporting on childhood experiences, family milieu etc, in a clinical fashion, terse and somewhat arid. I found it fascinating to get to know how the writers saw themselves. As some time had elapsed between the writing and the interview, they probably had no clear memory of what they had already told me. One aim of this particular method was to discover discrepancies between the confessions on paper and those at the interview. I naturally watched expressive behaviour attentively, as I am convinced through both instinct and my particular studies on gesture that persons reveal themselves not by what they say or do, but by their postures and gestures, by facial expression, by tone of voice. Although discrepancies could not be denied, the authenticity of the documents was never in doubt. The dawning of homosexual feelings, their development etc. were clearly and apparently truthfully conveyed. The importance of the structure of childhood life with its particular family background for homosexuality, had been grasped by all, whatever their I.Q. might be.

Both the interviews and the statistical research by way of questionnaires represent the material of this study. I give a detailed description of how I conducted the interviews in the next chapter.

The questionnaire was designed to allow for a general picture of lesbianism, or rather, as complete a survey as possible of its salient characteristics. The same questionnaire was answered by subjects and controls. It covered, first of all, data on the family and themselves, but I endeavoured also to extract as much information as possible about their personalities. Ninety questions were asked, and most subjects and controls answered all of them. The intimate details of sex life

D

are of greatest interest in the study of deviants. A separate questionnaire, which was answered by lesbians only, inquired about these. The information obtained from this questionnaire relates to the sexual role in undisguised sex dreams, in masturbation fantasies and so on.

The general questionnaire is tabulated in 27 tables. All data were processed at the Computer Centre of the Medical Research Council under the supervision of Dr Clive Spicer. He also undertook to apply the significance tests to them. The tables were designed to reflect the following situations:

1. The social, professional and family background.
2. The causes of lesbianism, apart from genetics, with reference to early childhood, and direct, as well as cross-relationships inside the family.
3. Emotional, sexual and social relationships outside the family.
4. The success or failure of marriages, and attitudes to children.
5. The incidence of neurotic or mental illness and alcoholism with particular reference to sexual trauma in childhood and later, and the numbers of those who had received psychotherapy or other psychiatric treatment, and those who had not.
6. The evaluation of psychosomatic diseases such as asthma, together with the factor of nervous and emotional stress which is connected with them.
7. The incidence of mental illness, alcoholism, and homosexuality in the family history.
8. A comprehensive picture of traits of temperament and personality, with special reference to aggression, suggestibility, social attitudes in general and social integration in particular.

The emotional autobiographies which I mentioned earlier in this chapter are a new departure in the investigation of lesbianism. I have incorporated three of them into this book. They are part of my method of research and they convey something of the *reality* of lesbian personalities and lives.

Chapter Five

The Interview

The thought of interviewing raises feelings of both curiosity and apprehension. Few interviewers, I think, can escape a mild attack of stage fright. This is as it should be, because if the interviewer does not feel anything at all, the job will not be well done. The word contact covers a very wide field of relationships, in fact it is the backbone of every relationship of every kind. Even in a transitory contact such as an interview, the basic conditions of success are sympathy between the two participants, and empathy on the part of the interviewer. I had made it clear that my subjects should not be patients but people. This made my situation more difficult. The professional interview runs on specific lines, which provide a structure for the dialogue. My position with the person who came to see me was that of meeting a stranger, and it was important that I should make a good impression on her in order to gain her confidence. Another problem was that I had to compress a complete acquaintance of my interviewee into a brief period of time.

I made no plan as to a method of procedure; it would have let me down and defeated the purpose of the project. I abandoned anticipation and followed my instinct and intuition which I thought would serve me best. In fact, I trusted to luck. I had a good starting point of contact with those who had sent their autobiographies, but most interviews were conducted with complete strangers. I had some surprises, not only about the people I met, but also about my own reactions.

A number of the interviewees came either by train or car from the country or the suburbs. Most of them appeared on the dot on my doorstep. I developed the habit of looking out of the window at the appointed time, so that I might catch a glimpse of the stranger. This first picture of the person received unknown to her gave me an impression of her personality, and released some intuitive knowledge in me. It was as if I had caught hold of the *gestalt* of the stranger in an uncanny, subconscious fashion, and this helped me to get some idea of my general approach and of what I would say to her. I went about my task by adapting myself to the situation as it presented itself. Everybody who came was received as a friend. This was as important for the purpose of the visit as it was natural to me. In every case it was I who opened the front door. Knowing the fear of lesbians to be spotted as such, I saw to it that no other person went near them.

The two interviews which follow are shortened versions of the originals. They focus on the salient points of the dialogues I held with two of the subjects. The first one had sent me her emotional autobiography. I shall call her Miss Smith.

The front door bell rang a few minutes before I expected Miss Smith to arrive. I knew she had to come up by train from the country. An anxious person, I thought, and regretted not having had time to get a glimpse of her beforehand through the window. A tall, thin woman stood at my front door. She looked straight at me, with no sign of anxiety or desire to make contact. Anyway, that was my first impression. I was wrong. She spoke first, holding herself erect, and as if in full control of herself and this unusual situation: 'I am glad to come to see you, because I never can speak to anybody about what concerns me most, the homosexual problem and my own personal feelings'.

Quite a speech, I thought, noticing at the same time her considerable nervous tension, which manifested itself in her voice and her stiff posture, apart from the general impression of strain, so intense that it seemed as if it were something tangible. I did not attempt any small talk. I said nothing but: 'Do look at the paintings in this room. I'll make you a cup of coffee'. I returned from the kitchen after a few minutes and found her somewhat relaxed. She gave a brief, tentative smile when I served the coffee. I could start the interview.

Qu. I know that you live with your mother, though you have reached the age of forty-one. Do you mind?

A. Yes and no. In some ways we're very close. She's frail and I want to look after her. I could never leave her as long as she lives.

Qu. You told me in your autobiography that your mother still treats you like a baby, and that she even calls you 'baby' in front of others. Does this worry you or not?

A. Of course I'm embarrassed when we're with friends or acquaintances. Otherwise no, it doesn't worry me. I know she likes to show that I'm completely her own, even more so since my brother married some years ago.

Qu. You mentioned that your mother wants you to give up your job as a solicitor's clerk, so that you could always be together.

A. No, I never would. I need my job, not only for financial reasons. I couldn't bear becoming isolated from the outside world. I'd have a nervous breakdown. My mother knows that and has to accept it. I'm obstinate as far as my job goes, (and also in other things, she added).

Qu. Tell me about your father. I know that he died two years ago. I would like to hear about your relationship with him and his with you, particularly when you were a child.

A. He was always a stranger to me. He preferred my brother who could talk to him openly. I never could. I was shy and embarrassed with him because I felt that I didn't come up to his expectations.

Qu. Why was that?

A. He wanted me to make up to him, to be feminine. I resented that. I've always wanted to be a boy for as long as I can remember. My parents are of Scottish origin. And though my mother never showed me her affection in words, I felt sure that she loved me. She didn't get on with my father. Neither of us could really communicate with him. I thought that he only communicated with my brother and that he was a very introspective man. I might have been wrong. People he met outside, acquaintances rather than friends, liked him a lot, we were told. They said that he was really popular.

Qu. Would you like to tell me about your brother; anything that comes into your mind about him?

A. Yes, I will. He's five years younger than me and much cleverer. I think that my mother made me her favourite because he and my father got on so well. I think that I envied him his intelligence. (Silence. I saw her face getting tense and there was a sad look in her eyes.) Suddenly she went on : We get on well now, since he got married. I'm staying with him and his wife at present. I visit them every year.

I felt her resistance, and I sensed, through her silence and her expressive behaviour, a great deal about this relationship.

Qu. You wrote to me about your school life and your first feelings for another girl. Would you tell me about this again?

A. Certainly. As you know, I was a solitary child and very imaginative. I loved reading. My school life was very unhappy because for some unknown reason I was persecuted by some girls in my form, a gang of them. They picked on me and followed me home. They used to stop me, and tease me, and even fight me. I hadn't done anything to anyone. I never defended myself. It would have made matters worse since it was one against five or six. I can't explain why that happened to me. Can you?

Qu. Did you work hard, or perhaps you were a favourite with your teachers?

A. Yes, I worked hard and I did get on well with most of my teachers. I couldn't say whether I was a favourite or not.

Qu. When the other girls played up teachers and that sort of thing, did you join in?

A. No, I never joined in with the rest of my form when they were giggling and playing practical jokes. I hated that kind of thing. Oh, I understand what you mean. They hated me for being 'good'.

Qu. How long did you have to put up with this persecution from the other girls?

A. Until I passed the eleven plus and went to Grammar school. It was there that I made the first friend I ever had. She was older than me and in a higher form. I can't remember how it happened that we got friendly. She was the sister of one of the girls who had persecuted me. We used to walk to school together every day, and come home together too. And we also met at the week-ends. Once, when we went out for a picnic, she put her arms round me. I was then about thirteen. I had never experienced anything like what went through my body at that moment and afterwards. I was all tingling with excitement and almost shivering. And I felt quite breathless. It changed my life, and I couldn't think of anything except that wonderful moment and the look in her eyes. She must have noticed that something had happened to me. She avoided me after that incident.

Qu. How did you take that?

A. I never mentioned her decision to give me up. I don't think I really suffered, but it was at that time that I began to masturbate.

Qu. Did you feel guilty about it? I mean, guilty about your friend putting her arms round you, and masturbating?

A. No, I didn't feel guilty about either. But I was unhappy about masturbating. I was afraid it might harm me somehow, that it might make me ill physically. And it left me feeling sad every time, the whole time, in fact.

Qu. How did you get on in school after this emotional upheaval?

A. There appeared to be a complete change in my school work. I lost my powers of concentration, and I worked harder and harder to make up for a kind of confusion which got hold of me when I tried to do my homework, and worse when I was asked questions in class. My work went down-hill. It worried me terribly, but it seemed that I couldn't do anything about it. Before that I'd been top of my form. My favourite subject had been science. I had hoped to go to university and do science or biology. Although I got my school certificate in the end, my dream of going up to university was shattered.

Qu. You wrote to me that after that first experience you were too afraid ever to show your feelings to any other girl or woman. Can you explain this more fully?

A. When I was attracted by someone, I always worshipped her too much and felt too much respect for her as a person. I couldn't possibly involve her in my desire and emotion. I always loved from afar. I felt that my emotions were too overwhelming. I was afraid of them. They seemed to have a terrible effect on my body, which also made me shy away. I didn't want others to notice it and I was afraid of making a fool of myself. I was terrified that I might start trembling and that my hands would get sweaty. I was even afraid that I might feel faint.

Qu. Have you religious convictions or beliefs?

A. Not really. We're C. of E. and I go to church with Mother, but I don't think that I'm a religious person. I only believe in love.

Qu. You mentioned in your autobiographical report and you told me just now that your respect for the other person was such that you could not possibly let them become involved with you emotionally and physically. Are you really content with such restraint?

A. Yes, I am. I believe in romance. It's the most beautiful and important thing in life, and physical love is nothing compared with it.

Qu. You told me in your letter that you met the love of your life only three years ago, and that she died a year ago. Did you keep to your principles when you really fell in love?

A. Yes, I did. I never made advances to her, or even told her that I loved and adored her. She was aware of it, I'm sure. She was far too sensitive not to realise what I felt.

Qu. Did you ever caress each other?

A. No, not really. It depends what you understand by caress. We looked at each other in peace. (I was struck by this expression.) And she approved of my plans and ambitions.

Qu. What were and what are your ambitions?

A. I wanted to get back to learning something, and to achieve something. She encouraged me to do practical things and I took driving lessons, which I was good at. I passed my test the first time. And I went to evening classes to learn German and French. I still go on with both.

Qu. Did you speak to her about homosexuality?

A. Yes, in an indirect way. I told her about the M.R.G., and she was interested and thought it an excellent thing. But I never mentioned to her that I had joined. I don't know why I kept that secret.

Qu. Were you afraid that she might look too closely into your feelings for her?

A. Yes, perhaps. I didn't want her to 'classify' me as a lesbian, although it is pretty certain that she understood that I am exclusively homosexual.

Qu. Was your friend married?

A. No. But there were several men in her life, though no women, and I think that I was her closest woman friend. (Miss Smith now turned right round and faced me, saying : Do you mind if I have a cigarette? Of course not, I answered.)

Qu. Did you see your friend a great deal?

A. She was a professional woman and very busy. We met once or twice a week. Three months before her death she went to stay with her sister. She had never told me she was ill. She must have known. I never saw her again after she left.

Qu. You wrote to me about it, and how you felt afterwards. How long did it take you to find your feet again? Do you know?

A. I've never been the same, but I haven't really changed either. I mean I can do my work and be interested in things I've always been interested in, but in a way it's different.

Qu. How is it different? Can you explain?

A. I'll try. I always feel the presence of my friend when I'm awake, and sometimes I dream of her. I live in her presence.

Qu. It sounds to me like a religious, almost a Christian attitude. It seems to be this rare thing Christians talk about, and some experience : the constant presence of Christ. Does this make sense to you?

A. Yes, it does. In the same way, her presence keeps me going.

Qu. Could you imagine ever finding anybody else with whom you might have a close relationship?

A. No. It wouldn't be fair in the first place, because of what I've told you. My love belongs to her. Anyway, I'm a self-sufficient person.

Qu. Do you think of yourself as an introspective person?

A. Yes, I'd say so. I live happily with only my own company. I don't want to meet strangers and make new relationships. I don't even want contact with people I have to meet professionally and otherwise.

Qu. You told me that you never wanted to be female. Can you explain this?

A. I think homosexuality is mainly biological. Anyway that's how it seems to me. I feel and have always felt male ever since my earliest memories. I always despised dolls and the sort of games girls play. I could never fall in love with a man. Yes, I would still prefer to be a man. I don't feel normal in skirts, but I have to wear them because of my job, and because my mother wouldn't like to see me in trousers.

Qu. Have you any other interests apart from driving and outdoor life?

A. I love ballet. I saw the Ballet Rambert, and I go to see every ballet that comes into town if I possibly can. I appreciate beautiful movements so keenly because I'm so clumsy myself. And ballet takes me out of myself.

Qu. Are there any artists in your family? You didn't mention your family background in your letter.

A. I come from a working-class family. My father was a taxi driver and my mother was a maid. As you know, my father wasn't happy at home, but was popular with people outside. He was an intelligent man. No, there's nothing artistic about us.

Qu. Are you content with your life as it is, professionally?

A. Yes, I am now. We have a little week-end cottage near the sea with a garden. I've taken up gardening and enjoy it.

Qu. Do you have any financial problems?

A. No. My father left us quite a bit of money and Mother has a pension. We don't need much because we live very simply. I earn quite good money in my job. Like me, my mother loves the country, gardening and the sea. I drive her down to the cottage every week-end.

Qu. You said that homosexuality is in your opinion mainly biological. Tell me any other ideas you have about lesbianism and male homosexuality.

A. To me it's natural. You're born that way. I believe that male and female homosexuals have a great part to play in society. They're not burdened with parenthood and other responsibilities of marriage. They can devote their time to culture. Homosexuals are very important people, or could be, in my opinion.

I ended the conversation, agreeing with what she had said. She answered willingly and without inhibition my detailed questionnaires. She gave me a warm handshake and asked if she could come to see me again when she was on holiday at her brother's.

COMMENT

This comment on the interview with Miss Smith was written the day I saw her. I must differentiate between my psychological diagnosis and my personal impression. One is an objective analysis, the other conveys my human reactions.

I diagnosed Miss Smith as a schizothym personality with infantile traits. She is a woman with masculine gender identity. The cause of it could not be satisfactorily evaluated as I was, for obvious reasons, unable to examine her physically. Only through a physical examination could I have known whether she represented a case of pseudo-hermaphroditism or even hermaphroditism. In both cases her masculine gender identity could have been explained through physical stigmata, and her conviction that her homosexuality was of a biological nature would have been given concrete substance.

Her lack of emotional desire after one overwhelming experience is probably due to her tendency to withdraw from reality. She flees into a world of books and her own imagination. This flight must be seen as a substitute for emotional experiences which represent catastrophic threats to her self. Her escapism is a safety valve against suffering, and at the same time it relieves her of the burden of adult responsibilities in close relationships.

Her inhibitory mechanism is working in a constructive way. She has an extremely narrow, but comparatively happy inner world. Her interest in intellectual pursuits has been helped by her emotional withdrawal. In middle age, she still furthers her education by attending evening classes. She attends classes to prepare herself for a number of ordinary and advanced level examinations, so that she might still be able to go to university and get a degree. She is well adjusted to her professional and family milieu.

I was deeply impressed by the immense capacity for love I

sensed in her. Here was a true idealist, a woman who had experienced platonic love of such significance and strength that her life was changed. It was transformed into something holy. She gave me the feeling of a nun with a true vocation for her calling. Indeed, Miss Smith seemed to be one in a million, or rather ten million. This woman, who had renounced physical pleasure and the search for a fulfilling experience because she kept faithful to her one and only love, sets an example of the beauty and reward of emotional solitude. Her integrity is of the very highest and, in accordance with it, her character is of the most admirable. A treasure to have as a friend, I thought. The restrictions and the narrowness of outlook are well compensated for by her reliability in the obligations she is able to take on.

She seemed to me as near a saint as a person can possibly be. Of course, the absence of charm and vivacity is a handicap for anyone, saintly or not. She is a marvellous person, but would be boring in social and closer personal acquaintance.

It is sad, I thought, that the people who glitter and bewitch us with their magnetism are, more often than not, the least reliable as friends and professional colleagues.

It is reassuring to see that the dutiful behaviour of this daughter towards her mother does not weigh her down, but gives her purpose. And her self-sufficiency is enviable. If she were left alone in the world, she would not be lost.

Perhaps Miss Smith is one of the luckiest women I have interviewed; she is certainly one whom I shall never forget.

The second interview concerns a woman of fifty-four, of whom I knew nothing beforehand. I had to see my subjects mainly in the evenings or at week-ends, and Miss Brown was no exception. Her appointment was on a Sunday morning at 11 a.m. I stood at the window at the right time. A good-looking woman of athletic build looked anxiously at the house numbers, and settled for a wrong one. After she had been told of her mistake, she rang my bell. I wondered if she were the masculine type: she looked shy and boyish. Good family, I noted, because of the manner in which she approached me. She was immediately at ease with me. Some conventional remarks were passed, as dictated by her upbringing, while going upstairs. We settled ourselves down. She said abruptly: 'I've only come in order to help you. I really hate talking about myself. I would never want to consult a psychiatrist'.

Qu. Why do you want to help me?

A. I'm sure that it's important that a scientific book on lesbianism should be written.

Qu. Thank you. (She turned her square handsome face towards me; her short blond hair fell over her forehead. There was alcohol on her breath.) Are you an only child?

A. No. I've got two younger brothers, one nearly ten years my junior.

Qu. Do you get on well with them?

A. No. I don't take any notice of them – I never have. I dislike my younger brother; he's a weakling, he's sick, really, and hangs on to Mother's apron strings. The older one is married. I never see him.

Qu. Are your parents alive?

A. Mother is. I wish she was dead. I really hate her.

Qu. Did you love your father?

A. No, never. But he liked me best of the children. He treated me like a son. He didn't think much of my brothers. He always wanted me with him. He enjoyed games and sport, and he taught me golf, riding, swimming and shooting. The trouble was he couldn't stand up to Mother – he was a weak man – and he drank. I despised him more for his lack of guts than his alcoholism.

Qu. Do you look like him?

A. Yes, I do. Not a bit like Mother.

Qu. What did she look like?

A. She was petite, smart, elegant and very pretty – oh, and so vivacious. She really was marvellous: everybody fell for her. Actually, come to think of it, she was very restless. Never sat still. And always full of new ideas – where to spend the next holidays, a visit to the theatre and so on. Anything to amuse herself.

Qu. She sounds fascinating. Were you close to her?

A. I admired her enormously, but I didn't respect her. She never cared for us children, except my younger brother. And she only discovered her love for him later in life when she was older. She was thoroughly selfish, you know.

Qu. What are your feelings for her now?

A. I told you, I hate her. She's a parasite. She probably ruined my father. I'm pretty certain that she had a series of lovers. One was always in the house. It made me wild. She was a hypocrite.

Qu. Didn't your father object?

A. That's just it, he didn't. He retired meekly into his shell and shut his eyes. I suppose he was afraid of a scandal, and then he didn't want to lose her altogether. That's probably why he paid so much attention to me.

Qu. Did you get away from home, I mean to a boarding school?

A. Yes, I went to a boarding school. That's where it first started.

Qu. Did you work hard at school?

A. Not at all. I got interested in girls at the age of twelve. I didn't know anything about sex. I'd never heard of lesbianism. We all had crushes on teachers and older girls. We wrote letters and kissed, on the mouth, of course. That sort of thing. We never slept with each other, though.

Qu. Did you get any training after leaving school?

A. None. I went to a finishing school in Paris. I was sixteen.

Qu. And after that?

A. I got engaged at seventeen to a very attractive man of twenty-six. He was a drinker.

Qu. Were you in love with him?

A. No. I felt physically attracted to him. He was my first lover. After six months he broke off the engagement without giving any reason.

Qu. How did you manage your life after that?

A. I didn't mind much. I started to have affairs with men and became quite promiscuous. And at eighteen I fell in love for the first time. It was with a woman. She was married with three children. Nobody would have thought of her as a lesbian. I didn't, but she was. She returned my feelings and we went all the way. It was fantastic. Her husband was a brute. I don't know if he found out or not, but my friend had a nervous breakdown and never really recovered.

Qu. How long did you see each other regularly?

A. Three years at least, until she had that breakdown. After that we ended that kind of relationship. But we always remained friends. It was a long time before I fell in love again.

(Her face showed signs of nervous strain: the lines around her mouth deepened, and she spoke hesitatingly. I gave her a glass of vodka. 'That's what I needed,' she said. 'What else do you want to know?' There was a hint of aggression in her voice.)

Qu. Don't go on if you are exhausted and tired of this. But if you would like to tell me more, how was your life at that point? What type of sexual experience did you have?

A. I slept around again. At times it was just like drinking champagne, at other times it was a bloody bore. I was an old bastard, a floater.

Qu. How long did that go on?

A. Until I was twenty-five, when war broke out. It saved me, really. I don't know why, but I couldn't get away from home. I was so dependent on Mother, although I hated her guts by then.

Qu. How did you like it in the services?

A. I became a Wren. I loved it. That is when my real life started.

Qu. What did you like about it?

A. I loved wearing uniform to start with. And I liked the idea of duty. I became an officer. I think that the war gave me an opportunity to show that I am as good as a man, or better. I love to compete with men. My greatest moment was when an admiral told me, and other people in the services too, that I was just as good as a man.

Qu. But what about your personal life?

A. It was happy too. I fell deeply in love with another woman in the services. In many ways she was like my first love. She was also married and had children. I was even more moved than with the first woman. I had the time of my life during the war in every way. But the affair ended with the return of her husband at the end of the war.

Qu. You obviously had to start your life again. Will you tell me about it?

A. Of course. I felt lost and went back to the life I'd led before the war. I compensated for my disappointment by being promiscuous. I started to drink heavily. I thought that nothing mattered any more.

Qu. Did you prefer women or men sexually?

A. I don't know really. I had about an equal number of both, until I fell in love again with a woman. I've never fallen in love with a man.

Qu. When did that happen?

A. Only six years ago. She dominated me completely. She's intelligent and domineering. We were well suited. We didn't like England and went by car to India. When we returned we bought some land and farmed. She once said to me, 'You're as weak as water and as hard as nails'.

Qu. Have you settled down now?

A. I don't know really. I like travelling abroad.

Qu. I see that you smoke rather a lot. Do you also drink a great deal?

A. I'm an alcoholic, I know. I don't care. I am just a bastard and I don't care what happens to me.

Qu. Would you care to answer my questionnaires?

A. Yes, I suppose so.

She did so and left.

COMMENT

Miss Brown is an example of the extrovert who finds it difficult, if not impossible, to live alone. She needs people and movement around her. A frequent change of scene satisfies her sensuous appetite. Her level of frustration tolerance is very low, which explains much of her impulsiveness and aggression. It points, in general, to a deficient inhibitory mechanism. And both are at the back of her easily aroused anger and her bad temper. She suffers from a marked sense of inferiority and insecurity. Her heavy drinking is not, in my view, true alcoholism, but a symptom of a psychological trauma – a trauma which has been caused by lack of maternal love and paternal support. The absence of ethical values in her family background aggravated her emotional plight. She considers her parents, and apparently with good reason, to be despicable hypocrites. She is a woman who suffers from a predominantly negative mother-fixation. In any case, her ambivalence of hate and love towards her mother shows, on the conscious level, only feelings of disgust and contempt. Her ensuing loneliness and her confused emotional reactions reflect on all her relationships, peripheral and intimate. Her aggression, her need to compete with men, indeed her lesbianism, can be explained in the light of the particular brand of her mother-fixation. Her heavy drinking could be explained, according to Freudian thought, on the same lines. I am inclined to see this addiction as an escape from depression and self-hate, but both *might* be connected with her mother-complex. Her intellectual endowment is certainly good, but her intellectual achievement is poor because of her emotional difficulties. She has insight into her condition, which accentuates her introjected aggression and, in consequence, her self-destructive drives.

My personal impression of Miss Brown left me with a feeling of sadness. Fine material gone to seed, I thought. She had a beautifully shaped head and the bone structure of her face was well proportioned. Her life had, however, played havoc with her features. The mouth was drawn down, the skin already wrinkled, and most of all, the coarseness and heaviness of the lower part of the face made her look almost unattractive. Her gestures showed impulsiveness, defiance and aggression. She certainly had difficulties in adaptation, and would find it hard to arouse sympathy in others. Nevertheless, I discovered traces of delicacy and sensitivity in her. She was very courteous towards me, and I believe that she possessed not only good manners, but also decent values. She stands for loyalty and for giving support to the right causes. She certainly is no fool. I was convinced of that through remarks she made about problems of lesbianism, and about herself.

The psychological interpretation may explain her self-hate, but it cannot convey the tragedy of a person whose every attempt in human relationships is thwarted by it, and who is thereby driven into depression. Like many other lesbians she keeps up a facade, but behind it lurks the abyss of self-destructive feelings.

The two women with whom I was engaged in these dialogues were poles apart in appearance and personality. Miss Smith looked like a nun, with a fine and feminine profile, but she felt entirely masculine. Her expressive movements were set and inhibited, but they too, did not suggest a masculine woman –

quite the opposite. Miss Smith gave the impression of a well-integrated person, and one could never have diagnosed her as a lesbian from appearance and behaviour.

Miss Brown revealed, through words and gestures, aggressiveness and other traits generally attributed to the male. She is, however, a dependent and fundamentally a feminine woman. The impression given by her expressive behaviour contradicts her real nature. She is a woman of the sporting type often found among the land-owning upper classes, and by conventional standards, she is the far more 'normal' of the two. She suggests, however, to the untrained eye, the typical masculine lesbian. In spite of her emotional dilemma and her liking for alcohol, she is able to pursue a job successfully. She too has managed to integrate herself, though with difficulty, into her social and professional milieu.

Chapter Six

The Impact of the Family

When we speak of the family we mean a groupage of people as it has evolved in a patrilineal society. The first immediate surroundings of a child in western civilisation consist of the towering figures of the father and mother, and, in most cases, siblings. Father comes first, not only in the conventional use of language, but in terms of law and authority. The real priority, however, often does not conform to the conventional model: it is shifted to the mother.

Although the word family suggests a stable entity, the fine facade of a family often covers nothing but ruins. In spite of a *laissez faire* attitude prevailing in many families, the bond between mother and child holds. The old saying that blood is thicker than water is always applicable to this elemental tie, except in very abnormal situations. The link between the father and the child is a looser one for the following reason: *what* we are constitutionally, we owe to both parents, but *that* we are at all, we owe to our mother alone. This truth is not going to be proved false, unless test tube babies become one day a reality. The debt for our very existence is no small matter, but it does not even tell the whole story of what we owe to the mother. The foetus is a part of the mother's body. It is nurtured through her blood-stream, and its first home is the womb. The union does not stop there. The mother's nervous and emotional reactions affect her circulatory system, and it is likely that repercussions of the former affect the embryo. From the unique union between mother and child from the time of foetal existence certain features of their relationship are the natural consequence. They are possessiveness and a special kind of loving. This is so when all is well and natural.

From the child's point of view, its sex cannot make any difference to the fundamental situation I described. I stressed this aspect in Chapter 3. The 'normal' girl child who suffers disappointment with her mother because she is a girl may turn to her father in order to fill an emotional void. The girl with lesbian tendencies may find it difficult to close this gap through an attachment to her father, even when he is a loving and strong personality. Her mother's love will always remain her priority.

It is therefore no wonder that the mother is the strongest force in the development of lesbianism, a fact which is clearly shown in my statistical tables dealing with family influences. Children are inclined to identify with one or other of their parents. Girls with lesbian tendencies imitate their fathers rather than their mothers. They sometimes follow in his footsteps when choosing a profession. This kind of behaviour is more that of a son than a daughter. The lesbian, however, cannot as a rule ever be won over emotionally by a male, even when she has close contact and a good relationship with her father. The 'good' father has in fact far less influence on lesbianism than the 'bad' one, who nevertheless still stands far behind the mother in this respect. In very extreme cases, when he is a criminal or a sexual maniac, a 'normal' girl may turn away from the male altogether and become homosexual. An incestuous approach of the father or step-father is, of course, one of the most traumatic experiences a girl can endure. Several homosexual women of my survey, whose step-father had approached them in this way, told me that this experience had made them 100 per cent homosexual. In cases like this, even if the girls do not become lesbians, they find the door shut to a real relationship with a man because of fear and contempt.

This brings me to the psycho-analytic concept of a 'natural' incestuous situation inside the family. I have dealt extensively with this subject in Chapter 3, but I want to underline here once more my view that a *primary* incest situation only exists between mother and child, or rather, child and mother, independent of the child's sex. A girl may have a *secondary* incest problem with a brother, arising from sexual curiosity and rivalry. It is arguable whether a potential incest situation *is* confined to the family. I do not believe it is. We know from the works of Konrad Lorenz, Tinbergen, Beach and Ford, Desmond Morris and others that animals *use* sexual seduction when they are threatened, or think they are threatened, by stronger members of their species. In other words, they employ sex as a form of defence, and once they have done so, they may have formed the habit of a submissive sexual approach for good. The same applies to man. Sexual reactions *and* attitudes can be roused by the need for security, particularly in the child, but also in adults whose psychosexual development remains immature. If children are placed in an environment where figures of authority are not blood relations, they may show the same defensive attitudes as animals do. The simulation of libidinous wishes and erotic feelings towards the powerful simply expresses the need for protection, because sexuality is in many ways a means of warding off anxiety.

It was advisable to match subjects and controls according to their family background. The difference in their social environment was so small that it can be discounted. It is a matter of fact that both subjects and controls not only came from a similar milieu, but also attained a similar social status themselves. Lesbianism cannot therefore be determined by the cultural and educational level of the family. The answer to the question why the children of one group became deviants while those of the other did not must be looked for elsewhere.

I inquired into the age of the mother at the birth of subjects and controls, which could reveal a genetic factor in homosexuality. Dr Eliot Slater and Dr F. Kenyon had already investigated the maternal age at the birth of homosexuals. The former extended his inquiry to men and women, the latter to lesbians only. Both came to the same conclusion, namely that mothers of homosexuals are frequently in the older age groups. Dr Kenyon treated his finding with reserve, saying that 'the data were insufficient to calculate the birth order in the same way as Slater'. The result of my own investigation is opposite to that of both authors. As the Table 3 shows, the maternal age at the birth of the lesbian group is significantly lower than in the control group. This result, taken as an isolated item, can only indicate a trend, but it gains in significance when seen in conjunction with other findings of my survey. They register destructive maternal attitudes, either indifference or downright neglect, disproportionately prevailing in the lesbian group. Such failings in a mother are related to serious psychological disturbances. Ambivalent behaviour to her girl child is another preponderant characteristic of mothers in the lesbian group. On the one hand homosexual girls frequently enjoyed the privileges of a favourite, while on the other they were victims of indifference or neglect. The mothers of the control group lived up to what one would expect of a normal woman's feelings and behaviour.

Every mother, the giver of life, appears to every child as the source of all nourishment, physical, emotional and mental. The inevitable consequence of her power is the child's complete dependency on her. Every child is meant to take its mother's love and absolute reliability for granted. This is nature's provision. The failure of the mother to fulfil her natural functions leads to traumatic disturbances in the child; the most frequent and obvious are anxiety states and depression. Fickleness of the mother, who is expected to be a rock of trustworthiness, undermines the *ground* on which the child builds its life, and leads to disorientation about its place with its mother, the family and the world. The word insecurity, much used and often vaguely used, is hardly adequate to describe the emotional and mental climate of a person so damaged.

The overall picture of the mother in the lesbian group suggests immaturity and unreliability. Young mothers who had not enough time to settle their adolescent longings and needs may resent a child for these reasons alone, and they will, as a rule, reject a daughter more readily than a son. It may be that the unconscious fear of having a future rival at her breast makes the young mother turn away emotionally from a daughter. But this psycho-analytic interpretation does not apply in every case, and represents only one possibility in the mosaic of all possibilities. The difference in the number of mothers in the lesbian and control groups who made their girl a favourite is as striking as the difference in the number of those who did not care. Maternal inadequacy, accentuated by an emotional bias against her daughter, adds to the dilemma of the lesbian. Mothers showed no difference in their treatment of all their children in the great majority of the control group, in striking contrast to mothers of the lesbian group (see Table 7). This means either stability or instability in the mother-daughter relationship, and it must reflect on the family as a whole.

The situations described, weighty as they are, do not exhaust the list of dangers. A girl can receive another serious, if not devastating, blow in her relationship with her mother: her preference for a brother. The realisation that her mother would have preferred her to be a male may have an even more injurious effect on her. These maternal attitudes strike at the root of a daughter's being, and are an essential cause of the development of lesbianism. Mothers of lesbians inclined to these preferences more often than the mothers of the 'normal' group. However, the difference is not very significant (see Table 8). When pondering over the generally greater strength of a mother's feelings for a male child, one may ask oneself, what is nature and what is second nature? Anthropology suggests that preference for the son can by no means be taken for granted, even in our day, as certain African peoples still give first place to a daughter—a fact which makes both father and mother prefer their female child. It seems that second nature can become 'first' nature when, over the centuries, habits grow deeper and deeper in human beings. Hundreds of years of a *definite idea* have worked their way through to the hypothalamus, the 'emotional' brain. The extent to which this particular habit formation has affected woman in our patrilineal society, is shown in my study through the comparatively slight difference which exists in this respect between the two groups.

Many girls must realise, either consciously or subconsciously, that they are a disappointment to their mothers from birth onwards. Because of this, a nagging feeling of guilt follows them through their childhood, their youth, and often throughout their whole life. A change may come when the daughter is grown up, as I mentioned earlier in this book, because mothers then turn about and give preference to the daughter with whom, by now, they identify.

A correlation exists between delinquency and broken homes.

Homosexuality follows the same pattern, but there is no suggestion that it predisposes merely thereby to delinquent behaviour. Divorce or separation of the parents represent the most obvious symptom of a broken home. But what about a home where the parents remain married while hating each other? A 'break' can take many forms, both obvious and subtle. Many of the latter variety may not be recognised by the outsider, nor consciously registered by the children. The family is a collective organism, although its shape has, to some extent, been artificially produced. It is largely the pressures of religion and society that have shaped the family unit. They were highly successful for many centuries, and the family is still the most important collective unit we have. But nobody can forecast how long it will stay that way. My own impression is that the ground on which family life is built has become sterile, and will be supplanted by a new order. The lesbian situation is one among many which has pin-pointed the limitations of this sacrosanct institution.

In every generation one lives with other periods of time. In some parts of Africa today, we still find traces of the neolithic age, and cannibalistic tribes still exist in the wilds of Brazil. We can encounter the middle ages in some countries of the Middle East, and even in the remoter parts of south-west France. I myself saw remnants of the Tsarist era in the U.S.S.R. when I visited spas on the Black Sea in the late twenties.

The broken family is perhaps the flag-bearer of a new era, in spite of its destructiveness. However, the stable family is still with us, and my study tells its story, made poignant through the contrast between the situation in the two groups. One look at the statistical tables is sufficient to make one aware of the difference in their family attitudes. The control subjects with their sound and, on the whole, caring and protective background, are living proof of the powerful influence which a 'stable' family can exert on character and behaviour. Table 25, dealing with personality characteristics, bears witness to this fact. The mothers of the lesbian group often failed their daughters and left them with an emotional void. These children felt as though they were living in a house where one wall was missing. It is common knowledge that the house symbolises both the mother and the sense of security which, in psycho-analytic language, are symbolically synonymous. I must stress once more that no absolute conclusions should be drawn from the picture I have conveyed, but the trend can be accepted as being highly significant.

Although 108 is an adequate number of subjects on which to base this kind of research, it might have been ideal to study 1000. But it would probably have taken twenty years or more to collect so many suitable subjects. Even in that span of time I doubt if one could find and interview that number of lesbians, except through institutes of sexology and psychiatric clinics. People who visit either of these places would not have been suitable, because my object was to obtain knowledge of the ordinary homosexual woman who is unlikely to visit clinics or institutes dealing with sexual pathology. The social stigma attached to lesbians makes her particularly wary of having anything to do with an institution associated with deviants.

Another point must be considered. Social and other pressures bring about reactions in lesbians, which produce a common denominator in certain aspects of their behaviour. Lesbians, although individually different from one another, just as 'normal' women are, have many common characteristics. One can therefore compare research on lesbianism to research on a specified neurosis where symptoms are similar, if not identical. It is because of this that smaller numbers suffice to reveal the *nature* of the condition investigated.

I must return to the heart of the matter – the mother and her influence on lesbianism. It may seem strange that the mother, in spite of her vacillating attitudes and behaviour, is significantly more often the dominant parent in the lesbian than in the control group (see Table 6). This finding suggests a self-willed and self-assertive personality, whose interests were not restricted to marriage and children. It does not automatically indicate that she was lacking in maternal love. Some of the powerful mothers in the lesbian group were, however, of a narcissistic, immature type, who had little or no motherly feeling. Both types showed a certain detachment from family bonds. Although born into the early years of this century, the independent mother is a modern type, signalling the change in the woman's place in family and society as it has, to some extent, come about in our time.

The dominant influence of the mother makes the diminution of the father's say in the family unavoidable. His image pales in comparison with hers. Father's negative image is not in itself a factor in the development of lesbianism, but if, through his behaviour and lack of moral principles, his influence is destructive, he may help to turn the wheels in the direction of full-blown homosexuality in his daughter. The step-father, who is found considerably more often in the lesbian than in the control group (see Table 14), is a potential source of traumatic experience in any event. Of the lesbians studied, there were five cases in which he manifested sadism not only in words but in actions. These ranged from sexual exposure to demands for mutual masturbation.

The position of the lesbian among siblings has been considered to be of possible significance by the American research workers Grundlach and Riess, in their paper, *Birth Order and Sex of Siblings in a Sample of Lesbians and Non-Lesbians* (1967). I am particularly interested in their investigation, as their results are similar to mine. The most striking of their findings and my own is the fact that so many lesbians are only children. In my survey, lesbians also belonged more often to the elder siblings, and were very seldom found to be the youngest children (see Table 4). The only child is, in any case, a problem, through its very position, because she (or he for that matter) has a restricted emotional horizon, certainly in childhood. It is obvious that an only girl child is bound to have difficulty in adapting herself to others, and particularly to boys. With most of the lesbians studied who were only children, the closeness of the emotional bond with their mother made them more or less unfit to face the world outside. An extreme example of this is the second autobiography in Chapter 9, the writer of which was a war child. A considerable number of the lesbian group belonged to the same generation, and those of her problems which related to the absence of the father during the war were not isolated ones. They made the natural rivalry with the father more acute, indeed traumatic. To the natural alienism of the male was added the sudden intrusion of a man who took mother's full attention away from the girl. She felt robbed of her birthright, and the sudden realisation of the changed position with her mother acted as a shock experience. Hostility to the father, and the development of a female inferiority feeling were the obvious consequences. The girl with lesbian tendencies is not, of course, alone in the situation. The 'normal' girl is bound to feel the same, but she tries to win the 'enemy', and represses her hostility, while the lesbian gives vent to it either openly or in roundabout ways.

It is interesting to note in this context that homosexual women who adopt children generally prefer boys. One of the lesbians I interviewed achieved the record of having adopted three boys. She and her friend devoted their whole lives to them, showing them the world for the purpose of educating and broadening their minds. According to this very interesting and intelligent woman, the educational efforts were successful. The boys turned out to be natural, well-mannered and ethically sound. I have no proof of the truth of this statement other than her word; but my impression of this *father-mother* was such that I believe that she was not fooled, and that she did not fool me. It is an interesting experiment, if one can call it that, to bring up boys without a father, and see them developing into men without any of the defects one would expect of a fatherless son. However, this successful case appears to be the exception rather than the rule. Two other instances of adoption of boys by homosexual women have come to my notice, and they had either a doubtful or unsuccessful outcome. The boys concerned not only made use of their 'mothers' in an underhand fashion, but one turned out to be delinquent and the other an unstable personality. Why did these women adopt boys? Their preference for a son exhibits particular problems of lesbianism. It does not only refer to a female inferiority complex, which some lesbians share with many heterosexual women. It relates to the frustration and insecurity which they experienced as children in their relationship with their mother. The 'son' represents a wish-fulfilment: the adopting mother would have preferred to have been born a male. As a son, she would have received all the love from her mother she is now giving to her 'child'. Hers is a case of identification. The great majority of homosexual women wanted to be boys when they were children. The reason they gave was that, as girls, it fell to their lot to do the domestic chores, while the boys were free from menial tasks, and spoiled by mother into the bargain. They resented this bitterly, as it not only proved their secondary position in the family, but was a symbol of mother's preference for the male.

The lesbians had been, with few exceptions, tomboys. They

were aggressive and very active children who preferred 'masculine' games and sports to 'feminine' pursuits. A small number of 'normal' girls also grow up as little tomboys, but they develop, nevertheless, into heterosexual women. The preference for so-called masculine attitudes and games does not, therefore, by itself indicate homosexual tendencies. It refers, in my view, to the bisexual nature of every human being. At the same time it shows the wish and need of girls, particularly those with lesbian tendencies, to prove that they are as good as any boy. Only 18 control subjects said they had wished to be male when they were children, while 81 lesbians had wanted to be boys. This discrepancy supports my theory that the girl who develops into a heterosexual woman tends to imitate her mother. She stresses her femininity in order to get the protection and admiration of her father and other males.

Lesbians rarely wished to be male when they were adults (see Table 15). This finding is of particular interest. First of all it shows the acceptance of their homosexuality without resentment or grudge, but, more important, it reveals that lesbianism in our time does not imply imitation of heterosexual relationships. Lesbianism has, so to speak, found its feet. It is a thing of its own, where partners live out their bisexual nature without adopting any special sexual attitudes or behaviour. Cynthia Reid, who is associated with biological research on lesbianism, mentioned at a lecture in February 1970, that she had circulated a questionnaire among a group of lesbians in which they were asked whether they would prefer to be male. Every one of them had answered 'No'. Her finding does not correspond to the result of my own inquiry, as there were 29 out of 108 lesbians who still wanted to be men as adults. The explanation of the discrepancy in our results is this: all but 3 of these 29 homosexual women, when asked the reason why they would prefer to be men, were in agreement: 'Because of the better professional opportunities accorded to men'. They would then also be spared the secretiveness of their private lives. This shows that their desire had nothing to do with a 'sex wish', but was the result of the inequality in the treatment of women still persisting in our society.

Their position as the eldest or elder sibling in the family gave lesbians a special role – that of the less fortunate child. Being the eldest or one of the elder girls, the burden of looking after one or more younger children fell on their shoulders, and in many cases it proved to be too heavy. The situation was highlighted during the interviews with a note of strong resentment. In cases where the mother lacked interest in her children and particularly in her daughter, a task already too difficult became emotionally unbearable. As one of my subjects put it: 'I had constantly to swim against the stream'. Flight from both the idea and the reality of family life was an outcome to be expected. With some this flight could be performed in the imagination only. With others it led to lesbian relationships while they still lived at home. The need to get away from the pressure of the family was an added reason for seeing the goal of their lives in a homosexual association with another woman. Simone de Beauvoir speaks in *The Second Sex* about lesbian relationships as a 'choice', a way of life chosen. Although her interpretation misses some essential aspects, she has pointed out an added reason for the lesbian's disregard of conventional relationships.

In spite of the lesbian's more uncomfortable position in the family, there was no significant difference in their emotional reactions to other siblings, except in one respect. It concerned the hostility of the lesbian girl to her younger brother(s) (see Table 11). This animosity had a strong motivation, because it combined two causes of resentment: the task of looking after him, and her jealousy of the male. The third autobiography in Chapter 9 is an extreme example of the wound inflicted through such a situation. It led to a complete break with the family.

I compared the incidence of mental illness, alcoholism and homosexuality in the family histories, and found them to be more numerous in the lesbian than in the control group (see Table 24). This was particularly so in the case of homosexuality, an interesting finding, probably of genetic significance. My concern here is with the impact of defective families on the development of lesbianism. Only an overall assessment is possible. It is this: I spoke earlier on of the frequency of bad relationships between the parents of lesbians, leading to broken homes. In the light of their family history, a number of families in the lesbian group were also cursed with the tragedy of a bad family history.

It is small wonder that children of families with a considerable load of mental abnormality mirror some of the defects of their parents. Cases of psychosis and alcoholism are proof of it. Both these conditions were much more frequent in the lesbian than in the control group, although I discovered through close scrutiny during the interviews that a number of the homosexual women who had been inmates of a mental hospital had not, in fact, been psychotic patients. The incidence of psychological illness, mainly anxiety neurosis, was however astonishingly high among the lesbians as compared with the controls (see Table 23). This finding serves as a valuable measure of the constructive or destructive impact of the family on the life of the child. Neurosis or other psychological disturbances are not necessarily caused by parents who are, in one way or another, abnormal. It is commonly known that these conditions can be produced through ignorance alone, ignorance in the handling of a child, both in a literal and a symbolic sense. Wrong handling means lack of contact, again in both senses of the word. It is not, of course, the only source of danger to the healthy development of a child. I need not go into detail about the many situations which can threaten the emotional equilibrium of the young. They are well known, and so is the fact that psychological illness becomes manifest, in many cases, long after its initial, unconscious beginning in childhood. Of course, lack of harmony between the parents or the break-up of the home cannot fail to be emotionally and mentally injurious to any child, and particularly to one who is an outsider as the lesbian is. Neurosis begins at home, but its roots also grow well outside its native soil, when emotional and social pressures take their toll. Both are the lesbian's particular problem. However skilfully one may turn round the 'picture' of a psychological illness, its basic structure is always designed during the first years of life.

The item in my questionnaire (Table 23) asking about hospitalisation in a mental hospital does not automatically imply that a positive answer is related to psychosis. In fact only four lesbians who had been in such places appeared to have been psychotic. The others had attempted suicide and were kept in a mental hospital for observation. They suffered from nervous breakdowns or reactive depression. None of them had been in hospital for longer than three months except one, who remained inside for four months because of an obsessional condition. This happened seven years ago. She was so much improved that she

did not need psychiatric after-treatment, as she coped satisfactorily with her professional and private life.

It was suggested to me by lesbians themselves that alcoholism
is one of the sad side-effects of female homosexuality. I have myself observed a considerable number of lesbians taking to drink,
but one could by no means call all of them alcoholics. Real
alcoholism is a most serious addiction, which could be classed
as mental illness. Alcoholism occurred significantly more often
in the lesbian than in the control group (see Table 23). In 24
out of 106 cases, the addiction ran in the family. One may therefore ask the question whether alcoholism has a genetic significance, or whether the example of the elders is imitated by the
offspring. Many lesbians drink in order to drown their depressive
feelings, their over-excitement or their conflicts. However, 16
homosexual women were real alcoholics.

We know that many illnesses have a psychogenic origin.
Allergies belong to this category, and asthma can be singled out
as a condition in which nervousness plays a significant part. The
anxious person is prone to it, and it is not surprising that sufferers
from asthma were found more often among the lesbian than
the control group (see Table 22). The impact of unsuitable family
conditions could be blamed for it.

The families of the two groups were closely matched according
to their background, and it would have been reasonable to expect
that they would exert similar influences on their respective children. My statistics show how erroneous such an assumption would
have been. The different attitudes of my two groups with regard
to guilt feelings about extra-marital sexual intercourse illustrate
this point (see Table 26). The families of the controls, seen as a
whole, must have had strong authoritarian and religious principles with repressive effects on their children. Feelings of sex
guilt originate from fear of disapproval by parents, with special
reference to the mother. The child adopts, as a rule, the principles it has been taught by word and example and for reasons
often mentioned in this book the 'normal' girl is apt to conform,
to be faithful to the example of her parents, in spite of a possible
rebellious adolescence. This is what appears to have happened
with the subjects of the control group. The situation is reversed
in the lesbian group. During every interview, I asked the
question: 'Have you any guilt feelings about your homosex-

uality?' Most of the lesbians answered simply and clearly: 'None'. As it was of great interest to assess this attitude because of the vital effect it had on their lives, I was 'all ears' as I listened to the answers. I wanted to detect any note either of exhibitionism or perhaps of defiance. There was neither. Only 19 homosexual women admitted feeling guilty about their homosexuality (see Table 26), twelve because 'Mother was so disappointed', and the rest for religious reasons. The freedom from guilt feelings about sex, expressed by the lesbian group, is an obvious protest against family life. The overriding cause, however, may be found in the lesbian's defiance of convention, and her sense of independence. Homosexuality is synonymous, in her eyes, with being herself. The freedom from conscious guilt feelings is a facade, hiding the real thing: unconscious guilt feelings. These, as we know, are a great danger to psychical equilibrium, and are likely to have contributed to the many cases of psychological illness in the lesbian group.

Chapter Seven

The Characteristic Lesbian

When I was young I saw the differences in individuals so
strongly that I underrated what all of us have in common. As
time went on I realised more and more how alike people are,
and individual differences appeared to me to be more the varnish
than the essence of human beings. The fact that there are
similarities between people makes it possible to devise types of
personality. Personality is one of those words which are either
vaguely used or differently interpreted. A definition is therefore
desirable. One by John Bowlby has the merit of being both
concrete and simple. He writes in *Personality and Mental Illness*
p. 2 :

> The term is commonly used to describe what a person is like,
> how he feels, thinks and behaves in the circumstances of life,
> in much the same way as the term 'shape' is used to describe
> the spatial qualities of an object. Personal qualities are those
> which tell us whether a person is easy to get on with, or is
> angular and difficult, whether he is conventional or eccentric,
> apathetic or ambitious. Personality is the sum total of all these
> qualities, a synthesis of various and often contradictory
> trends.

E

A quotation from Bowlby's latest book, *Attachment and Loss* p. 177 is particularly relevant to my theme.

> Psycho-analysts have recognised that the child's first human relationship with his mother is the foundation stone of his personality.

Bowlby emphasises that the whole of psycho-analytic theory is an attempt to explain the functioning of personality.

D. W. Winnicott stresses what is, in my view, the essential quality of personality when he speaks about its 'core' in his *The Maturational Processes and the Facilitating Environment* (p. 187). I have myself written about the 'essence' of personality in *On the Way to Myself*. It is the quintessence of that book. Winnicott, in line with psycho-analytic thinking, sees the beginning of the 'inner self' in early infancy. It starts with a kind of solitude when the baby is with himself in peace and no outside stimuli divert or disturb him. At the same time, so Winnicott maintains, the undisturbing, distant presence of someone else is necessary for the process to succeed.

I am not sure whether the 'inner self' comes into existence in early infancy, but I know that it grows through reflection and meditation. It can become stronger and firmer throughout all phases of life. It is incommunicative and incommunicable – it is the silence which expresses what we *really* are. And the intangible effect a person can have on others comes from this source. The power of the 'unspeaking' self is perhaps the greatest power invested in man.

To complete my excursion into definitions of personality, I should like to quote a non-Freudian one by G. Alport. It comes from his *Personality: a Psychological Interpretation*, p. 48:

> Personality is the dynamic organisation within the individual of those psychophysical systems that determine his unique adjustment to his environment.

This is a broad, and at the same time, precise sweep over the vast canvas of personality.

Character is of course part of personality, and its definition must be included here. The psycho-analyst Otto Fenichel defined character in *The Psycho-analytic Theory of Neurosis* like this (p. 467):

> Character is necessarily a function of the constant organised and integrating part of the personality which is the Ego. Indeed Ego was defined as that part of the organism that handles the communication between the instinctual demands and the external world.

Temperament is intrinsically linked with personality, and is more basic than character. Temperament is, in my own definition, the individual 'tuning' of a person's reactions on which the expression of his feelings and emotions depends. Temperament is part of man's biopsychical constitution, and it has a particularly close link with endocrine function. Obviously temperament is an innate endowment and lies at the roots of personality. It never changes fundamentally, while other aspects of personality are modified by environmental influences, in the first place by those of the family. It may be of interest to add to my definition one by Bowlby. He says in *Attachment and Loss* (p. 121):

> In some cases, mood words are used to refer to the style of behaviour predicted of a person over longer periods of time – they are then regarded as temperament.

The 'inner self', character and temperament belong to the structure of the person itself. But how is this person moved into action? The dynamics of aggression are probably its chief driving force.

AGGRESSION (see Table 25)

Ordinary people get alarmed when one questions them about their aggressiveness, as if one touches a taboo. They equate aggression with hostility, and feel not only guilty, but ashamed of it. I had therefore explained to the participants of my research that everybody is aggressive, and that it is nonsensical to view part of our nature, and a foremost part at that, in a moralistic way. I put the question: 'Highly aggressive: Yes or No', at the head of the list in my questionnaire dealing with personality traits because of its paramount importance. Aggression is one of those mechanically used and misused words. Its real meaning is either unknown to ordinary people, or has been repressed through feelings of anxiety and guilt. Ignorance may mainly account for the lack of clarity on this subject. Anthony Storr's *Human Aggression* has the merit of emphasising its *positive* aspects. D. W. Winnicott speaks of aggressiveness in the book already mentioned as 'an evidence of life'. He connects its very beginning with the beginning of life. In his *The Family and Individual Development*, Winnicott points to the embryo's *motility*, which is, according to him, the precursor of aggression. Psycho-analytic thinking certainly goes to the bitter-beginning. The fact that aggressiveness is part of the erotic drive has, of course, been stressed by psychologists and is common knowledge.

I understand aggression as *élan vital*, which implies not only a state of constant alertness, but also the capacity to focus on a target. Aggressiveness is an instinctual drive because of its unpremeditated and absolute sureness.

The answers to my question: 'Highly aggressive: Yes or No' (see Table 25) show a considerable discrepancy between the lesbian and the control group, so much so that a comment about this difference is required. We must be aware that a long-standing 'mechanical' interpretation of aggression as being a 'bad thing' cannot easily be replaced by the understanding of its real meaning. Education by parents and teachers, and by religious instructors, is mainly responsible for equating aggression with hostility only.

Another point of importance is the fact that *overt* aggression does not reveal the whole of it. It is only the tip of the iceberg which a person can see. I pointed out in the preceding chapter that the families of the control subjects were more inclined to restrictive and repressive attitudes towards their daughters than those of the lesbian group. Because of it, the controls were probably less conscious of their aggressiveness than the homosexual subjects. 42 of 106 lesbians thought of themselves as being highly aggressive, as being in constant 'Kampfbereitschaft', compared with 14 of the controls. Many of the lesbians took up arms for both collective and personal aims, of which Emotional Autobiography I is an example. Collective aggressiveness of the lesbian group was and is directed towards *constructive* goals. I am thinking of organisations like Kenric and the Minorities Research Trust in this country, and the Daughters of Bilitis in America. They do constructive work in several directions. They provide a congenial milieu for lesbians who can never really be themselves in heterosexual society, and they encourage by word and active help research into homosexuality. It is in the nature of most collective endeavours to aim at constructive targets, but it is far more difficult to adopt this attitude in the personal life of an individual. There, negative aggression all too often takes the upper hand, a fact sadly confirmed by many of the lesbian subjects. Lesbians are not earmarked in this way, but for reasons which I shall try to sketch very briefly, the lesbian's situation in life has more sharp edges than that of the heterosexual woman, a fact which engenders aggression.

Aggression is aroused by suppression or rejection of spontaneous expression. This is a tall order for any human being to cope with. Thus aggression seeps out of every corner of one's being, and can take as many shapes or forms as a chameleon. Much aggressiveness *must* be suppressed to make life bearable at all. Enough of it remains active to lead us towards either creativeness or destruction. Among the many forms aggression can take, I single out three :

1. aggression which stems from insecurity or downright rejection,
2. aggression that is the consequence of frustration,
3. aggression which is part of the erotic drive.

The first has a completely negative character, while the second and particularly the third are directed towards both constructive and destructive goals. I adhere to psycho-analytic thought about the origin of insecurity-aggression. It originates in early childhood, and its source is the mother's relationship with her baby. The most injurious situation is the physical separation of the mother from the infant, but any form of defective – or no – contact, in both the physical and emotional sense, arouses insecurity-aggression. Other situations, as for example rejection by the father in childhood and adolescence and by society in adulthood, become dangerous causes of aggression because they open old wounds. It is obvious that a girl with lesbian tendencies, who has not transferred her affections from the mother to the male, will be a girl who particularly suffered from early insecurity, and will react against it with accentuated aggressiveness.

It is no exaggeration to say that frustration-aggression is an inevitable consequence of living, and is with us throughout life. Overt frustration-aggression is paramount in childhood. It decreases, as a rule, with age. Frustration is one of the foremost teachers of the art of learning and living. Aggressive reactions against frustration can lead to the consolidation of knowledge and the progressive integration of personality. Accumulated and overpowering frustration stimulates destructive aggression, which can cause depressive states if it is directed against the self.

One may ask why the lesbian should be singled out to suffer frustration and its consequences more acutely and more deeply than the normal woman. The answer is that the ground of her whole existence is far more fragile. In addition, many lesbians have a weak ego, which makes control of aggression problematic, if not impossible. It is understandable that homosexual women have special difficulties in building integrating defences against unacceptable drives. This is both the cause and consequence of their emotional dilemma. No lesbian has ever been able to solve the problem of her mother fixation and therefore dependency on another woman. The frustrations and insecurity entailed in her mother-fixation make the proper consolidation of the ego haphazard. Twenty-five of the lesbian group were married (see Table 21) and most did not consciously realise their homosexuality before marriage – a fact which did not exclude them from the same difficulty. Although their dependency on members of their own sex remained unconscious until later in life, it was there all the time, and with few exceptions, their 'normal' relationship with men had been deceptive and superficial.

I let D. W. Winnicott have the first word on erotic aggressiveness. He writes in his *The Maturational Processes and the Facilitating Environment*, p. 17 :

In the early psycho-analytic statement there is but little reference to the destructive aims of the love impulse, or to the aggressive drives that only in health become fully fused with the erotic.

Winnicott uses the term erotic in its real meaning as Ferenczi did, and I apply it in the same sense. The word erotic encompasses the areas of sexuality, sensuousness and aesthetics, and aggression is inherent in different forms in all three. An attack of one kind or other is required even to get near the object of love, not to speak of gaining possession of it. And men and women exhibit no difference in this respect.

Erotic love per se, with its wide range of emotions and sensations, grows stronger when sexual love becomes difficult. However happy physical relations between homosexual women may be, they are deprived of the last step, and have to come to terms with a void. With lesbians, both the sensuous and the aesthetic aspects of erotic love are predominant. These are inseparable from emotion, while sexual love by itself can function without emotion. Destructive aggression is part of sexuality, but not necessarily of erotic love. During the preamble of erotic contact, aggression finds constructive and sophisticated outlets in teasing, wit and *sous-entendus*. Every lover, be it man or woman, must have experienced the delights of love's teasings. The poison of destructive aggressive drives is produced by an overdose of eroticism, when intimate contact becomes overpowering. The poison is effective the moment possessiveness rules out all else. As far as any love is built on ownership, it is aggressively-destructive. Jealousy which accompanies possessive love is negative aggression with the face of a gargoyle.

Lesbian love is essentially emotional and erotic, and because of it, aggressive impulses are dispersed over wide areas. Firstly, there is aggression ingrained in possessiveness. Secondly, inimical influences, be they real or imaginary, present a constant threat to the emotional equilibrium of many lesbians, and can evoke vicious attacks against possible and real persecutors, as well as against the loved person.

ABUSE, BAD TEMPER AND VIOLENCE (see Table 25)

The incidence of abuse and violence, the paroxysms of aggression, was significantly higher in the lesbian than in the control group. Abusive language is a haranguing flow of insulting words. It stands midway between bad temper and violence.

Bad temper can be considered to be an infantile hangover. The tantrums of the child, the kickings against the 'Don'ts', are transformed either into verbal attacks, or in extremes, into pseudo-violent acts. In the latter case, objects at hand are thrown to the floor etc. Such actions are protests against a person or an object, but lack of motor co-ordination generally prevents them from being hit. The bad-tempered individual wants to miss the target. The outburst is a ritual rather than the real thing, which sets it apart from violence itself. Bad temper was found in both groups without significant difference, while violence occurred more often among the homosexual women. It is not feasible within the framework of this book to investigate the possible origins of violence. Suffice it to say they are manifold. I must however mention violence as a consequence of alcoholism, because the latter seems to have some significance in lesbianism. It occurred significantly often in the families of the lesbian group, as well as in the homosexual subjects themselves. I had occasion to witness (outside this research) violence aroused through alcoholism in three lesbian couples. Their physical onslaughts ranged from hard hits over the face to attempts at strangling. Obscene, abusive language generally accompanies these outbursts and it did so in the cases which came to my notice. The attacks were repeated at intervals, and many a time a doctor was called in, and the police appeared, summoned by one of the victims. One can argue that the same happens between heterosexual couples, but with them it is almost without exception the male who commits the attack. Heterosexual women are rarely physically violent, and a comparison could only be made between them and homosexual women. The main reason for violent behaviour in the lesbian subjects was jealousy, as evidenced by the interviews. The fear of losing their partner went so far with some of them that they avoided going to social meetings of the lesbian organisation to which they belonged. Their anticipated, morbid jealousy was a symptom of an obsession. They guarded each other like prison warders.

To sum up: aggressiveness which is either part of love, or a reaction against rejection, insecurity and frustration, is more extensive and more intense in lesbians than in heterosexual women.

I mentioned earlier that aggressiveness as a reaction to frustration can be of high value, and that all teaching contains, of necessity, an element of frustration because the pupil advances through his errors. We vacillate in our emotional and mental development between frustrations and rewards. The former make us aggressive in a creative way, when the latter are properly dealt out each time we take a step forward in our 'lessons'. Reward is as necessary to achievement as frustration.

INHIBITION (see Table 25)

Frustration is linked with inhibitory processes. A human being without inhibitions could hardly, if at all, survive. He would break down in the chaos of disintegration. Inhibitory systems are part of the biopsychical structure of man. Animal psychology has taught us a great deal about innate behaviour-systems which, of course, entail inhibitions. Behaviour patterns in man are also predesigned; they develop and alter through learning. The same is true of the animal within the boundaries of its brain capacity. Behaviour is both physiologically and psychologically conditioned. In man, for example, the hormone levels at certain periods of life, in puberty, climacterium and age, or under circumstances of stress, influence behaviour, and with it, certain inhibitory reactions. The general state of health, disease, hunger etc. can do likewise. One type of behaviour automatically excludes others. Any situation, be it an external or an internal one, calls for a special behavioural attitude. One must be favoured at the cost of others. The one chosen will be, in ideal cases, the most advantageous in the circumstances. The healthy person has the greatest chance of behaving with circumspection, and avoiding emotional pitfalls, contrary impulses and confusion. The immature individual may be unable to adopt adequate behavioural patterns. The neurotic regresses to faulty, or, in severe cases, to infantile ones. Children find it most difficult, if not impossible, to come to grips with their contrary impulses. This accounts for their ambivalent and fragmentary behaviour. They consequently change from one attitude to another in no time.

The human being learns more slowly than the animal how to use his behavioural systems and he has to be taught by his elders when and what impulses to inhibit. According to D. W. Winnicott, inhibitions are learnt by the infant during the first year of life. Already at that time, it begins to use caution and starts to build up its super-ego. In *The Family and Individual Development* p. 11, he says: 'It (the super-ego) starts as the result of crude fears of retaliation'. This statement points to the infant's drive for shelter and security which is, in my view, its absolute priority. Winnicott implies that the development of the super-ego partly precedes that of the ego. The super-ego, which I prefer to call conscience, is based on fears which head the list of influences developing morality. It is a sobering thought that fear is the mason of human ethics. The Old Testament showed the wisdom of the ages in teaching the fear of God as the basis of the good life.

Obviously inhibitions are the prop of life. They are essential to our existence. Concealment of destructive feelings unavoidably makes hypocrites of us all, and so does the projection of ourselves as good and desirable people. Both our super-ego and our ego demand that we should do so. Otherwise we would go to pieces. But man develops, in time, a second conscience which is a guardian protecting the core of the personality – the inner self – and with it, the sense of identity. Guilt feelings proper arise from *this* source, and are not imposed by outside agents and fear of retaliation. In doing wrong, the greatest harm is done to our own self and sense of identity.

It would be erroneous to assume that only destructive feelings must be hidden from others. All impulses of vital importance need secrecy, and the wish to make them public must be inhibited. The desire to communicate with others is elementary, as it relieves the sense of loneliness. Man is both an individual and communal animal. Confession of secrets is an excellent means of getting attention from others. The young girl or boy who whispers into another's ear: "I'll tell you a secret", wants attention and friendship in order not to be alone. Adults apply the same method in more sophisticated ways. We learn, however, from an early age onwards, that inner nakedness can have fatal results. Inhibitions enable man to compromise and to choose, though they do not get him out of a dilemma; he either compromises because he fears that he may lose the esteem and love of others, or he does not do so because he values his integrity and self-respect more than his reputation and need of friendship.

A division between a true and a false self is unavoidable. Everybody who is not a hermit has, in this sense, a divided self or a double personality. Inhibitions reinforce both the real and the false self. We inhibit those impulses, the expression of which would undermine our security and deform the image we want others to have of us. Famous stage personalities, for example, must live up to the image the public wants to have of them. Their public appearance may bear little resemblance to their private face, their real selves. The personality all of us show to the world is of necessity a synthetic one. It is impossible to be as honest with others as with ourselves.

Inhibitions which reinforce the true self are vital to inner development, and to the real joy of living. Most important for the integrity of the personality is secrecy about things most precious. They concern love and creativity. The latter is rooted in the former but transcends it. Verbal communication of either would harm their growth and could even be lethal to them. This is certainly so in the initial stages. The best inner experiences must be kept secret, as we would otherwise become diminished. Siegfried Lenz, the German novelist and playwright, illustrates this point in his recent play *Augenbinde* : 'Sie wissen doch : Jeder ist soviel wert wie seine Geheimnisse', which can be translated : 'You undoubtedly know that a person's "worth" is equal to his secrets'.

I have written at length about inhibition in order to elucidate certain personality traits in the homosexual women of my study who were more inhibited than the control subjects. Their inhibitions covered both the areas of defence against the milieu and the safe-guarding of their identity – their inner self. Defensive aggressiveness is the principal cause of inhibitions extending over wide areas of the psyche. Aggression was a significant mark of the lesbian group as compared with the controls, and their stronger inhibitive processes were therefore a natural consequence. The question : 'Are you very tense?' (see Table 25) relates to the intensity of inhibitory function in general, while the question : 'Are you extremely shy?" is concerned with a special area of it. A high degree of nervous tension represents a perpetual inner posture of defence, a defence which is directed against fear of one's own aggression and that of being attacked by others. Defensive attitudes reveal themselves in psycho-motor behaviour. Stiffness of posture, for example, (if not due to physical causes) is a sign of inhibition, of nervous tension. A person who always sits on the edge of a chair, or does not automatically turn her head to face her vis-à-vis, expresses nervous tension which inhibits spontaneous psycho-motor behaviour. The lesbian has good reason to be on the defensive against aggressiveness, her own and that of others. She must preserve her homosexual identity, but is afraid of giving herself away as a deviant because of the hostility she might provoke. Most of the lesbian subjects told me at the interviews that they had suffered aggression from others because of their inclination. They also had to tolerate particular forms of frustration, to which normal girls and women are not exposed. All the vetoes of the past and present created emotional hurdles for them which they found in many, though not in all, cases difficult to jump.

The fact that they were more often abusive and violent than the controls seems to contradict their very inhibited behaviour. These traits apparently show a remarkable lack of inhibition. How then is one to understand this apparent contradiction? A naturally relaxed person has no need to be pushed into any crisis of expressive behaviour or violent action. He would not build up an inner tension so unbearable that he has to break through it perforce. The inhibited individual grapples with and grasps at extreme attitudes.

Lack of inhibition is the result of inhibition.

Discomfort is the forerunner of nervous tension. Its roots go back to infancy, to a mother's faulty holding of her baby. An anxious, a reluctant and worst of all a rejecting mother cannot hold her infant naturally in her arms, and she makes it feel insecure. Failure in holding attitudes causes immediate distress, but its consequences can be both far-reaching and severe. A baby who has not been safely enfolded but stiffly held is likely to grow into a person who is in constant apprehension of inner discomfort and outer threats.

One can assume that many lesbians suffered from the traumatic experience of faulty holding by their mother when they were infants. This laid the foundation of their nervous tension which developed, in time, through fights with their milieu and their own inner conflicts. Nervous tension is always expressed through inhibited psycho-motor behaviour.

SHYNESS (see Table 25)

This brings me to a defined area of inhibition : to shyness. I have so far never met people who have not told me that they were basically rather shy. Even those whose behaviour is brazen admit to shyness when put to the test.

A person who suffers acutely from shyness, and therefore has difficulty in making contact, is faced with both an emotional and social problem. Extreme shyness predominated in the lesbian group as compared with the controls. Why? Shyness is a composite inhibition. Its roots generally go back to childhood. Many small children cannot bear to be looked at. They either cry or hide. I knew a little boy aged 3 who always went about with a towel which he put over his face at the sight of any stranger. Shyness is linked with the sense of touch. Adults who think it fit to tickle a child, and get it excited to the point of laughter or tears, may lay the foundation for emotional disturbances which go with extreme shyness. The child may develop hypersensitivity to touch, which can lead to aversion to physical contact in later life.

Fear and excitement at being touched by others, as well as touching oneself, are both sources of self-consciousness and shyness. A niggling feeling of discomfort and unease follows masturbation, even in those who do not feel guilty about it. The sexual activities of homosexual women explain much of their accentuated shyness.

Fear of the 'other' is understandable, but it implies a somewhat paranoid attitude. Hostility inside one's milieu leads to subterfuge, hypocrisy, and last but not least, to the withdrawal reaction of shyness. Fear of the 'other', which is with us from birth to death, makes good collective (and personal) contacts a necessity. The formation of groups of like-minded people is the antidote to the hostility of society at large. The lesbian situation puts this into relief. Although many homosexual women of my study denied any difficulty in social integration, their behaviour seen as a whole changes from guarded, self-conscious attitudes when with heterosexual people to spontaneity when they are among themselves. Some of my subjects made a division between their official and private self which, in my view, was self-deceptive. It is a way of camouflaging the discomfort of being an alien, and lesbians are aliens in any heterosexual group whether they admit it or not. If they exhibit brazen behaviour in heterosexual society, they over-compensate for fears, self-consciousness and shyness.

SUGGESTIBILITY (see Table 25)

Suggestibility can be regarded as a counterpoise to inhibition. Suggestible people are open to the influence of others. The fact that suggestibility is linked with anxiety states provides the key to its understanding. It is a sign of ego weakness, an infirmity which dates back to early childhood when the mother either supported or suppressed the developing ego. The suggestible person retains the need for encouragement and approval more than others. Instead of fighting against, he ingratiates himself with the 'other'. Suggestibility is essentially an imitative process : one mimics someone else in adopting suggestions. The anxious, suggestible individual is inclined to turn aggression against himself, inhibiting hostility against the 'other'.

The incidence of high suggestibility was only slightly more pronounced in the homosexual women than in the control subjects. Although its origin lies in early emotional disturbances, social pressures are bound to play their part too. The statistical result indicates a persistent social insecurity in working women, be they hetero- or homosexual. They appear not to be strong enough to face the world of men with self-confidence and assuredness. Their social insecurity is understandable. Exceptional women only are given a proper place in our patrilineal society. Others, particularly those who work in industry and government departments, do not get to the top. But their male bosses may entirely depend on them. Their influence on society, via the male, is typically feminine. Equality of the sexes will depend more on *male* than on female emancipation. Unless men change certain personal, ethical and social values, women cannot feel accepted by them as their equals. The following will illustrate my point. In a recent nation-wide survey, a bulky questionnaire had to be answered by nurses. A few of them raised the question whether they would be paid for this additional work, as several hours were involved in its completion. The answer was, of course, in the negative. The militants pointed out that no male doctor would do such a job without payment. They felt, and rightly, indignant at being treated as second class people. 'We would not be asked to give services of this kind if we were men', they said.

ADAPTABILITY (see Table 25)

The elementary repertoire of education includes the pruning of impulses in order to make a child adapt himself to others. The way in which man fits or does not fit into his milieu is a measure of his adaptability. But what must he adapt to? We have moved so far away from a homogeneous society that 'adaptation to society' is no more than an empty phrase. Man must first adapt to his family, then, outside it, to school life and his playmates. Later on the circle widens, and he has to adapt to the social group into which he places himself, or rather, has been placed.

The word society is on a par with words like normal or ordinary which are practically meaningless. Society can be considered as an abstract force only in so far as it regulates people's lives through the rules of conventions. When I speak of adaptability I refer to the way in which the subjects of this study found a niche in personal groupings, in their professional milieu and their social environment. Adaptation or maladaptation to these concrete, tangible entities can make or mar a person's fitness to live with others. The immediate milieu has, as a rule, ramifications into a larger community, and this helps to reinforce collective identity and participation. One must ask the question : which part of ourselves, if not the whole, has to adapt to others? The whole person is engaged in the process of adaptation, and physical health or disease, youth and age, emotional and mental well-being or the opposite, intelligence, ego strength or weakness are all involved in it. Although the whole of us is engaged in this process the milieu must not swallow us whole, or we should cease to exist as individuals. Adaptability demands the interplay of engagement and reserve, or participation and detachment. We must give ourselves without losing ourselves.

Adaptability is conditioned by early relationships. Motherly love, harmony between the parents, paternal concern, stable family inter-relationships are the best school for its development. Someone who goes out into the world with a grudge against his mother or his father or siblings automatically transfers resentments to other relationships, be they personal or collective.

Adaptability belongs to the equipment essential for the survival of all living creatures. The animal has a set and simple goal, the survival of the species, and it adapts itself to its environment for this purpose. Man's adaptability is a much more complex affair. He may be useless at producing offspring, but highly successful in adapting to his surroundings. One of the lesbians I interviewed saw a definite advantage in homosexuality with regard to cultural advance. She said that homosexuals were not, in the majority of cases, bothered with family responsibilities, and could therefore give themselves whole-heartedly to other tasks, which implies adaptability of some kind.

Social adaptation implies an already sophisticated mental process, namely the capacity to conceive of goals beyond immediate and concrete situations. This is a faculty of abstraction which is not developed before the maturation of the brain is complete. To quote from John Bowlby's latest book, (p. 156):

> Even by the time the second birthday is reached, the prefrontal lobes remain very little developed. These parts of the brain, evidence suggests, are necessary if an individual is to inhibit immediate response so that a plan of action, dependent on factors not present in the immediate environment, can be carried to completion. Consistent with that, it is found that only towards the end of the pre-school years are most children able to make a choice that gives substantial weight to factors not present in the here and now.

The child who has grown up in a harmonious milieu will be able to step out naturally and confidently, provided it is healthy and endowed with a suitable temperament and a good intelligence. The predominantly extravert personality has herein an advantage over the predominantly introvert; or to adopt Sheldon's terminology, viscerotonic and somatotonic individuals are more adaptable than those with a cerebrotonic temperament. Flexibility of the mind, that is, intelligence, plays a considerable part in adaptation. One must however differentiate between two kinds of mental flexibility. Presence of mind grasps a situation in a flash and acts accordingly, but it is not necessarily associated with remarkable intellectual endowment. It operates on a semi-intuitive level. For example, a driver who foresees a danger unnoticed by others and acts accordingly possesses presence of mind which is a form of kinaesthetic intelligence, as it is linked with both perceptiveness and movement. Presence of mind is a *superficial* form of adaptation, reacting to circumstances of emergency or hidden danger. Real adaptability requires insight into the structure of the milieu to which one must adapt. It is a slow process of growth in a new soil, which is its essential difference from a superficial or pseudo-adaptation. It is common knowledge that pseudo-adaptation is practised by people all over the world in human relationships.

The most poignant cause of pseudo-adaptation to others is our divided self, which makes some dishonesty inevitable in every human relationship. The psychical structure of man is such that ethical super-structures are necessary to cement human associations, and to counteract as much as possible the ambivalence of his emotions and attitudes. Written and unwritten laws watch over people's behaviour, whether in intimate groupings such as marriage, or professional institutions and national and international organisations. An absolutely stable environment exists only in the abstract, which means that man has to fight on two fronts in his endeavour to adapt. His own instability would possibly be matched by that of the milieu, if pseudo-adaptation and the law did not come to the rescue.

It came as no surprise to me that the lesbians were significantly less adaptable than the controls, except in social contacts. Their adaptability to their professional milieu and in intimate relationships was poor in comparison with the controls. Most lesbians had a particularly disturbed relationship with their mothers. This was the *fundamental* cause of their deficient adaptability. It fully explains their difficulties in coping with intimate relationships. Many among them were unable to find peace and real relaxation with their partners. They went on hunting for the ideal mother or high-powered romance. The cause of their difficulty in feeling at home in their professional environment has been largely discussed in the third chapter. It was mainly due to fear of giving themselves away as homosexual, and of running the risk of losing their job.

This brings me to their comparatively good adaptation in social contacts. A lesbian must act a part, and she learns to do so through fear. Her social ease is put on in heterosexual company, but is spontaneous when she is with her own kind. The wish to be accepted by society makes lesbians observant of the 'other' and aware of his or her idiosyncrasies. This attitude is pleasing and creates good will. Married lesbians who have or had a family have no apparent difficulty in adapting to 'normal' people as long as they are unconscious of their homosexuality. Many lesbians had affairs with men and while these lasted they felt easier in normal society. But the moment they reverted to full-blown homosexuality they encountered difficulty in integrating into heterosexual groups.

STRESS SYMPTOMS (see Table 27)

Stress symptoms accompany maladaptation, and can cause psychosomatic illnesses – from endocrine dysfunction to high blood-pressure, etc. The emotional symptoms of continuous nervous strain are as manifold as they are variable. In order to relieve them, people escape into drug-taking, drink or an intensified imaginative life. The majority of the lesbian subjects wrote and spoke of their vivid imagination. They mentioned that much of their love, their hate and their aggressiveness was lived out in imagination. The fact that they more frequently *dreamed* about sex than was the case with the controls tends to underline the stronger motives they have for escaping from reality.

Stress symptoms arise from low tolerance of stress situations, which was a marked feature of the lesbian group. The frequency of their loss of composure and emotional equilibrium was much higher than in the control group. Enjoyment of leisure and joie de vivre provide a barometer for gauging a person's capacity for relaxation in every sense : muscular, nervous, emotional and mental. As was to be expected, the lesbian group again fared badly in comparison with the control subjects.

SEXUALITY (see Table 28)

This table lists sexual manifestations in lesbians which throw light on their intimate life. They pertain, at the same time, to the lesbian personality as a whole.

Imagination plays a dominant part in everybody's life whatever their personality type may be, but it becomes a salient factor in the introvert. Imagination is an extension of and a compensation for what we call reality, and much more besides. Lesbians need its compensatory functions more than heterosexual people : the reasons for this are discussed throughout this book. Most of the lesbians I saw were introspective individuals, and sexual fantasies as well as dreams represented significant components of their sex life. One could detect a theme running through its different manifestations, a theme with variations. They bring into the open a characteristic aspect of lesbianism. All but eleven of the subjects had undisguised sex dreams. This is not in itself peculiar to lesbians, but the dream-contents are. I have mentioned many times that the *emotional* bond represents the essence of female homosexuality, and I have proposed that a more appropriate name for lesbians would be homoemotional women. The statistical results of Table 28 confirm my assertion. They show that most lesbians have no complete fixation on the female sexual organs. Many of them had been physically attracted to men, and most of them had heterosexual experiences (see Tables 17 and 20). The same inclinations were revealed in their dreams, day-dreams and in masturbation fantasies. The reverse was true for strong emotional attachments. 90 out of 106 lesbians were exclusively homoemotional, while only 14 felt also emotional about men (see Table 18). The fact that 10 of the lesbian subjects had, in their dreams, sexual intercourse with men only, and 33 with either sex, clearly points to persisting *bisexual* reactions in homoemotional women. If one also takes the 25 cases of voyeur dreams into account, it is evident that the *real* crux of lesbianism lies in emotional and not in sexual fixation. The subjects emphasised that their voyeur dreams were about copulation between men and women. The dreamers witnessed, in other words, the primal scene. Unconscious memory traces of intercourse between their parents or parent substitutes, either seen or imagined, break through in voyeur dreams. This is a possible interpretation, but a more convincing explanation was put forward by two lesbians. They maintained that voyeur dreams were dreams of wish-fulfilment. They expressed envy of heterosexuality, mainly because of the procreation of children. With some, the act itself was enviable to the dreamer, but the sense of deprivation through childlessness seemed to be the more significant point. I have no statistical evidence as to whether pets are child substitutes for lesbians. Although no appropriate question was included in the questionnaire, I interrogated the subjects about it during the interviews. Most of them possessed one or more animals. All but four had one or two cats. One kept white mice in addition to a cat. Four lesbians who loved and reared dogs lived in the country. It must be remembered that this study is mainly concerned with working women, and their home conditions were possibly responsible for the absence of dogs in their ménages. The question whether the cat, symbol of the female, enjoys special favour with lesbians cannot be answered. It is conjecture to say that this might be so.

All lesbians expressed nostalgia for a proper home. They wanted to live a kind of family life, although most of them resented their own family. A reasonable stability of life is still seen by most people, be they 'normal' or deviant, in the model of a family. This idea persists in spite of the many signs that the harmonious and stable family unit is on the way out. It looks as if it is going to be replaced by new forms of intimate partnerships, which may be integrated into larger communal units. Lesbians appeared to be old-fashioned in their ideal of a family because they are so insecure as to fear any kind of sharing which might invite the disaster of loss. All the homosexual women I saw wanted to have a settled life with another woman, but insisted that they did not wish to ape heterosexual marriage.

In the twenties and thirties many lesbians dressed in a quasi-male uniform. They still were, at that period, so uncertain of themselves as to imitate men. The accent of lesbianism appeared to be on false heterosexuality. This attitude stunted the natural reactions and the social behaviour of homosexual women. The lesbian situation of today, according to this study, is different. The old model of competing with the male is practically gone. Comparatively few lesbians would have changed their sex if they could, and those who still preferred to be men did so because of better professional prospects and a less furtive life. The new attitude is reflected in greater self-confidence and less fear of being a woman, a fact which was evidenced by the sexual reactions of the lesbian subjects. The answers to the question whether they experienced orgasm either as 'male' or 'female', or were functioning both ways, throw light on their erotic imagination and their sexual identity. A considerable number of women, be they hetero- or homosexual, are unable to experience vaginal orgasm. They are fixated on clitoral release. This may be the outcome of masturbatory habits, or it may be due to various psychological causes. Infantilism of the sexual organs can be an obvious physical impediment to vaginal orgasm. Another similarity between homo- and heterosexual women is the fact that some need the help of fantasy to achieve orgasm.

When a lesbian gets sexual satisfaction as a 'male', nothing else is meant but that she reacts to stimulation of the clitoris only. No real difference exists, therefore, in the *sexual functioning itself* between the normal and the deviant woman. They differ only in the content of their fantasies. A lesbian imagines herself to be a man making love to a woman. When fantasy plays a part in sexual function, the person concerned applies the technique of the voyeur through the mind's eye.

One of the outstanding findings listed in Table 28 is that 46 lesbians easily changed over from 'male' to 'female' sexual reactions. It is also of interest that 27 of the homosexual subjects experienced only vaginal orgasm, in any case as a final release. The sexual foreplay involves stimulation of the clitoris in all women. One can thus state that the homosexual subjects reacted sexually in every way as 'normal' women do. They differed in two aspects only, apart from their fantasies:

1. their ease in changing from sexual aggressiveness to feminine surrender,
2. the rare occurrence of frigidity.

The second point gives substance to my view that lesbians are sexually highly responsive and virile.

Masturbation and fantasy are linked; they get more and more closely connected as time goes on. In childhood and adolescence self-stimulation can be a simple and direct act to relieve tension, without the involvement of the imagination. Anxious and lonely children masturbate *unconsciously*, and adolescents may have *unconscious* fantasies at the act, but may be *consciously* blank. This auto-erotic pursuit releases and expresses a variety of impulses, of which aggression and eroticism head the list. Masturbation is an essentially introspective activity, which explains why fantasy plays a part in it. Only 22 of the lesbian subjects denied that they indulged in this form of auto-eroticism. It is common knowledge that most people masturbate, even when they have sexual partners. Homosexuality in both men and women entails masturbatory activities. Heterosexual people may employ similar techniques, but not, as a rule, to the same extent. However, any sex act can be called masturbation when it is performed for self-gratification only. In other words, all sexual life degenerates into masturbation when it is devoid of the experience of, and concentration on, the 'other'.

The sexual act in itself is a loss, unless it originates from a deep-seated emotion for another person. Heterosexual people can find release from tension in futile, unemotional copulations if they can separate their sex life from their emotions. It is well known that many homosexual men are also inclined to transitory or one-night affairs that are purely physical, but I do not believe that the same is true of lesbians. Masturbation plays a more important part in the life of homosexual than heterosexual women for obvious physical reasons, which contributes to the fact that with lesbians emotion is the conditio sine qua non for sexual expression. I am aware that there are women on the fringes of lesbian organisations who are promiscuous. They count the number of those whom they seduce in brief, one-night encounters, as immature men do. Their behaviour is not characteristic of lesbianism.

It is of great interest that the number of lesbians who imagined themselves either as male or female during masturbation was in reverse proportion to those who did so in their sex dreams. Comparatively few lesbians saw themselves as women during self-stimulation. The number who experienced vaginal orgasm only shrank accordingly in connection with masturbation fantasy. Only ten women belonged to this category.

SUMMARY

I want to sum up the characteristic personality traits of the lesbians of my study. It is hardly necessary to mention that I can only give a schematic outline. The finer individual differences cannot be assessed by this or any statistical study. They escape pigeon-holes through the very nature of the method.

Both lesbians and control subjects had common denominators. Firstly, they earned their own living in similar occupations. Secondly, they came from a similar family background, and their average age was roughly the same. Most of them were what one might call an average kind of person. Mentally brilliant or otherwise unusual people were few and far between. It is therefore reasonable to assume that the results appertaining to this particular inquiry indicate characteristic personality traits of the lesbian in our midst.

The lesbian's aggressiveness stands out, not only as a characteristic of behaviour, but as the very soil on which she strives and thrives. Her aggressiveness provides clues to her personality. The range of aggressiveness is, as we know, an all-embracing one. It manifests itself in everything alive, be it constructive or destructive. The lesbian's sense of freedom and independence, her emotional curiosity and sense of adventure, indeed her virility, express the positive side of her aggressiveness. Its destructive qualities were, however, those which predominated. Abusive and violent behaviour, for example, were significantly prevailing in the homosexual group. Lesbians appear to be constantly on the qui vive to defend themselves. Their sense of insecurity is responsible for their defensive-aggressive reactions. The fear of being cast out or being attacked accounts for much of the lesbian's uninhibited aggression on the one hand, and for her strongly inhibited behaviour on the other. The latter is the other side of the former. Highly aggressive persons are afraid of their own hostility, and of what might happen when they let go. They must therefore try to inhibit these destructive impulses, even if they know that they may be unsuccessful in holding them down. A similar mechanism can explain extreme shyness, another personality characteristic of the lesbian. She has to put a brake on her natural impulses, be they of an erotic nature or not, because she never loses the fear of giving herself away. There are of course other causes for extreme shyness, for instance, unconscious (and conscious) feelings of guilt about homosexuality or masturbation or both.

A difficulty in adaptation makes homosexual women awkward for their colleagues at work, and more than awkward in their personal relationships. An atmosphere of drama, suggestive of both high-powered emotivity and low tolerance against stress, is the psychical climate in which lesbians live. Their powers of relaxation and of enjoyment of life are often lower than in others, which is an obvious sequitur of what has been said. To mention it once more : the lesbian is at a considerable disadvantage in every milieu. A possible gain from her vicissitudes is tolerance and understanding of the suffering of other people.

The sexual and emotional life of some lesbians remains frustrated because of their childlessness. Although this is not the case with the majority, it counts with some of the feminine type. While the lesbian's sex life is more restricted than that of the heterosexual woman, her eroticism is likely to be not only stronger but more imaginative. Girls and boys who go through homosexual phases become, as a rule, good lovers in heterosexual relationships because they retain a higher degree of erotic playfulness. The lesbian's curriculum of love gives Eros a predominant place.

It depends on one's attitude to Eros whether one considers the lesbian's erotic playfulness to be a positive aspect of her personality or not. Norman O. Brown advocates in his *Life against Death* that people should give more to Eros in order to have less of Thanatos in their lives. I am inclined to his point of view.

Chapter Eight

Lesbians—a Minority Group

The first lesbian organisation in Great Britain called itself a minority group, and this expresses the way many homosexual women look at themselves. The word minority evokes associations of an ethnical and political kind. Minorities are groups of people who at best are tolerated and may even be persecuted. They have their own codes of behaviour, their own ideals, habits and *sous-entendus*. Political extremists such as the Trotzkyites and anarchists for example are international minorities, and certain religious and semi-religious sects belong to the same category. The Freemasons are an example of the latter. One of my interviewees expressed the view that lesbianism had much in common with Freemasonry. They both represent international fraternities, the members of which help one another and further their mutual interests because of personal and collective identification. I wondered whether her views were biased through her own place in society. She belonged to the upper class and noblesse still obliged, so she told me, in her own circle of friends and acquaintances. She was convinced that lesbians recognise one another at a glance, wherever they are, at home and abroad. I think that there is truth in her statement, which was confirmed by other homosexual women. They know, in a rather uncanny way, who belongs to the fraternity and who does not. They sense the kindred soul and get the signal, even when the appearance of the other woman is perfectly 'normal'.

Lesbian groups do not account for the sum total of homosexual women. Many remain incognito and would neither dare nor wish to join a lesbian organisation for a number of reasons, the most important of which is fear of being thrown to the wolves by their own class. Feminine diplomacy must cover up their true inclination, an attitude which may add to their mystique for both women and men. The *anonymous* lesbian leads a double life, being of necessity a hypocrite. Her situation calls for strict discipline in behaviour and most of all for camouflage, which adds to the strain of a constant vigilance. She can under no circumstances run the risk of being found out. Lesbians are generally successful in hiding their secret from their family, but they are not so lucky where their friends are concerned, many of whom are aware of their inclination. One of my interviewees put it this way : 'I am aware that most of my heterosexual friends know about me, but as long as I am not found out, I am all right'. Both the reason for and the means of camouflage are different in different countries, depending on the prevailing political and social structure. Mimicry of some kind or other is necessary in all countries, because of the patrilineal system which is worldwide and which dictates society's attitudes to the lesbian. Lesbianism can be understood as an international, underground society and in this way it resembles Freemasonry. The similarity ends however at this point. No comparison can be made between lesbians and national minorities because of the fact that *nature* has made them what they are, and human nature is the same all over the world. Although lesbianism has the same ingredients everywhere, the framework of country and language gives a distinctly national flavour to the manners and behaviour of homosexual women. In some countries, such as Great Britain and America, lesbianism arouses a special if not sensational interest. In others its problems, indeed, its very existence is swept under the carpet. It is *totgeschwiegen*, as far as I know, behind the Iron Curtain, in spite of the fact that attitudes to homosexuality are far-sighted and tolerant there, according to the East German psychiatrist, Dr Rudolf Klimmer. Wherever they live and in whatever way they are looked at (if not ignored) by their respective governments and the population, the lesbian's style of life is out of tune with that of 'normal' people. The majority of these consider them to be a foreign body in the organism of society. A human organism tries to free itself of such an invader either through its natural powers, or with the help of surgery. The social organism imitates these attempts at a cure where minorities are concerned. As no country could afford to punish thousands of its workers through the isolation of imprisonment, it could not possibly proceed to have millions of homosexual women ostracised and banned from public life. Society cannot in any case touch those who remain successfully camouflaged, but the state could make life very difficult for those who come into the open. As well we know, this was the case for nearly 2000 years. Although laws against lesbianism have been dropped in most countries, persecution of lesbian minorities still continues through different forms of mental cruelty. Lesbians are always at risk of isolation through being either ridiculed or ignored. They are made to feel that they are unnatural women of vice. This is so even today in our so-called permissive society. The fact that homosexual women are persecuted by the majority, even though it is done in a subtle way, forges a link between them and other minority groups, with whom they have otherwise nothing in common. I cannot resist pointing out once more a certain resemblance in the fate of Jews and lesbians. Both are found in all parts of the world, and both are made to feel, in either a ruthless or a subtle way, that they are out of place. Although the physical persecution of Jews has been dropped in most civilised countries, a tenuous form of anti-semitism persists everywhere. The latter holds good for the lesbian minority also. But their lot is worse than that of the Jews because they are rejected wholesale by society, except for those who excel in the arts, literature and the professions. They are accepted and sometimes revered by the public. Comparisons serve to illustrate a point, but they must not be pursued beyond that point. Two situations are never identical. The comparison between the lesbian and the Jewish situation must be understood in this way. It is obvious that the two groups differ in the influence they exert on the communities in which they live and in the range of international contacts and communication. The Jews are a necessity to their countries, and they are, as a rule, though often reluctantly, accepted as such. Jews are internationally linked through their common history, and their common interests in the present. The span of international contact between lesbians is limited, and communication is correspondingly restricted. The axis of lesbian alliance extends over many countries : but is strongest in Great Britain, the United States of America and last but not least, Holland.

The common language makes contact between the lesbian organisations in America and Great Britain particularly easy. Periodicals such as *Arena Three* in Britain and *The Ladder* in America keep members informed about activities, and help to further knowledge of and research into female homosexuality in the two countries. Reciprocal visits strengthen and enliven contacts between the two organisations.

Holland, although outside the English speaking fraternity, merits special mention. Its second city, Amsterdam, has become the metropolis of homosexual freedom. The Netherlands have proved to be the most advanced nation in regard to the understanding of the homosexual woman and man and their problems. Many Dutch people are multilingual because of their colonial past, their trade, and an altogether international outlook. English is spoken as a second language by the educated and this facilitates contact between the homosexuals of both countries. Many English lesbians (and homosexual men) visit Amsterdam to enjoy the feeling of freedom and the social facilities at the C.O.C. The three letters stand for Cultuur en Ontspannunscentrum (Cultural and Relaxation Centre). This organisation has unusual merits and I should like to give a brief outline of its history and activities. Its beginnings go back to the end of the war, to the departure of the Nazis from Holland. Homosexuals had a special reason for thankfulness because of the cruel laws introduced by the Nazi régime against them. Free from the fear of persecution, intellectuals of homosexual inclination formed a group which they named the Shakespeare Circle. They held regular meetings where literary subjects and problems of homosexuality were discussed. The discussion group was soon transformed into a place for social gatherings and pleasure. Before they dared do this, permission was sought from the police to found a club for homosexual people. The request was granted after a few days of deliberation, because the police saw no danger to public welfare in the undertaking. A club for homosexuals was of course a sensation in Holland, and it soon attracted many deviant men and women of all social classes. What had started as a small group of intellectuals broadened in a few years into the largest European community of homosexuals. In 1948 the Club could afford an administrative Centre with workers on full-time pay. The Samaritan phase of the C.O.C. had begun. The employees at the Centre were on call at every hour of the day to give help to homosexuals, members or not. This was not all. Approaches made to churches, medical organisations, individual psychiatrists and organisations for social services had found a wholehearted response and an army of competent counsellors and helpers was at the ready. The club had found an open ear everywhere, and the government of the Netherlands itself supported the services rendered to its homosexual population. Everyone engaged in specialist work for the C.O.C. gave his services free of charge. It was to be expected that Amsterdam would become a focal point of attraction for homosexuals from all over the world, and it did. The C.O.C. Club is only a hundred yards away from the American Hotel in Amsterdam, and next to a famous cabaret where women impersonators perform. Apart from a bar, reception rooms, a dance hall for both homosexual men and lesbians, the club offers facilities for art exhibitions and conferences. All these activities provide the necessary funds for the upkeep of the organisation. The growing membership, now standing at about 4000, of which nearly 1000 are women, contributes to the financial needs.

The C.O.C. was built on the principles of the American Declaration of Human Rights. It was in the natural course of events that the organisation would encompass a wider field than the national one, and in 1951 the International Committee for Sexual Equality was founded. The I.C.S.E. held conferences in Amsterdam, Frankfurt am Main, Copenhagen, Brussels and Paris, under the direction and with the participation of leading European psychiatrists and sexologists. This organisation regrettably folded up after about seven years, but it had in the meantime spread knowledge and a wider understanding of homosexuality throughout Europe.

Organisations for homosexuals also exist in France, Belgium, the Scandinavian countries, Iceland and Switzerland. The one in Switzerland can boast that it is the oldest homosexual organisation in Europe. It is also of particular interest to my subject, because its founder was a lesbian. In 1932 she published, with the help of a number of homosexual women and men, a periodical called *Schweizerischer Freundschaftbanner*. The subscribers belonged at the same time to the organisation *Der Kreis*. The journal was edited under the founder's own name. She had to pay for her courage because she lost several jobs on account of it. The periodical changed hands after 1938, but it is still in existence.

Germany has no lesbian organisations. Male homosexuals have some kind of contact with one another through a periodical *Der Weg*, which, according to Dr Rudolf Klimmer, has a wide and international circulation. Although lesbians are not collectively gathered together through an organisation, two of my interviewees who had spent some years in Germany told me that lesbianism is widespread there, though it remains underground.

Apart from the C.O.C. in Holland, it is Great Britain which possesses the most comprehensive organisation of help for homosexual women and men, the Albany Trust. This has a history and structure very different from the C.O.C., which it resembles only in its counselling service. The Albany Trust calls itself a referral agency. It is a registered charity which works to 'promote psychological health through education, research and social action', to quote from one of its leaflets. Its origin goes back to the year 1958, when it was set up by members of the executive committee of the Law Reform Society. It concentrated its services on homosexuals only until 1967, the year of the Sexual Offences Act, which legalised the private homosexual behaviour of two consenting adults. Since the act had, up to a point, come to the aid of homosexuals, the Albany Trust extended its care to *all* deviants. Its membership of about 1500 comprises hetero- as well as homosexual people. Some of the patrons of the organisation are household names, known through their reputation in religious, scientific and humanitarian work. Two trends can be discerned in the principal objectives of the Albany Trust: active aid to those in need, and a wide programme of scientific research into psycho-sexual dispositions and difficulties. Last but not least, the organisation is concerned to promote a better understanding and more tolerance of the deviant by society.

Antony Grey, the then Director of the Albany Trust, has over seven years done everything to achieve the goal set out in its programme. He did so in Britain and also in America, through personal contacts as well as through lectures and television interviews. The interest aroused in the States led to collaboration between the American Erickson Educational Foundation and the Albany Trust. This is only one example of the international outlook and aspirations of the Trust. There are many others which I cannot refer to in the framework of this book. The intellectual quality prevailing in the Albany Trust is reflected in *Man and Society*, a periodical published twice yearly. Its contributors are specialists in the fields of psychiatry, psychology, sociology etc. A news sheet is circulated every two months among the members, informing them about new projects of research and other enterprises. The organisation is entirely dependent on voluntary support, another difference from the C.O.C. It has managed to survive financial crises through the help of people with a progressive and humanitarian outlook.

I cannot go into detail about all branches of activity of the Albany Trust, but I want to speak about two of them : the extent of collaboration with other organisations, and their active help in individual cases.

The Albany Trust collaborates with several universities in furthering research and assisting in conferences. Both lesbianism and male homosexuality were discussed, for example, at Aston University, Birmingham, on Antony Grey's initiative. Further research, particularly on social problems of homosexuals, is planned by Aston University in collaboration with the Albany Trust and a research worker from the Kinsey Institute of New York. A large survey on social conditions of homosexual women and men has recently been carried out by the Trust itself. The number of participants was surprisingly high. The Trust is also in touch with research projects with government departments. The Social Science Research Council expressed interest in large-scale surveys on community adjustments of homosexual men and lesbians.

Information is education. The medical and legal professions need and want information about homosexuality and the Albany Trust is in contact with both to provide it. The Probation Service has shown interest in the Trust's work and its helpful advisory function. Certain teaching hospitals are particularly interested in homosexuality and transsexualism, and communication with them is reciprocally fruitful. Discussions about collaboration were held with the Department of Health, the Health Education Council, the Marriage Guidance Council and other official organisations. In short, the Trust has been able to organise a network of communication and collaboration with relevant institutions and individuals. It carries out a great task in an area of life where we need more scientific knowledge and human understanding.

The immediate help for the individual has, of course, priority in the Trust's activities. In 1968, 530 people, 103 of them lesbians, visited the offices and were interviewed by the case-worker Doreen Cordell.

Everybody who seeks the help of the Albany Trust is bound to have psychological difficulties, whatever the nature of his or her actual problem may be. The case-worker considers it her primary task to give psychological first aid : to listen to the person she interviews with sympathy and understanding. Her counsel on the social problem may be the answer needed, but in many cases it is not. Mrs Cordell's psycho-therapeutic understanding will relieve tension, but it cannot be curative in itself. The help of others has to be engaged and the links forged by the Albany Trust with the relevant organisations and specialists, which I have mentioned, provide it.

Although the exclusively lesbian organisations are built on different principles from those of the Albany Trust, there is much common ground between them. Their long-term aims are the same, such as the furthering of biological and psychological research and the education of the public about homosexuality. They are however distinctly different in one respect : the Albany Trust is an organisation which deals with the *problems* of its clients, either directly or indirectly. The lesbian organisations focus their attention on the relief from loneliness. They deal with ordinary people, not with cases.

The Minorities Research Group was the first lesbian organisation in Great Britain. It was founded in 1963. At the start, lesbians with psychological problems came to the private flat from which the organisation functioned. They received as much help through friendship and understanding as the helpers were able to give. These did what they could, but in the majority of cases, this line of action did not succeed because it neither satisfied the helper nor the one who wanted help. The Group had no backing from official bodies, nor financial resources other than the contributions from members. All services were rendered voluntarily and under the pin-pricks of a subtle persecution. When the owners of the premises realised that a lesbian journal was issued from them, they forbade the address to be used for this purpose. In the end, the Minorities Research Group had to find another address from which to distribute their journal and receive correspondence. One of the great services of the Group was the monthly publication of *Arena Three*. Every member received the journal, which kept her informed about a wide variety of items related to lesbianism, from literary reviews of relevant fiction and non-fiction to announcements of social meetings and advertisements for personal acquaintanceships.

The Minorities Research Group's humble beginnings and considerable difficulties did not damp the spirit of its founders. They participated in research projects on lesbianism through appeals for subjects in *Arena Three* and by the distribution of questionnaires. Psychiatry owes them a considerable debt. They also talked and wrote about lesbianism. Esmé Langley for example, gave a lecture to members of Mensa in Cambridge. Diana Chapman wrote an article 'What is a Lesbian?', first published in the *Family Doctor* and later reprinted by the Albany Trust in *Man and Society*. One of the main objectives, namely to find a place for regular meetings of members, seemed to succeed for a while. A well-known pub in Carnaby Street made a room available for social gatherings of the Group. However the garb of some of the members might have aroused misgivings in the owner of the pub who cancelled the arrangement. The Minorities Research Group had bad luck with excursions into the world outside, but undaunted, the members moved on to another pub in a less fashionable area. Although no outward difficulties were put in their way there, the gatherings themselves lost impetus after a time and finally ceased.

Regional groups had by now been established in many counties outside London. But the social gatherings of the Minorities Research Group in London folded up in 1965. *Arena Three* became the only focus of its activity. Some of the founder

F

members were so dissatisfied with the failure to give a collective home to members that they broke away from the Group altogether. They saw no possibility of mending differences and decided therefore to create a new group, which they called Kenric. The name is a combination of two London districts, Kensington and Richmond, where many of the members had their homes.

Kenric filled a gap, which the Minorities Research Group, called the Minorities Research Trust since 1968, had left. It was able to form a solid, well-organised association with the principal aim of fighting the isolation and loneliness of lesbians, through bringing them regularly together in private homes and once monthly at a night club. At the Annual General Meeting, a committee of six is elected to organise and arrange meetings and further research and to invite outside people to talk on current investigations about lesbianism or other topics of general interest. The group's programme of meetings, which is tabulated in a monthly newsletter, reflects its circumspect and useful activities. It comprises intellectual, artistic, sporting and social activities. A literary evening as well as a music group take place once a month and discussions are held in private homes and after lectures by outside research workers in public halls. Visits to the theatre and art galleries, treasure hunts in the country, walking tours, trips on the river mirror the variety of needs and interests of this lesbian community. The library has its *jour* once a month in the house of two friends and the exchange of books is combined with a social evening. Kenric has more than doubled its membership in the last two years and has not so far failed in any of its enterprises. The membership consists mainly of women who work as employees of one kind or another, but there are also university graduates and professional people among them. One of them gave talks at several universities about lesbianism in general and Kenric in particular. All members are in agreement about helping in research projects. They follow herein the line of the Minorities Research Trust and the Albany Trust.

Most of my interviewees told me that their life had been changed through Kenric. Many spoke of another benefit. Their sense of identity and self-esteem had been strengthened. They did not any longer feel inferior to heterosexual people. Although not all of them had shed the gloom and humiliation of being considered second-class citizens, I recognised their determination not to form a ghetto and a ghetto-mentality. They wanted to be accepted as equal partners in any group. In fact, they *resent* being a minority group. They aspire to be fully recognised by, and integrated into, the community. I think that this goal is still far from becoming reality. But the trend is healthy, and the same attitude prevails among male homosexuals particularly in Holland and France.

I had seen 108 lesbians as individuals and had made contact beyond the interview with a number of them. I thought it important that I should also become acquainted with their collective behaviour. I had access to their private homes and their more public gatherings, and I took advantage of both. I visited some couples for dinner and conversation, I went to discussion groups, gave a talk myself, and last but not least, I attended monthly evenings at a night club. My impressions as well as the conclusions I drew from them must, because of the nature of impressions, be subjective. But I think they may nevertheless contribute to the knowledge of lesbianism from another angle. Lesbians vary in individual differences and character as much as 'normal' women, which hardly needs to be emphasised. Those who came into my orbit of observation struck me however as distinctly 'other' in one respect. In a crowd of women, one generally has a certain feeling of claustrophobia. The effect produced by a group of women alone is different from that of a group of men alone. Women by themselves appear to be incomplete, as if a limb were missing. They do not come into their proper place and function without the male. They seem to suggest a herd which is on the point of losing direction, or a substance without a proper structure.

I never felt anything like this at Kenric meetings, whether they were discussion groups or social gatherings. I noticed many times that people were rather enclosed in themselves because of strong emotional preoccupations, but they never suggested incompleteness. Men were neither felt to be missing nor missed. At the talks and discussions in which I participated, one could have heard a pin drop, such was the attention and concentration. A strange event, I thought, as many of the listeners were obviously emotionally overwrought people. I noticed reserve and restraint in their attitude to others and no respect for authority.

If anything, they were highly critical if not aggressive in discussion. The word atmosphere conveys the intangible, and perhaps the most telling characteristic of the atmosphere in the lesbian group was virility of mind. The homosexual women I observed were neither hesitant nor apparently inhibited in any way when *en masse*. I thought that they had shed their mask the moment they found themselves among their own kind. No cosiness, no chit-chat recalled a feminine world.

Fashion has come to the aid of both the female and male homosexual. Casual clothes, such as pullover and slacks, is no longer a symptom of lesbian protest against men. Most girls wore that comfortable uniform on different occasions. I saw them in the same garb at private parties, official gatherings and dances. Comfort of dress may be a lingering protest against the decorative discomfort women had to suffer over the centuries, but if so, this protest is not the monopoly of lesbians. Heterosexual women can now indulge in the same freedom, but with them clothes are still chosen to please men. They consider their sex-appeal for the male a priority and they shape their appearance for his eyes. This is a necessity not only for the fulfilment of their own sexual and emotional needs, but also for their professional advancement. The latter dilemma affects the lesbian too. She dresses up when at her job, but she *acts* the part.

I watched with particular keenness the appearance of lesbians at club evenings, when they had paid special attention to their clothes. Only two out of about 120 were dressed in men's trousers and shirts. The rest wore the same clothes as on other occasions, but one noticed how much care all of them had given to accessories and particularly to their hair style. A small number wore mini-skirts and their hair hanging loose down to their waists.

Apart from the colourful picture of everybody spruced up in dress and coiffure, I was fascinated by the gradual development of events during the evening. To start with, nothing at all appeared to happen. People sat, drank and talked, as in any other pub. After a while, very gingerly, some life came into the party. One, then two couples made strange, ritual movements at each other but not with one another. The evening had really begun. The confined floor was soon filled by one pair after another making similar stereotyped movements, which recalled Eastern dances. Women dancing together are not an uncommon spectacle. It does not look unnatural, although it generally strikes one that they are dancing together for want of male partners. This was not the case here. As the evening progressed and the atmosphere got hotter and hotter, the couples abandoned the ritual narcissistic gyrations and moved in closest contact. Once more, nothing seemed to be missing. They were a fulfilled community – fulfilled without the male. Why? This phenomenon is related to the fact that gender identity is not only not the same as sex identity, but that it generates a person's erotic magnetism. The lesbian women with their mixed or masculine gender identity related to one another with complete naturalness. Erotic and emotional tensions between them were analogous to those between well-suited heterosexual couples. And their capacity for abandonment could not be surpassed. They can rightly claim to be self-contained in their erotic and emotional life.

One wonders why they are so much resented by men and women. Because of the pride and vanity of the male, only few men would consider lesbians to be serious rivals. Men's dislike of them goes back to a fundamental psychological cause : the need for the mother in a woman. The male wants to be 'fed' by the female. He needs ego support throughout his life. A lesbian who 'feeds' (loves) another woman puts him and his world into chaos; she is a rival because she takes away maternal support which should be HIS not HERS.

Women loathe lesbians for reasons of their own. Lesbianism is close to the surface in every woman. A woman is afraid of it because of her own propensity. It affects her sense of security in relation to both herself and the male. The world of the homosexual woman is topsy-turvy in the eyes of the 'normal' female. She avoids association with lesbians for fear that she might be considered to be freakish herself.

Lesbians are isolated people because they are outsiders. This fact increases their sense of insecurity, which arises in the first place from a difficult and painful relationship with their mother. The most disturbing aspect of it is that most homosexual women feel that their mother would have loved them more if they had been born male.

The emotional autobiographies of three lesbians form the content of Chapter IX, so that life itself can make its comment on the findings of this study.

Chapter Nine

Three Lesbian Autobiographies

EMOTIONAL AUTOBIOGRAPHY I

Those who are even superficially acquainted with psychology will, on reading this brief summary of my life, find in it a textbook case of maladjustment. Insecurity is there, a lack of proper mother love, perhaps an over-identification with my father, and yet although I think that these things have contributed to making me an insecure human being, I doubt that they have made me a homosexual. I do however think that the difficulty of being homosexual in present-day society has exacerbated my basic emotional troubles.

There are plenty of women who have suffered very similar psychological traumata to mine who are not homosexual. Neurotic they may be, nymphomaniacs perhaps, alcoholics, or even seemingly normal wives and mothers, but homosexual they are not.

There are plenty of men who look desperately for mothers and find them in their wives. This provides a socially approved way of meeting their emotional needs. Almost all lesbians are looking for mother love: their relationship with their mother can only in very rare cases be adequate. Their relationship with their father is often deficient too. This does not however send them out looking for father substitutes in the form of husbands.

'Are we born or are we made?' someone asked me only the other day. I answered that I did not really know; that no one knew. I started off by thinking that I was born that way, then I went through a phase of thinking that it was nurture not nature, now I have returned to nature again.

I am more masculine than the average woman: so are a lot of lesbians. It is not that we have rejected femininity, it is simply that femininity is outweighed in our make-up by masculinity. This means that from our earliest years we have lived our lives at odds with our basic natures. The aggressiveness, for example, which men can show freely in competing with other men in sport or business or getting themselves a wife, we have to suppress, and it turns against ourselves. We feel insecure, we feel guilty, we consult psychotherapists, a lot of us even attempt suicide. Then because we show these tendencies to a higher degree probably (I have no statistics to support them) than heterosexual women, we think of ourselves as neurotic. It isn't surprising that we're neurotic, but we're not homosexual because we're neurotic. We're made neurotic through the pressure of living against our true natures.

In *The Marsh Arabs*, Wilfred Thesiger describes a tribe who do in fact accept that some women are basically masculine. They are allowed to become warriors and hunters, and are not forced to stay at home with the women. How much greater wisdom do these primitive people show than modern civilisation!

Next birthday I shall be 42. Growing up has been a long and painful process, and is still far from complete. I wouldn't dare to describe myself as a mature person. When I discovered at the age of five or thereabouts that I had been born into the wrong body I raged impotently – how appropriate a word. At times I still do. I still say that I have done nothing in my life that I couldn't have done as well or better had I been a man, and God knows the things I might have done had I been born male instead of female.

I was born physically in a nursing home in a large provincial town. My mother was thirty-nine, my father about forty-two, and I their first and only child. My mother's story – and so brainwashed was I by her that I accepted it until a year or so ago – was that all the decent men (decent was a great word of hers) were killed off in the first war, and she had been forced to defer marriage until this late age, when she more or less reluctantly decided to make do with my bargain-basement father in order that she could have a child, which was apparently her life's ambition.

It was only recently that I did a simple sum in my head, namely that my mother was born in 1889. When the first war broke out in 1914 she was twenty-five! Plenty of time in which to get married. Since she was a very good-looking woman with no shortage of admirers, it would seem more likely that her reluctance to marry lay within herself rather than in external circumstances. Indeed, when she spoke of the intense Puritanism of her own father, of whom she was fond, and of the bitter resentment of her own mother against him – because she in her turn had been prevented from marrying the man of her choice – it is not difficult to see what a hotbed of neurosis her family life had been. When I think of my mother and her sister, it is as though a kind of brooding spiritual darkness lay over them – as though passionate and emotional natures had been utterly frustrated. I believe this to be the case. They both died of cancer in their mid-fifties, and fanciful though it may be, I sometimes wonder if it wasn't their own creativity which in the end broke out in this malignant form and killed them.

My father was a far more extravert character. A man's man. A bibulous ex-sailor, and frustrated intellectual, and in many ways an excellent husband. He, as a youngster, had had no family life at all. What happened to his mother I had no idea, but at the age of about five or so he and his brother were farmed out: he to a bachelor who sent him to a good grammar school, where apparently he did very well. At the age of sixteen he became, in his own words, 'sick of being a charity brat' and ran away to sea on the lower deck. In the navy he remained for sixteen years and reached the rank of Chief Petty Officer. He left the navy, took a clerical job, lived in digs. In some mysterious way unknown to me, he met my mother. They went for bicycle rides together. One thing about him that my mother liked was that he made no physical advances to her. However, this he must have remedied fairly smartly after the wedding, because eleven months later I arrived.

Shortly after achieving her life's ambition of producing a baby, my mother had a nervous breakdown. She went to the country for a few weeks' holiday and I back to the nursing home. Whether this early separation had any effect on my future psychological development I leave to those better qualified than I to ponder. I do know that as a very small child I wouldn't willingly have her out of my sight. I remember even now children's parties during which I spent the whole time clinging to her, not daring to play with the others. At that time it was thought to be a sign of devotion. Today, so much more sophisticated are we that we would see in it a symptom of acute anxiety.

My mother in her turn was excessively solicitous about me, and I have often wondered why, considering how much fuss was made of me, I should find in myself evidence of lack of proper mother-love. I came across the answer one day in Ian Suttie's *The Origins of Love and Hate* – at least it seemed to me the answer then, and I have had no reason to think otherwise since. It is to be read in full in Chapter 4. He is speaking of a mother who herself suffers from love-anxiety, as I should well imagine mine did, and he says : 'It seems to me that a mother whose love-need is of this constant, urgent character is able to achieve a para-doxical reaction in her child by over-indulging it, so that it comes to take services and attention for granted, while in spite of her love she leaves the primary separation-anxiety unappeased or even aggravated by the rejection of its uncultural "gifts" (e.g. cleanliness training) and by her demands upon a demonstrative love and consideration which are beyond the child's feelings and power. The importance of this lies in the fact that it can explain love-anxiety in the best loved child, and also account for the perpetuation of neurosis from generation to generation.'

My parents lived at this time in a house whose upper part was occupied by my maternal grandmother and my mother's youngest sister, Vera. She was called 'Auntie Tiny' because of her small stature and frail physique. Indeed she died when only thirty-three from pneumonia. There was a gentleness about her to which I responded, and I spent as much time as I could with her. She would talk to me for hours – stories, sagas, bits of history – and she herself wrote plays and poetry. I was very fond of her. She died when I was seven. There was great grief and mourning all around me, but I remained unmoved. I shrugged off the fact of her death. A few years ago, when I was thirty-nine, at a party when I had without doubt had a few drinks, I started to talk about my Aunt Vera, and to my horror burst into tears! It happened several times after that but now I seem to have worked my way through it.

When I was four, we moved house, and it was here, when I was about five, that I made the dreadful discovery that I had been born into the wrong body. I remember quite clearly how it came about. Next door lived two boys of about my age, who weren't averse to climbing on to the garden wall and urinating. For the first time – or at least the first time it took on any significance – I saw this interesting pink protuberance. I remember distinctly thinking : 'It isn't fair.' (The classical Freudian penis envy. No one has yet explained why *all* girls do not suffer from this.) I think that until this time I was living in a sort of infant fool's paradise. I knew virtually no children of my own age, and I don't recall having ever seen a naked male. Sexual differentiation had never entered my head. Now suddenly the basic difference between my own body and that of a male was thrust upon me. I realised that I was – of all things – a GIRL! I was appalled, affronted. From that day I rejected everything that was feminine. I would wear only shorts. I remember clearly my mother trying to make me wear some frilly dress that she had made for me. I was adamant. Everyone thought that I was being difficult, peculiar and stubborn. I was not. No one would expect a normal boy of five to wear a green frilly dress, and I was reacting as a normal boy. To this day, and all through my life, if I put on a feminine sort of dress, lots of make-up and high heels, I feel as though I'm in 'drag'. To me, normality is wearing slacks and a shirt or sweater.

And so I embarked upon a life-long battle, alienated both from my own body and from its social environment. Things were made worse by the fact that I had a male cousin, whom I will call Eric, seven years older than I. For various reasons too numerous to be gone into now, Eric began to impinge on my life. My father used to take him for cycle rides, my mother and her sister spent hours discussing his future. I developed a kind of love-hate for him. One half of me admired him because he was male and could box and swim. The other half bitterly resented him for being able to do these things so much better than I. He seemed to me to personify masculine freedom and physical prowess, whereas I was bogged down in the restriction of petty femininity from

which, by virtue of my physical sex, not even age would free me.
And indeed, when I began to menstruate at the age of twelve, I
was bogged down even more thoroughly, and remained so until
the merciful release by hysterectomy at the age of thirty-five. If
at that age someone had told me that there are advantages in
being a woman, I would not have believed them, and now at my
present age I can only say that if there are, they haven't yet been
revealed to me!

Time passed. The country headed into war, and I into
adolescence. My school work reflected my discouragement. 'Elizabeth has the ability but will not try' is the theme that runs
through every school report. I developed a stoop, for which they
gave me physiotherapy at school! The war came, and I was
scared stiff, bored to tears, sullen and depressed. My parents and
I were like three strangers under the same roof. My only passions
were for other girls at school, but there was nothing strange in
this because, for some peculiar reason, it was not only common-
place at my school, but more or less expected. If you weren't
'keen' on someone you were thought odd. As it was a day school
we did not translate our emotions into any physical action:
distant worship was the thing.

Sex reared its head when I was about fourteen. I remember
going through a period of the most intense concupiscence,
though had anyone of either sex approached me with a view to
satisfying it, I would have recoiled in horror. Had not my mother
instilled into me the need to be 'decent'? 'Decent' girls did not
allow men to touch them. So I thrashed about on the bed in
agonies of sexual desire, not even knowledgeable enough to
masturbate. Or I lay in the bath gently squeezing water from the
sponge on to my clitoris, enjoying the sensation, but much too
ignorant and unanalytical to connect this with any kind of action
between men and women or women and women. As far as I was
concerned, sex was sex and love was love, and never the twain
shall meet.

If I am asked, 'When did you first realise that you were a
lesbian?', I find it difficult to answer. The clarity of my childish
perception about my nature blurred with the onset of the miseries
of adolescence. As I grew older I felt totally incapable of attracting
the opposite sex, though I knew that society put a high premium
on sexual attractiveness in women. Of course, eventually, I

did attract them for a while, but they didn't attract me. My sexual instincts had gone right underground, and so they aroused in me neither an erotic nor an emotional response. My father died when I was almost eighteen, and my mother exactly a year later. A burden fell from my shoulders. I felt neither grief nor loss, only a profound relief. Looking back, I see no reason to apologise for my feelings. When I was looking after my mother in her last illness, I was often visited by a contemporary with whom I had been at school. In my loneliness and misery I fell in love with her. I would have fallen in love with the devil himself at that time. I was nineteen. I was astonished at myself, because I had honestly supposed that this was a phase of my life that I had outgrown, and that I would sooner or later fall in love with a man. I never have.

It was then that I decided that I was a lesbian, and when, a couple of years later, I read *The Well of Loneliness* it fell upon me like a revelation. I identified with every line. I wept floods of tears over it, and it confirmed my belief in my homosexuality.

The thing I find extraordinary about my life is that men have been singularly absent from it except in the most ephemeral way. Whereas other lesbians I know have acquired male lovers, even husbands, no significant male has ever appeared in mine, but every turn in my life has been engineered by some female lover. The story of my life is the story of my loves, and now they begin to stretch out, like Macbeth's ghosts, to the crack of doom!

If at any time of my life, some man began to show interest in, or affection, for me, it would be at this point that some hitherto absent girl-friend would turn up and drag him away. Of course the reason for this is, I suppose, that whereas her libido was centred on him, mine was focused on my current passion, and I never cared enough about the man to bother.

My affair with Jane lasted for about four years. Although we did in fact have a physical relationship, it was of small significance. I was totally ignorant of love-making, and supposed, as indeed a great many still do, that a penis was necessary for the proper satisfaction of a woman. No, my ignorance was even more profound than that. The concept of erotic arousal and sexual satisfaction just did not enter my mind at that time. Love was an emotion, nothing more. Physical contact to me, at that time, was symbolic not erotic. Indeed, in some respects it has for me remained at that, although I have with time and experience become a better lover for my partners. And perhaps it has been my misfortune in this present life to miss out on one of the great basic pleasures of physical existence. Well, I am probably not alone in this, and it is better to face the fact than torture oneself with thoughts of one's own inadequacy in this respect, though it is only recently that I have come to this decision.

The time came when Jane decided to spend a year in France. She had graduated from university, where I too had spent a couple of years doing social studies. I was not especially interested in them, but I couldn't remotely think of anything at all that I really wanted to do. I had my school certificate, but had failed in maths, thereby not matriculating, so a degree course was not open to me. Looking back now, it was a very pleasant two years. The work was well within my grasp, I made some good friends, I spent a lot of time drinking coffee and chatting. In fact I did what one is supposed to do with a university education, as opposed to the driving rat-race to obtain a technical qualification, which is what it has mostly become now. (And indeed what it was to me when I finally embarked on my degree course, but that was a long way in the future.)

Jane went to France, and I could not stand the thought of my home town without her. This was 1950. At this time those who could did, and those who couldn't took a secretarial course which, for some peculiar reason, was supposed to be the open sesame to a vast variety of interesting jobs. I decided to take my secretarial course in London, and at random chose a secretarial school in the West End.

I came to London, found myself a room, and walked in ten minutes late to the first class in typing. Sitting amongst a row of students was a very dark, very exotic woman. She was to be my second love; but better, she is still my friend. We have known each other now for nineteen years – a fact upon which we commented with astonishment when I went to have drinks with her and her husband a couple of days ago on Christmas Day!

I still do not know how such an ill-assorted pair got together. This, however, I must make clear. She was not, and never has been homosexual, and there was never anything physical between us. I adored her, she accepted it. She handled me very well, but being more than usually attractive she was well used to handling admirers. Also, she and her husband love each other dearly, and this gives a security which is not easily disturbed. This strange relationship, a variation upon the eternal triangle, lasted in that particular form for a further four years or so. In some respects it was beneficial. Under Andrea's tutelage I became more polished, lost some of my hairy-heeled provincialism, acquired more social self-confidence. In other ways perhaps, in retrospect, it was not so good. First, there were the torments of passion and jealousy, for although I still had incredibly little notion of the nature of physical sex, nevertheless some instinct told me that it was something I wanted, even if only symbolically. (At this stage in my life I am now profoundly thankful that she and I never did go to bed together, for at the time I would not have had a clue how to cope, and would have made an utter fool of myself.) Secondly, for someone who considered herself to be unattractive to the opposite sex, to live constantly under the aegis of someone so blatantly and obviously attractive is very diminishing. To be fair though, Andrea constantly sought to present me to men, or men to me, and it was because of her that I first tried going to bed with them. There were two in the running. I tried one the first week, and the other the second. Both attempts were signal failures on my part. I had been afraid that I might 'die wondering', and I perceived that I was still going to 'die wondering'. I made a third attempt a year or so later, and my period failed to materialise! The agony and panic I went through – I was fortunate enough to take some stilboestrol, and it appeared three days later – put me off sex with men for several years to come. When I think how fertile my mother must have been to have conceived so quickly at the age of thirty-nine, I sometimes feel that Providence must have been kind to have kept my sexual instincts in abeyance for so long. Had this not been so, I shudder to think what might have happened.

After leaving typing school I took a clerical job, but it soon became apparent that I was not cut out for this kind of work. Worse than this, I was supplementing my income by drawing on such capital as remained from my mother's none-too-grand legacy. I could not, I realised, live on the scale to which I had become accustomed (though it was modest enough) on a clerk's wages. One day, in a mood of depression, I went to Andrea, 'What the hell am I to do with my life? Here I am, in love with you, and where's that ever going to lead me?' Andrea was brisk, and suggested to me that I should raise a loan on a reversionary legacy which would come to me on the death of my great-aunt, and put myself through university and get a professional training. I raised the loan. I then had to go right back to square one, and take ordinary level Physics, Chemistry and Maths, because these were needed before I could enter the faculty of my choice. Having done this, I did 'A' level Physics, Chemistry and Biology, and entered London University to start training for a professional career. Once again, Providence intervened.

I was living on my own. I was (though I did not realise it) suffering from anaemia as a result of excessively heavy menstruation. The work I had started was far more difficult than anything I had done before, and things were going badly. Into the house where I had my room, came a Canadian widow, on a prolonged visit to England. She had never been in love with a woman before, but was very experienced with men, and had loved her late husband dearly. She was lonely and so was I. We fell in love, and I returned to Canada with her to continue my degree course at a Canadian university.

Without her looking after me, supporting me, cherishing me, I could not have coped at all, for the work was very difficult. Our relationship soon passed from that of lovers to one more like mother-child. During my time in Canada, I fell romantically and abortively in love with a woman younger than myself, who, being quite heterosexual, rejected me. As part of the cure I tried sex with a man again. Whilst I feel that I probably became a bit less inhibited as a result of this, and I liked him and enjoyed his company, I cannot say that I was in any way emotionally stirred by him. Eventually I decided to make a return trip to England, although I felt by this time that I had adjusted to Canada and had put down roots there.

I had only been back in England a few weeks when I realised how very much more at home I felt here. I felt most reluctant to return to Canada at the end of a year, although I fully realised how very hurt and lonely my friend would be if I did not.

By this time my menstrual troubles had become so severe that I went to a gynaecologist, with the result that I went into hospital for a hysterectomy. My stay there was prolonged due to complications, and whilst there, a friend (the Jane of my early years, now married) brought me a copy of a magazine in which there was an article about lesbians. It is hard to realise now that even this short time ago female homosexuality was scarcely ever mentioned. *The Well of Loneliness* and *The Children's Hour* were the only two bits of literature on the subject of which I had ever heard. Even male homosexuality was virtually unmentionable, although there had been Mary Renault's marvellous book *The Charioteer*, which I had read avidly a few years previously. Therefore to see The Word even mentioned was quite astonishing. The article was atrocious. During my convalescence I re-read it several times, and in the end wrote a reply to it. With trepidation I signed the article and posted it to the editor. I was terrified. To admit to being a lesbian and to sign one's name! I do not know what I thought would happen, but I have since discovered that this kind of unreasonable panic is very common amongst lesbians even today. At that time, although I was thirty-five, I had never actually met another lesbian, though I had seen in passing the odd obvious one. I had lived for years in Chelsea, and had known of the existence of the Gateways Club, but for some odd reason I never sought it out. I suppose being basically a rather solitary person, the idea of lesbians en masse rather appalled me, although had I made the effort to go there my life story might have been very different. I don't care for parties and I don't much like clubs, so I never did what so many other lonely types have done, got themselves into 'The Gates' and gone on from there.

The upshot was that my reply was published anonymously in the next issue of the magazine. In the meantime, I had returned to Canada for a short time to convalesce, and to say my final good-bye to the friend who had been so good to me – and still is, though we are thousands of miles apart and unlikely to meet again in this life. While I was there I received a letter from a woman who had read my article, and who had the idea of starting a magazine for lesbians. Again my life took another turn. I provided background support, and also wrote a fair number of articles, and so *Arena Three* and the Minority Research Group was born.

We had no idea when we launched the little magazine what would happen. We thought we might be prosecuted for putting out an obscene publication, or that we might get bricks through the window. In fact we got all sorts of extraordinary things, including quite a few men under the impression that we were producing pornography. So naïve were we that it never occurred to us that lesbianism is featured in pornographic literature. We got married women writing in by the dozens. We got sad life histories over the telephone. We got people so obviously disturbed that being homosexual was the least of their problems. And we got a constant demand for social activities. 'Why can't you have meetings?' was the cry. So, reluctantly, as we were not very social, we started to organise gatherings. Then sub-groups were started, and the whole thing snow-balled.

At this stage, after about two years, I was afflicted with one of my periodic lunacies, and became obsessed with a girl years younger than myself. Changes occurred in the Minorities Research Group, and it is now known as the Minorities Research Trust and continues to publish *Arena Three*. An entirely new group based on the older Kensington-Richmond sub-group, was formed. It called itself Kenric, and it is a thriving and highly respectable social organisation for lesbians. I had the privilege to be one of the founder members.

Since that time I have had another three-year association with an older woman, which finished when we each fell in love with 'normal' women. Hers has so far proved to be successful, mine not.

So, at the age of forty-two, I have these last few months had more than enough time and more than enough misery to force myself into an intense introspective analysis of myself, my life, and my motives, and to ask myself several questions. Has it been worth it? Would you have had it any other way? What have you been looking for? What do you really want?

When I look back on my life I see a distinct pattern in the jumble of seeming chances. I loved Jane, and because of this, fled to London and met Andrea, who gave me the push into getting myself properly qualified. But without meeting Sally, my Canadian friend, I would probably never have made the grade with my degree. The other night a friend rang me and said: 'Oh, we went to a good party last night, A. was there with B. – they seem to be making a go of it. C. was there with D., they're buying a house on a mortgage . . .' I said: 'Look at all these lonely people who have been able to get together, who never would have done if I hadn't helped to get Kenric going. If I die tomorrow, at least I've done that much.'

More than that, through meeting so many hundreds of lesbians and having made some good friends among them, I've been able to come to terms with my homosexuality in a way that wasn't possible before. Now it's no longer some dread guilty secret, like carrying a stigma – it's just the way I am. Also I no longer feel a false sense of solidarity with someone simply because they are homosexual too. So, on the whole, both on my own account and other people's, it has been worth it.

Would I have it any other way? Yes, to have been born a man. Though what sort of man I would have been I sometimes wonder! Often when I observe men acting in a deplorable way, I know only too well their motivation, because I can see it in myself. Women are a mystery to me, but not men. So often I find myself resenting the way men act because I am a woman, yet knowing that if I'd been born male I'd probably be acting in the same way. So in one way it is perhaps better that I was born a woman.

Would I not have preferred to be a normal heterosexual woman? I find this concept so alien that I cannot imagine it. To want children and to love men is beyond my comprehension. To be the father of children of the woman one loves – that I can understand, but to be a mother, no.

What would have happened if at the age of nineteen say, some nice lad had come along and in my unhappiness I'd married him and had a family? I don't know. Would I have settled down to provincial married life? Given my restless and romantic nature it seems unlikely. I can only thank Providence that the question never arose, for like my mother and grandmother before me, I would most certainly have made both husband and children unhappy.

What have I been looking for? What a whole generation of us, brainwashed by Hollywood trash, have been looking for. To fall madly and beautifully in love, to totter hand in hand into the sunset while an orchestra plays Tchaikovsky's *Romeo and Juliet* overture in the background, and to live happily ever after together in a cottage with roses round the door! An unlikely event but a powerful myth, and one cannot base one's life on myths. To some extent I have the love-death myth, whereby I have periodically felt impelled by what I thought to be love towards some individual who was in some way unattainable. If what I thought I 'loved' reciprocated and came towards me, then I became highly nervous and promptly fell out of love. If, on the other hand, she remained out of reach through being married, or unfaithful, or heterosexual, then my romantic anguish knew no bounds, and stalwart friends braced themselves for long sessions on the phone, punctuated by sobs.

I have often said that one year of a homosexual partnership is equal to five of a marriage, and really is this surprising? Far from making pledges to each other in public a lot of couples have to pretend that they are no more than flat-mates. Some even have to spend Christmas apart because their families have no idea of the true situation. Also, lesbians demand far more from each other than married couples do. Women are conditioned to put up with a lot from a man, and they will, because he is the provider and the father of the children. Women demand from each other love, kindness, tolerance, understanding, sex – the lot. And if they don't think they are getting it, it's easy enough to get out. What is surprising is not that so many lesbian partnerships break up, but that so many survive, in spite of, not because of, any social pressure.

What then do I *really* want? A succession of more or less disastrous idylls, or a settled life? One cannot have both, and one has to make a choice. At least, by my age one has to make a choice.

Whether I have achieved sufficient insight to be able to dispense with the first, and if so, whether I shall be lucky enough to find a person with whom I can attempt the second, I do not know.

COMMENT

Psychological interpretation

The outstanding psychological feature is Miss X's obsession of having been born into the wrong sex – her male gender identity. She seems convinced of a biological root in her homosexuality. This must remain an open question, but it might be answered by an investigation into chromosome aberration in lesbians, which is currently being carried out at a London hospital. Miss X participated in the research : she may however not be told whether her chromosomes are normal or not. It is a matter of fact that Miss X, in spite of her broad shoulders and well-developed musculature, looks feminine, and shows no secondary male characteristics. Her expressive behaviour, particularly hand gestures and gait, alone betray her identification with the male. In short, her psycho-motor behaviour is masculine, her physique feminine. This points to a strongly *psychological* causation of her homosexuality, which, indeed, she demonstrates throughout the pages of her tale. How far she is conscious of the psychological impact of her childhood experiences, which paved the way to her lesbianism, remains doubtful. She does know that she suffers from separation-anxiety, which she rightly connects with her difficulties in her emotional relationships.

Psycho-analytical interpretation has its place in regard to her condition. Miss X is mother-fixated, but completely insecure with her mother. She resents her insecurity brought about by both separation in early infancy from her mother, and the fact that the latter was an anxiety-prone person herself. Miss X's emotional ambivalence towards mother-figures arises from this fundamental situation. Her life is overshadowed by her sense of insecurity, manifested in her state of perpetual anxiety, at times increasing to panic.

Miss X is a woman of considerable intelligence, with some insight into her condition. Her resentment against nature (or her parents for that matter) which gave her the wrong body, keeps her in perpetual self-torment and self-analysis. The latter remains, for obvious reasons, rather fruitless. Her frustration tolerance is low, which increases impulsiveness and gets her inhibitory mechanism out of gear. She shows lack of inhibition on the verbal level, and aggressiveness in general, though not in her sexual behaviour.

Personal impression

This lively, intelligent woman would be an asset to any group, not only a homosexual one. In spite of her introspective tendencies, she is observant of others and possesses a high degree of empathy. She is very capable, not only in her profession, but in sports and games as well as in the art of cooking. She opened up even more during the interview than in her script, and I am sure of a wealth of affection and passion underneath her many inhibitions, and obvious emotional repressions. Her pride (as well as her aggressiveness) prevents her from taking a 'masochistic' role towards others. In order to compensate for her unending complaints against the world and her own fate, she has cultivated a natural gift as a mimic. Clownishness is her way of protecting herself against being labelled by anybody as 'pathetic'.

She is a woman who is both burdened and enlivened by an insoluble problem.

EMOTIONAL AUTOBIOGRAPHY II

I was born just after the outbreak of war. When my father was called up, my mother and I went to live with his parents. My father and I are both only children. My grandmother spoilt me and used to allow me to do things like going to bed without cleaning my teeth, so that I would like her better than I liked Mummy. Mummy was not very demonstrative, but Granny was always kissing and cuddling me. Mummy would sit with me until I went to sleep, and I used to misbehave to make her cry so that I could comfort her.

When I was four I had a serious illness and have been rather delicate ever since. Because of this I did not go to school very much, and when I did I always felt out of it. I could not tie my shoelaces, button up my coat or go to the lavatory by myself, and the headmistress complained to Mummy that the other girls did not like having to look after me.

My grandfather had several strokes, and eventually became speechless and paralysed. Once, while he could still walk, he went to the lavatory and I went in, not knowing he was there. He chased me out with his pyjamas undone, and I half fell downstairs. He stood at the top making a roaring noise.

Granny went to the local repertory theatre every week, and I used to stay awake until she came back, so that she could tell me the story of the play (suitably edited) and describe what the actresses had worn. I would pretend to be them, and act out the plays or stories I had made up.

When Daddy came back from the war I was very jealous, as Mummy and Granny made such a fuss of him. He is not a communicative person, and we were never at ease with each other until recently. I used to try to please him, and he would try to please me, but we never really managed it.

Mummy, Daddy and I then moved to another town, and had four pleasant years together. I was a finnicky eater and would not stay for school dinner, so Mummy fetched me at lunch time. Sometimes she was late and I would be terrified that I would have to stay for the meal. Later I was allowed to go on the bus, and I made friends with a pretty girl who must, I suppose, have been about nineteen. One day I got off with her at the stop before mine and proudly escorted her to the door of her office! I always had to have one special friend, and had a nasty habit of breaking up other people's friendships. I was very possessive about my best friend, and hated her even to speak to anyone else. I used to make a point of singling out some unpopular girl so that I could look after her.

I can only remember being unhappy twice while we lived there. Once was when Mummy and I went to buy me a party dress, and the one I wanted was too expensive. I was very disappointed and when we got home Mummy cried. I always wanted a pet, and after I'd kept a large stone with a blue ribbon round it, which I called 'Hedgie', fed a rat under the shed, and adopted a mangy stray cat that had to be put to sleep, I was given a kitten. I was devoted to it, but a year later it was run over. I was heartbroken and cried myself to sleep every night for months.

We regularly spent week-ends with Granny. She used to persuade me to tell her that Mummy and Daddy were unkind to me. She must have repeated something I said, because Daddy was very angry and gave me a serious talking-to.

Then my grandfather died, and Daddy lost his job, so we went back to live with Granny again. My father always wanted to work with cars, but his father wanted him to be a professional man. They sent him to train and he had a nervous breakdown. He has never had a good job, and feels he is a failure and is very bitter.

Although I knew Mummy was upset, I did not mind going back because I was old enough to go to the theatre, and there was a little boy for me to play with who lived near Granny. He and I were friends from the age of six to eleven. I liked playing with boys' toys, although I was also very fond of my dolls and woolly animals. I had most of them in bed with me at night, and there was a strict rota governing who slept next to me and who slept on the edge! The little boy insisted we should examine each other's bodies (I preferred mine) and told me what the big boys did to the big girls at his school. I thought this was a way of fighting, and was quite disappointed some years later when I discovered that it was, in fact, making love.

I passed the eleven-plus examination, but it was decided that I was too delicate for the grammar school, so Granny paid for me to go to a private school. It was much larger than my previous school and it took me a long time to settle down, particularly as I arrived in the middle of a term. All the other girls came from much wealthier homes, and I felt this very much in my teens. My only consolation was that at least none of them went to the theatre, so I had something which they had not.

Granny bought my clothes and dressed me very childishly. I knew I looked different from the others and that they laughed at me, and from the age of fourteen I would hide in shop doorways if I saw anyone from school wearing smart teenage clothes. I still feel like doing this if I unexpectedly see anyone I know – though I do try not to! It gives me enormous pleasure now if someone says I look nice.

Granny and Mummy disliked each other, and Mummy often told me how unhappy she was. I was very religious until I was seventeen, and used to pray for her, but it did not seem to help either of us. If I did anything Granny disapproved of, she would nag Mummy about it. There was always a terrific fuss about what I should wear, do or eat. If I did not want any pudding, Granny would say: 'I made it specially for you', so I ate it and felt sick. I had to sleep with my bedroom door open, so that Granny could come in if she heard me moving or coughing. Until I was fifteen, and homework made it necessary for me to go to the theatre on Saturdays instead of during the week, Granny used to bathe me. As I grew older I preferred to sit in my bedroom in the evenings, studying or playing records, but she was constantly knocking on the door (which I had locked) asking if I was too cold, too hot, thirsty or hungry. When I decided I wanted to wash my own underclothes, she would creep in and take them away. If I hid them and washed them in the bathroom, she used to re-do them. I had little sex instruction. My mother gave me booklets on childbirth and menstruation, and the rest I found out for myself from the public library and other people.

I had my first violent crush on a teacher when I was fourteen. I longed to confide in her, and when I handed her a book I used to put my fingers underneath it so that her hand would touch mine when she took it.

Then my current best friend, Jane, started to come to the theatre with me and we both developed a crush on the same actress, Lindsey. We waited around the stage door and her lodgings, and when we saw her coming we used to walk towards her. At last, one lovely sunny day, she said 'Hallo' to me. For the first time in my life I felt ecstatically happy, and rushed home to tell my mother. She was furious. I kept getting into trouble after this, as people would see us waiting around and tell my mother. In spite of this, and teasing from the girls at school (we were even mocked by a teacher in front of the whole class), Jane and I were wonderfully happy.

Then Lindsey left and we were heart-broken. Jane lost interest, but I could not stop thinking about her and missing her. Jane and I used to make up stories and act them. We lay on the bed (always pretending to be other people) and kissed each other's necks as we thought kissing on the mouth was wrong. Once we were embracing in the kitchen, and my mother saw us through the window. She did not say anything until Jane had gone, and then there was a terrible row.

To please my mother, I had joined the Girl Guides when I was twelve. I hated it, and later went on to the Rangers, which I liked no better. I became very friendly with a rather tomboyish girl. We used to hold hands when we were alone, and I think she wanted to kiss me.

When I was sixteen I was allowed to go abroad with a school party. I had never been away from home even for a night before, and I loved it. A very beautiful woman visited the house where I was staying, and she used to come to sit with me while the family were at church. We did not talk much, but used to smile at each other. She was rather an outcast because she had an illegitimate child by a married man. The day I left she took me in her arms and kissed me very gently on the cheek. I wrote to her when I got home, but she did not reply.

Jane and I became friendly with an older girl, Terry, who went around with one of the actresses from the theatre. She always made me feel rather odd, and kept throwing out hints which we eventually discovered to mean that she was homosexual and thought we were too. Jane and I were drifting slightly apart, because I was hurt that she had forgotten Lindsey, and had a crush on another actress, Amanda. Terry began to go out with Amanda and she and Jane would talk about her together, so that I felt left out. I was very miserable and decided that they were sordid and horrible, and that I would grow up and become heterosexual. I made myself believe I had a crush on a young actor and my family were very pleased.

Jane had started to go out with a boy – the son of friends of her parents – but she thought he was silly. A boy from the grammar school asked me out. I found him terribly young and boring, and could not respond to him sexually, though I kept trying as I did want to be heterosexual. It worried him that he could not make me respond, and he thought there was something wrong with him. I wanted people to see me with him, so that they would know I had a boy-friend, but at the same time I felt embarrassed. I would not hold hands with him in the street unless it was dark, and when I got home I used to wash all over because I felt dirty after he had been near me.

After Lindsey had left, I decided that as I was never going to be happy again (!), I had better be useful, so I started to take out a disabled girl. Actually I enjoyed it, and had a lot of fun with her and her friends. I felt I had something in common with them because we all had sexual desires which we could not gratify.

I went to see Lindsey, who was now married with a baby, and had a wonderful afternoon with her. I felt more strongly than ever afterwards that I wanted to be 'normal' so that I could be friends with her on equal terms. I tried very hard during my last year at school to be like the others, and take part in local sixth-form activities, but all the time I felt I was just pretending, and the time I spent with Jane was more real.

Until I was fourteen, I had always thought I would go into the theatre when I left school. When the headmistress asked us all what we wanted to do I told her, and she roared with laughter. I told my parents and they were surprised that I had taken the theatre idea so seriously. There were long discussions with numerous people about what I should do, but I was not really interested. Eventually it was decided that I should go to university. I pointed out that I hated studying and that the idea of being cooped up with people of my own age was horrifying, but no one took any notice. I tried to tell my once-adored teacher about it, and she listened but did nothing. I had stopped liking her just before I first saw Lindsey, because I once said a poem in class very dramatically, specially to please her, and she was sarcastic about my showing off. For the rest of the time I was at school, I never put the slightest expression into anything I read for her, and she could never understand why.

I was determined to make a fresh start at university. I went out with a boy and imagined I was in love with him, until one day I came face to face with an older girl, Sarah, who looked terribly like Lindsey. All my old feelings came rushing back, and I realised I had been fooling myself. I made friends with a girl of my own age, Camilla. We seemed to be at ease in each other's company from the start, and one day I sensed that she was in love with Sarah. After this we were able to talk about it. Camilla had lots of personality and soon made Sarah notice her. I worshipped from afar. Camilla was miserable, because, like me, she did not want to be queer. She attracted men easily and used to go out with them. I hated everything. I could not cope with the work, and having to share a bedroom with a stranger, eat with hundreds of other people, and being constantly surrounded by hordes of young incomprehensible people was a nightmare.

When I went home for the Christmas holidays there was a new actress at the theatre, a married woman called Maria. The moment I saw her I felt warm all over, as if I had known and liked her for a long time. Jane and I also visited Lindsey, and were able to talk about her together again.

One evening after I went back to university, I had a bad headache, and went to Camilla's room for some aspirin. She was going out, but as my lodgings were cold and I felt lousy, she suggested I should stay there. I cuddled down in a chair and she put a rug round me. As she tucked it in, she kissed the top of my head and I felt a rush of feeling all over me, unlike anything I'd ever felt before. I realised then that I had never had any sexual feelings before, and that I was in love with her. It was a month before I told her, but I stopped seeing the boy I had been going out with as I felt I just could not make the effort any more. I did not go out with anyone regularly after that, although I did have one or two odd experiences.

There were two men at college whom I quite liked. One, who seemed more adult, was the brother of a friend. I found him easy to talk to, and he only once bothered me physically. Then he said he could tell I did not like it and he would never force himself on a girl. The other was a man I met at a dance. He was very drunk and could hardly walk when we left. I draped him over a wall and went back to my lodgings. The next day he came round to apologise and we went out occasionally. He hardly ever kissed me and I found him easy to talk to.

I had told Camilla I was in love with her, and though she said she could never feel the same about me, she kept hinting that we might get drunk alone together and 'see what happens'. We never did. I hated watching her fawning on Sarah, but could not stop myself seeing her. I was in a state of nerves the whole time, smoked thirty or forty cigarettes a day, and lived mainly on black coffee and Phensic. I cannot cry easily, and the more I wanted to, the less I was able to do so.

One glorious sunny morning, Camilla and I went out into the country to study, and while we lay on the grass I gently stroked her hair. I felt so wonderfully happy that I wanted to kill us both, so that there should be no anti-climax!

I went home at the end of the summer term and managed to meet Maria, who was very friendly. Jane, whose term was longer than mine, got me a job near her college. We were very close and caressed each other affectionately. Once or twice we almost went further, but somehow we did not. While I was there I heard that I had failed my exams. I was more relieved than anything else that I did not have to go back to university. I made up my mind to get over Camilla, and told myself I had three things on which to concentrate: the theatre, Maria, and a kitten I had planned to buy.

The week I arrived home, Maria left. I went to a secretarial school where the rest of the pupils were about fifteen, so I was very lonely. Jane was still at college, and anyway she was only interested in Terry. The kitten plan did not work either, as Granny insisted on feeding it, so it liked her better than me. Then I heard that the theatre was to be closed within a month and pulled down. That was the worst blow. I felt as if everything had been taken away from me. I could not cry, and there was no one to understand how I felt.

Camilla came to stay after Christmas. She was very sweet to me and we held hands and she stroked my hair. Then I threw myself into a futile campaign to try to save the theatre. I got wet, tired and cold delivering leaflets, and was ill for two months. I suppose it was a sort of breakdown. I did not want to do anything at all, I could not get better and I could not stop crying. The doctor suggested that a part-time job would give me some independence, and Mummy found one for me.

I heard from Maria, and Jane and I arranged to go on holiday to the place where she was acting; but after weeks of indecision, Terry persuaded Jane to go away with her instead.

After this I felt numb and nothing seemed real. Through the girls at work I met a boy who asked me out. He used to drive me from pub to pub, then we would park and I would put on the radio and smoke a cigarette while he kissed my breasts. This happened four or five times, but it made me feel sick, so I stopped seeing him. I still longed for Camilla, and every Saturday night I would burn a joss stick in front of her photograph, play all the records that reminded me of her, and cry myself to sleep.

I went to see Lindsey during this time. She was rather depressed and confided in me, which was wonderful. I also went to stay with Camilla who took me to see two lesbian friends. I had never met a settled couple before, and it was reassuring to see their cosy home. I had been afraid that all lesbians were like Terry, who lived with her parents and mostly had affairs with married women.

The next time Camilla came to stay, I introduced her to Jane and Terry. We went to Terry's house for the evening and got drunk. I suddenly started to cry about the theatre, and Terry put her arms round me and kissed me on the mouth. It was the first time I had ever been kissed by a woman and it was wonderful, but I knew Jane would be upset so I pushed her away. Then Terry and Camilla went upstairs and stayed there for ages. Jane was crying. In the end I walked out of the house and Camilla had to run after me. We did not speak all the way home, but when we got to bed I was furious with her for hurting Jane. She said it was awful of me to think that she and Terry had been having sex. I cried for ages and apologised. In the morning I saw that her neck was covered with love-bites.

I started full-time work after that. Jane had left college and was working locally, but she was absorbed in Terry, who made her unhappy. One day she told me that Terry had met a butch girl called Philippa. I said I would like to meet her, but Jane said she was living with someone, so I decided it would be no use. One day I saw Philippa coming out of Terry's office. She looked sad and rather attractive. A few days later I saw her in the library, but although I stood beside her and reached in front of her for a book – carefully displaying the black-stoned ring on my little finger – she did not notice me. She even held the door open for me when I went out, without registering my fluttering eyelashes and sweetly murmured 'Thank you'! I did not like the very butch way she was dressed, but I thought that all lesbians (except Jane and me) wanted to look masculine.

I did not see Philippa again for several weeks and gave the matter no further thought. Then Terry told her that she knew a girl who was 'mad about her'. She told her my name and where I worked. By a coincidence, Philippa passed my office a few moments later, just as I was coming out. I smiled at her, she followed me up the road and we made a date. I was terribly thrilled as I was going to see Maria the next day. I accidentally met Philippa on the way to the station and she gave me a lift. As Terry had told her I was mad about her, she was rather flirty with me. I did not take her seriously, but as she was the first woman who seemed really interested in me, I thought I would like to have an affair with her to get some experience. Terry had told me that no one wanted a virgin. Philippa said that the person she was living with was just a relation, so I know I was not doing anything wrong.

I had a lovely day with Maria and felt very attracted to her, but as she was married I thought I could only daydream about loving her. I was amazed some years later, when I wrote and told her I was a lesbian, to receive her reply that she had been very attracted to me, although she had never had other than heterosexual feelings before.

Philippa and I met for a drink. She seemed rather shy but we got on very well. Terry asked us to go up to her house for the week-end. I told my parents I was staying with my disabled friend. They hated Terry and Jane and although I was twenty-one, I was not allowed to stay out after eleven p.m., and always had to say where I was going. I was terribly nervous about the whole thing. I loathe having to tell lies – which is one of the reasons why I shun heterosexual company – and as Philippa had been with lots of girls, I was afraid she would find me inexperienced and boring.

When we got to Terry's, she and Jane rather pointedly went out to buy cigarettes. Philippa and I sat listening to records. Unfortunately they were singles, and every time I thought she was going to kiss me I had to get up and change the record! After about ten minutes of this I found an LP and everything was all right.

It was a ghastly evening. We all got drunk, I was sick and Terry made Jane cry. When we went up to bed, Terry tried to have sex with me, but I would not because of Jane. She went off and left me with Philippa. She hugged and kissed me and then went to sleep. In the morning I woke her up and tried to seduce her. She resisted at first, saying I was too young, but then gave in. She felt awful afterwards and would hardly speak to me. As Terry and Jane were also being unpleasant, I left as soon as I could, feeling utterly wretched. I did not think Philippa would want to have anything more to do with me, but the next day I had a letter from her, saying she had been thinking of me. We met a couple of days later: she had on a skirt which I found much more attractive. We felt rather awkward with each other, but went for a walk by the river, holding hands (it was dark). Then we stopped and began to kiss each other. We lay down on Philippa's coat and went on kissing and caressing. It was not until we got up that we realised that it had been raining and we were both wet through!

Now that we were in love, we both regretted having had such a sordid first night. We wrote to each other every evening and met before work to exchange the notes. We had difficulty in finding anywhere to meet. Philippa lived out of town and the last train went very early. If we went to a pub, not only were we stared at because of Philippa's clothes, but obviously we could not even hold hands.

Of course I wanted to introduce Philippa to my family. I did not *exactly* think they would throw an engagement party for me, but I did hope they would like her, although I was afraid that the fact that she was a good deal older than I was would go against her. However, on the evening she was supposed to come round, my mother said she did not feel well and did not want to see her. I was shattered because she had *never* done anything like that before.

Soon after this Philippa took a room in town. It was lovely to be there together, and I stayed later and later. One night I did not leave until 2 a.m. When I got home my parents called me into their bedroom. My father accused me of having 'perverted sexual relations with that woman'. I said I was. He then said that if I did not stop seeing her, I must leave the house by the end of the month. I replied that I had been wanting to go for years and would leave that night. Then my mother began to cry and that made me cry too. I told them that I loved Philippa, and asked them to try to understand. My father said that we all had these instincts, but we must try to control them. I said I did not have any other instincts, and that their sort of sex was revolting to me. Then my father began to cry and said it was his fault, and that if I went on seeing Philippa he would kill himself. My mother implored me to tell her where they had gone wrong in my upbringing. In the end I went to my room and the matter was not mentioned again. It was one of the most awful nights of my life – to know that I had made my parents so desperately unhappy – and yet it was not my fault and there was nothing I could do about it. I had always hoped that I would not fall in love with someone who loved me until after I had left home; then perhaps they would never have found out. I feel I have disappointed my parents. My mother kept her wedding dress for me and I know she would have loved grandchildren; or they could have been proud of a career-girl daughter, but it was obvious that I was not going to be that either.

When I told Philippa about the row, I was hurt because she was not pleased that I had refused to deny our love. She said

I should have laughed and told them they were being ridiculous.

In the summer I told my parents I was going away alone, and Philippa and I went for our 'honeymoon' to a town where we knew there was quite a lot of gay life. We found a pub and from there were taken to a club. Neither of us had ever been to a gay club before, and I immediately felt at home. For the first time in my life I had the feeling of 'belonging' and knowing that I was in a place where I was the same as everyone else, instead of being the one who was different.

We spent the last part of the holiday with Philippa's mother. She was ill and wanted Philippa to go back and live with her, so naturally she resented me. I told Philippa I would be faithful to her and join her as soon as I could get a job, but she had been deceived by so many girls that she could not trust me that far. I did not get on with any of her friends, homosexual or heterosexual.

Some time later Philippa's mother died and she was terribly upset. I wanted to live with her and make a home for her, so I decided to get a job away. I managed to get one in the town where we had had our honeymoon.

When I told my parents I was going, they made an appointment for me to see the doctor, so that he could give me a letter for a psychiatrist. He had been my doctor for about ten years, and I liked him. I thought I might be able to talk to him so that he could explain things to my parents, but when I went to see him he was horrible. He told me I was stupid and that the psychiatrist would soon 'knock all this nonsense' out of me. The psychiatrist asked me what the trouble was, and I told him that my parents had just found out that I was a lesbian. He asked me how I knew that I was, and I explained that I was only attracted to women and just could not get interested in boys. He then wanted to know if I was attracted to little girls! I said I usually liked women older than myself. He said they did not 'really know very much about this sort of thing', so I offered to answer any questions he might have, but he refused. He asked if I was worried about it, and I said I was only sorry that my parents were so upset. He suggested I should leave home and send my mother money every week. I exclaimed: 'But she wants grandchildren'. He did not answer. He sent the doctor a report saying nothing could be done for me.

I took Philippa to meet Lindsey. It was lovely to see them together and they seemed to like each other, but then I had a vague letter from Lindsey saying that Philippa could be a better friend to me than she ever could. After that she deliberately lost touch with me. I was very sad about this as I always felt so wonderful after seeing her – calm and self-confident – perhaps the sort of person I would have been had I not been homosexual.

Philippa and I finally moved and it was wonderful to be together at last. I had told my parents that she had gone back to her home town, but I do not think they believed me.

Then one night I was rushed to hospital, and Philippa had to telephone my parents and tell them I was on the danger list. They all met round my bed the next morning! Everyone was very stilted and formal and there was the most frightful atmosphere. Gradually, however, when they saw how well Philippa looked after me, they began to change their opinion, and after several years they at last accepted her.

Apart from visiting my family and going to work, I spend all my time in homosexual company. I have deliberately lost touch with all my relations, and childhood and school friends.

I have two heterosexual friends who know about me, but I do not see them often. I feel fairly comfortable with them, but otherwise when I am in heterosexual company I feel wary and tense. As I do not look obviously queer, sooner or later someone makes a sneering remark about 'pansies' or 'homos', and I think : 'That's me they're talking about – that's how they'd feel about me if they knew'. I never join in derogatory remarks about homosexuals, but on the other hand I have never had the courage to defend them.

I suppose the present public interest in homosexuality will have a beneficial effect in the end, but at the moment I am sick and tired of it. Every play, every book, every film, if not exclusively devoted to the subject, has to bring it in through a minor character. This means that quite ordinary people, who a few years ago would not have known what the words meant, are rushing around spotting 'pouves' and 'leses', and feeling terribly sophisticated.

I feel that my homosexuality has hampered me at work. I have no self-confidence, and am always sure that everyone is

G

thinking there is something odd about me. I find it difficult to get involved, because I always feel that I am an alien, trying to conform in foreign company. It takes me a long time to make friends in the office, partly because I very rarely find anyone I like, and partly because even the simplest of conversations is full of pitfalls. My favourite stage, film and record stars are all women, and I obviously cannot mention the names of the clubs and pubs I frequent. I do not want people to think I am homosexual, but I hate the idea that they think I am heterosexual! Luckily I do not attract men. I do not mind talking to them about work, but I hate it if they come too near me or try to flirt. I do not even like to spend too much time in the company of gay boys, and I only feel comfortable with them if they are in drag. I always feel inferior in the company of heterosexuals because I think that if they knew I was homosexual they would feel I was inferior to them. After all, society is organised by them, for them, and the only place where I belong is in my own or friends' homes or in clubs.

COMMENT

Psychological interpretation

Miss Y is one of the few lesbians who never wanted to be a boy. Her gender identity was and is unquestionably female. When she was about seven years old, her then boy-friend suggested a mutual inspection of their bodies. The exploration ended with this verdict of hers: 'I liked my body better'.

The abnormality of her early environment puts the psychological factor of her homosexuality into relief. The absence of the father during the first four years of her life enhanced the overpowering pampering by two mothers, her own and her grandmother. The latter was the stronger personality of the two. Both mothers kept her a baby right into adolescence, thus making the outside world a hostile playground for her. She felt an outsider from her school-days onwards, and her adaptability to other people was very poor. She has never been able to overcome this failing, and she has always to rely on a 'mother-figure' to soothe her anxieties and to protect her. She got over the initial hostility against her father, and they managed to achieve a tolerable and, at times, even a good relationship. This astonishing adaptation was, in my view, dictated by the super-ego rather than by natural affection.

She was a girl who did not want to be a homosexual. On the contrary, she tried to fall in love with boys and failed. Neither boys nor men could rouse her sexually and emotionally. Her lesbianism became evident to her when, in her later teens, she experienced both physical and emotional reactions through other women. She must have realised then where her future lay, but her perceptions appear to have been vague, as if she were walking through air rather than on terra firma.

The desire to escape played and plays an overwhelming part in her interests and in her life. Her grandmother had been the strongest influence in her childhood, and it was obviously she who gave her the taste for the stage. As a lonely and badly adjusted child, she lived in her imagination, and in the world of the theatre. She had *Schwaermereien* for actresses, and these natural, adolescent feelings went further with her than mere fancies. They affected her way of life, and she is still in the throes of this particular romanticism.

The psychological situation has certainly been the major cause of the development of her homosexuality, but a physical factor has also played a part in it. She belongs to the infantile type of woman, who is predisposed psycho-sexually to lesbianism.

Personal impression

Nobody, not even an experienced person with a sharp eye for the deviant, would ever think of Miss Y as a lesbian. This very pretty, feminine, well-dressed person is the picture of a 'normal' girl. Her marked youthfulness, which gives her the appearance of a woman of twenty, could, perhaps, make one suspicious as to her feminine maturity.

Miss Y is a highly anxious, nervous creature, who easily arouses feelings of sympathy and protection. She is painfully shy, but once put at her ease, she shows intelligence and a witty, sharp edge to her conversation. I am sure that she has high principles in behaviour and action. She lives up to the rare virtues of steadfastness, loyalty and stability in human relationships. She would never let anybody down, nor betray a confidence. A social misfit, not by necessity but through her upbringing, she has not found a professional or social place in accordance with her abilities. She could do better than take jobs as a shorthand typist. She compensates for her professional frustration through her interest in the theatre and literature. She identifies with those who are unfortunate through physical handicaps or other defects, and applies a practical religion : she goes and helps them.

EMOTIONAL AUTOBIOGRAPHY III

I was born twenty-eight years ago in a London suburb, where my parents are still living. I cannot remember much of my first four years, as my mother had a son when I was two, and from that time I took second place. I think my parents tried to be fair to both of us, but they definitely favoured my brother Donald. If he and I argued about anything, Mum always wanted to interfere, and usually took his side. I can remember at one stage I had the urge to murder him when I was very young, but cannot remember the reason why : probably because I was continually in the background.

I lived at my parents' house for eighteen years, during which time I attended school (I will return to these years later) after which I joined the WRAF Police. My ambition was to enter the Metropolitan Police on the River Squad, but of course women are not accepted in this branch of police work. (I had even dreamed of going to Canada and becoming a Mountie!) At 18 I was too young anyway for the Metropolitan Police, and the policewoman interviewing me suggested I joined one of the Forces first.

I chose the air force as I am fascinated by anything mechanical, especially cars and planes, and the prospect of flying added incentive. Really I was too young for the WRAF Police, but as I had good educational qualifications I was accepted, to my delight and relief. During my four years service I had a posting to Germany which I thoroughly enjoyed.

Whilst abroad I met Iris, who was my first affair. We made plans to live together when we were demobbed. When I finished my service I lived at my parents' home for about nine months, and then lived with Iris when she was demobbed. Our life together lasted about two years after which time we discovered that we are both 'butch', and fell for the same 'femme' who worked at our place of employment at that time! This realisation came as a shock as we had both imagined that we had a life-long relationship. However we remain extremely good friends. We continued to live together, but following our own pattern of life.

Then Iris met and became involved with a woman, and has recently gone to live with her. (Incidentally, Iris is four years older than myself.) I am at present a 'bachelor gay', taking life as it comes. Being on my own does not bother me in the slightest – I am able to live with myself. I have a great love for serious music, and spend much of my time listening to, reading and writing about music. I also play the piano, but at present my own instrument is in store unfortunately, and I hardly seem to be able to find time to go to the studios to practise. I like company. I belong to the London Philharmonic Society, and attend meetings and rehearsals when possible, which prove very interesting, and of course I am a member of Kenric, which, in my opinion, is a decidedly necessary organisation for lesbians. It gives us something and somewhere to meet people as ourselves. Although I am happy on my own, the company of friends and people (that isn't to say that friends are *not* people, you understand!) prevents my world from becoming too introspective, as I am too interested in life to allow this to happen. I also read philosophy, and stemming from this have studied a little psychology.

Since my air force days I have held a number of jobs, adding many strings to my bow. I have been in my present employment three years, and hope to obtain a music post with a record company sometime next year, as I feel I would like to work with music. Seeing that one spends one third of one's life working, one might as well be doing something one enjoys.

My first recollection that my feelings are for women came at the age of five or six when I was at school. I imagined that I was a man, dressed in a smart suit and peaked cap, and going out with one of the teachers. As my thoughts bordered on reality, I consoled myself that perhaps I could purchase an imitation male organ, although I had no idea where, but maybe I would find out when I got older. (Having got older I don't hanker after this now, as I feel any woman wanting it on a woman really needs a man and not a woman.)

After reading about *The Water Babies*, I fell in love with one of the lovely women pictured in the book, a Mrs Do-as-you-would-be-done-by, and again imagined that I was a man. (Fantastic, the things one remembers when one begins to write: I didn't imagine I had anything to say.)

At the age of seven or eight I remember a picture strip in the *Daily Express* about a detective, featuring a girl in distress named Flossie Frost. I used to conjure up all manner of situations from which I as the hero would rescue her and be suitably rewarded.

All through my school days I fell in and out of love with various teachers and mistresses of the schools I attended. To me this was quite natural, although I did overhear two girls talking about my love for a certain gym mistress, Miss P., as being 'a bit queer', which I ignored. I was seventeen or eighteen at the time. Needless to say this love was not returned; in fact, I'm certain she was gay herself and having an affair with another woman I met in connection with cricket. I used to play a lot of sport. I kept in contact with Miss P. when I joined the air force, and arranged to meet her for lunch just before being posted to Germany. After eating we walked along the Embankment in silence. I couldn't think of much to say. We sat on a bench and she said: 'We'd better sort this out', and asked me what I wanted of her. I replied her friendship, to which she said we had nothing in common. I was thoroughly flattened – that was the end of that.

During my WRAF days I kept myself pretty much to myself, saying I was studying (which I was, of course). I don't give a damn what anyone thinks, but I had to be careful in the Force, because if anyone had had any idea about me I would have been instantly dismissed from the Service. I organised a Music Circle which met weekly (whilst in Germany) and also sang in the Münchengladbach choir, so I imagine people saw me as a mad musician if they thought anything odd about me!

The people at my job know I am gay and accept me as I am. If they didn't it would be their hard luck, as far as I am concerned, not mine. Anyone who attempts to make life uncomfortable for me ends up extremely miserable!

It was during my Service career that I began to see just how possessive Donald was over me. Living at my parents' home for 18 years, he just about had everything he asked for and more besides, whilst I had to fight. In anything I did or possessed, Donald had to go one better. I did not realise his feelings for me were something they should not be, but being away for four years made me see how his mind was working. He imagined that eventually I would live with him (he admitted this during a fearful row which I will mention further on) and he would not have to lift a finger to do anything for himself, being thoroughly spoilt. The final illumination appeared when I met Iris, and Donald became very jealous. I was living with my parents at the time, before moving into a flat with Iris, and he would not leave us alone together for two minutes. If Iris and I went into one room to be alone, listening to music or talking, he would come in and refuse to take any hint to leave. He was thoroughly jealous.

He kept all the letters I had written to him during the early part of my air force days tied up in ribbon. I did not know this until much later, when I told him to burn them. He was most upset, but I did not leave until he had done so. I told him to leave me alone and let me live my life, and that I did not want any more contact with him, saying that I did not want cards at Christmas or on my birthday from him. This was in September. The following Christmas he sent me a card, after which I had a fierce scene at home involving Mum, Dad and Iris as well. I decided that the only way I could be free of him was to sever all contact with my family. I even sought the advice of a solicitor to see if there was any legal way in which I could ostracise him from my life.

For three years I did not see or contact any of my family. This was a very bitter period in my life, and I got things a bit out of perspective as regards the male sex, not seeing them as human beings at all. Do not misunderstand me – I don't like men, in fact I positively detest them, but I usually get along with them quite amicably on a friendly basis, nothing more. But during the period of my life to which I refer, I was so filled with nausea at the very fact that they are on this earth, that I imagine I was working myself up to a nervous breakdown. Fortunately this did not occur, and I managed to bring my mind into line about two years ago. My motto nowadays is live and let live, providing of course that no harm is caused.

Last Christmas I phoned my grandmother who is quite old and whom I love. I see her about every five or six weeks, and have met Mum a few times, once with Dad. My parents know I am gay and accept this. I have told them I do not wish to see Donald again and the reasons why. They accept this. (Actually, I am sure he is homosexual, but does not realise it himself. He still lives at my parents' home.)

I have tried not to make this too long, and have crammed a great deal into a few sentences. Maybe I can expand (not literally of course) at the interview if you wish. Briefly that is the story of my life. I will now attempt to put on paper my views on being homosexual.

First and foremost, I am proud to be gay. I've thought about this for many hours during the past ten years, always reaching the same conclusion. I would not want to be heterosexual unless I were a man. The life of heterosexual woman is hardly an existence, whereas a man has everything he wants, when and where and how.

The only difficulty in being lesbian is the fact of falling perhaps for a woman and not knowing whether she is also gay. This can be tricky and not always turn out satisfactorily. Heterosexuals do not have this trouble. Man meets woman and vice versa, and there is nothing to bar their way if they wish to have an affair. However, when woman meets woman there is an interim period of uncertainty, unless of course one meets within an organisation like Kenric.

I would like to settle down with a woman eventually, someone about the same age as myself with whom I am able to share my life and its interests, becoming part of and sharing hers. Early this year I met a French girl at the 'Gates' and took her home. The next day she informed me she had been out for a good time, and that she really preferred men. Looking back, I think I realised this earlier. I don't like one-night stands – they can be cheap and often one can be hurt. Relationships in the homosexual world should have a time for courting as heterosexuals do. Maybe I am old-fashioned in having this view, but it's the way I see things. After all I would not like my future partner to be a pawn in someone else's game.

I prefer wearing trousers to a skirt, and sometimes even wear them to concerts and rehearsals. The conversations I overhear like: 'What is it?' 'Is it a boy or a girl?' 'I thought it was a man' (in the ladies' cloakroom) go in at one ear and out of the other, (sometimes they don't get as far as that!)

The reasons I am lesbian are (I think) partly because I probably have more male than female hormones (I am awaiting the chromosomes tests at Lambeth and shall be curious to know the results,) and the fact that my brother was given more attention than myself. Therefore the male being a symbol of superiority I associated/associate myself with this.

I am interested to know what your opinion is, Dr Wolff.

COMMENT

Psychological interpretation

Miss Z has made a neat diagnosis of her own case, and I cannot but agree with her assessment. I shall therefore only explain certain implications of her statement that her lesbianism is caused by both biological and psychological factors.

This woman is by far the most masculine in physique and expressive behaviour of the whole group of lesbians I interviewed. If aberrations of chromosomes should be found in some lesbians, she might be one of them, according to her pheno-type. Her masculine gender identity carries conviction, not only for herself but also for others. She could easily pass for a young man. She was able to express her masculinity in jobs and interests when she was younger. She had an active, adventurous life, and her wish to be a member of the Metropolitan Police on the River Squad tells much about her nature. It also shows marked aggressiveness and the need for outdoor activity.

The relationship with her brother and her mother's preference for him, turned the emotional scales towards complete homosexuality, and flight from the family. Her refusal to compromise is, in psychological terms, a mixture of aggressiveness and avoidance of too painful a situation.

psychological experience →

Personal impression

Miss Z struck me as an idealistic, romantic person, who would not hesitate to sacrifice herself for her beliefs and convictions. Outwardly very quiet and measured in speech and gesture, one felt an inner volcano, held back by excellent manners and natural courtesy. She behaves like a chivalrous young man who always thinks of the other person first. Her narrow hips, broad shoulders, masculine hands and handsome face make her an attractive 'young man'. She is a self-sufficient person, with a tendency to look after the underdog. Her courtesy and her nobility of principles have an almost old-fashioned flavour. Miss Z could easily be exploited, but whatever may happen to her, I am sure she can take it.

Appendix 1:

28 statistical tables with explanatory notes

TABLE 1 Professions of Subjects and their Fathers. Tabulated according to the Classification of Occupations into Social Classes I to V, issued by the General Register Office, London.

SUBJECTS' PROFESSIONS	I	*Social Class* II & III	IV	V	*None*	*Unknown*	*Total*
Controls	5	114	1	–	3	–	123
Lesbians	8	86	7	1	6	–	108

FATHERS' PROFESSIONS							
Controls	9	105	6	–		3	123
Lesbians	14	76	5	6		7	108

Table 1 and Table 28 have been done by hand. They refer to 108 lesbians, while all other tables refer to 106. Two questionnaires of the lesbian group were sent separately to the Computor Centre of the Medical Research Council and must have gone astray.

TABLE 2 Age of Subjects

Age Groups	*Controls* No.	*Lesbians* No.
20 – 29	19	29
30 – 39	59	24
40 – 49	27	27
50 – 59	16	19
60+	2	7
	$\bar{x} = 38.24$	$\bar{x} = 39.96$

There is no significant difference in the average age of lesbians and controls.

TABLE 3 Age of Parents at Birth of Subjects

Mother's Age	Controls No.	Lesbians No.
Under 20	2	13
20 – 24	21	47
25 – 30	43	21
31 – 35	35	16
36 – 40	16	8
Over 40	5	–
Unknown	1	1

x^2 significant at 0.1% level. $P < 0.001$

The age of the mother at birth of subject is significantly lower in the lesbian than in the control group.

Father's Age		
20 – 29	41	40
30 – 39	59	47
40 – 49	12	11
50 – 59	5	3
60+	5	1
Unknown	1	4

x^2 not significant. $P < 0.05$

There is no difference in the father's age at birth of subjects in the two groups.

TABLE 4 Subjects' Position in Family

	Controls No.	Lesbians No.
* Only child	20	39
Illegitimate	1	5
Eldest	33	35
Second	37	22
Third	15	6
Fourth	9	2
Fifth	6	1
** Youngest	38	19

* x^2 significant at 0.1% level. $P < 0.001$
** x^2 significant at 5% level. $P < 0.05$

Lesbians are very significantly more often *only children*. They also tend to be more often the *elder ones* than the controls. They are significantly less often the youngest.

TABLE 5 Brothers and Sisters

			Controls No.	Lesbians No.
*	Had older brothers	Yes	43	18
		No	80	87
		Unknown		1
**	Had older sisters	Yes	49	21
		No	74	84
		Unknown		1
***	Had younger brothers	Yes	51	32
		No	72	73
		Unknown		1
****	Had younger sisters	Yes	41	23
		No	82	82
		Unknown		1

* χ^2 significant at 1% level. $0.001 < P < 0.01$
** χ^2 significant at 1% level. $0.001 < P < 0.01$
*** χ^2 not significant. $P > 0.05$
**** χ^2 not significant. $P > 0.05$

While lesbians had older brothers and sisters less often than the control group, there was no significant difference in the numbers of younger siblings between the two groups.

TABLE 6 Relative Dominance of Parents

	Controls No.	Lesbians No.
Mother	63	72
Father	55	33
Unknown	5	1

χ^2 significant at 5% level. $0.01 < P < 0.05$

The mother was the dominant parent more often among lesbians than in the control group.

TABLE 7 Positive Emotional Response of Mother to Subjects

		Controls No.	Lesbians No.
*	Mother's favourite	5	15
**	Mother loving	106	66
***	No preference for any child	66	13
	Unknown	4	1

* $\chi^2 = 7.266$ χ^2 significant at 1% level. $0.001 < P < 0.01$
** χ^2 significant at 0.1% level. $P < 0.001$
*** χ^2 significant at 0.1% level. $P < 0.001$

The lesbians were more often mothers' favourites than the controls, but as a whole, mothers were recorded to be *less loving* in the case of the lesbians. The mothers also showed much less preference for any child in the control group than in the lesbian group.

TABLE 8 Negative Emotional Responses of Mother to Subjects

			Controls No.	Lesbians No.
*	Mother preferred a brother		20	31
**	Mother would have preferred subject to be male	Yes	21	31
		No	99	75
	Unknown		3	

* χ^2 significant at 5% level. $0.01 < P < 0.05$
** χ^2 significant at 5% level. $0.01 < P < 0.05$

The mother showed a preference for a son more often in the case of lesbians, and she would also have preferred them to be male more often than in the control group.

TABLE 9 Negative Emotional Responses of Mother to Subjects (continued)

		Controls No.	Lesbians No.
*	Mother indifferent	12	29
**	Mother negligent	0	11
	Unknown	5	

* χ^2 significant at 0.1% level. $P < 0.001$
** χ^2 significant at 0.1% level. $P < 0.001$

The mother was far more often either indifferent or outright negligent in the lesbian than in the control group.

TABLE 10 Positive and Negative Emotional Responses of Father to Subjects

		Controls No.	Lesbians No.
*	Father's favourite	27	29
**	Father loving	104	62
***	Father negligent	3	14
	Unknown	2	3

    * χ^2 not significant. $P > 0.05$
    ** χ^2 significant at 0.1% level. $P < 0.001$
    *** χ^2 significant at 1% level. $0.01 < P < 0.01$

The father was much more often loving in the control group than in the lesbian group. The father more often showed a negligent attitude in the lesbian than in the control group.

TABLE 11 Subjects' Emotional Responses to Siblings

	Controls No.	Lesbians No.
Positive (close)		
Older brother(s)	8	4
Younger ,,	14	8
Older sister(s)	12	11
Younger ,,	6	10
Negative (antagonistic)		
Older brother(s)	3	6
Younger ,,	5	13
Older sister(s)	3	3
Younger ,,	6	10

The emotional responses to siblings showed no significant differences in the two groups, except for a trend towards hostility against younger brothers among the lesbians.

TABLE 12 Parents of Subjects Unhappily Married

	Controls No.	Lesbians No.
*Unhappily married	23	50
Unknown		2
Separated	4	11
Divorced	10	9
Neither	9	30

    * $\chi^2 = 17.5$ Idf χ^2 significant at 0.1% level. $P < 0.001$

The proportion of unhappily married parents is much higher in the lesbian than in the control group.

TABLE 13 Incidence of Death of a Parent before age of 18

Death of Mother at age of	Controls No.	Lesbians No.
0 – 3	2	–
4 – 7	1	3
8 – 12	3	1
13 – 18	1	–
Death of Father at age of		
0 – 3	1	3
4 – 7	6	4
8 – 12	1	4
13 – 18	6	15

χ^2 not significant. $P > 0.05$

TABLE 14 Data on Step-parents before age of 18

		Controls No.	Lesbians No.
* Stepmother before 18	Yes	7	5
	No	116	101
** Stepfather before 18	Yes	3	10
	No	120	96

* not significant. $P > 0.05$
** significant at 5% level. $0.01 < P < 0.05$

While the incidence of the death of a parent was not significantly different in the two groups, the lesbians more often had a step-father than the controls.

TABLE 15 Subjects' Wish to be Made a Male

		Controls No.	Lesbians No.
* As a child			
	Yes	18	81
	No	105	25
** Now			
	Yes	3	29
	No	120	77

* χ^2 significant at 0.1% level. $P < 0.001$
** χ^2 significant at 0.1% level. $P < 0.001$

Although the proportion of lesbians wanting to be a male is smaller in adulthood than in youth, it is still significantly higher than with the controls. A small number of controls wanted to be boys, and only 3 out of 123 wished to be male as grown-ups.

TABLE 16 Emotional Attachments of Subjects Outside the Family

	Controls No.	Lesbians No.
To women only	12	86
To men and women	88	17
To men only	21	–
Not known	2	3

χ^2 significant at 0.1% level. P < 0.001

The proportion of lesbians emotionally attached to women far outweighs that of the control group.

TABLE 17 Homo- and Heterosexual Feelings of Subjects

		Controls No.	Lesbians No.
* Physically attracted to men			
	Yes	87	58
	No	34	48
	Not known	2	
Physically attracted to women			
	Yes	11	106
	No	111	
	Not known	1	
** Fear of men			
	Yes	9	41
	No	113	65
	Not known	1	

* χ^2 significant at 1% level. 0.001 < P < 0.01
** χ^2 significant at 0.1% level. P < 0.001

The proportion of lesbians attracted to men was lower than in the control group, but not to a highly significant degree. Fear of men was greater in lesbians to a highly significant degree compared with the control group.

TABLE 18 Strong Emotional Relations with Either Sex

	Controls No.	Lesbians No.
Women only	14	90
Men and women	14	14
Men only	38	–
None	56	2
Not known	1	–

$\chi^2 = 135.102$ 3df χ^2 significant at 0.1% level. P < 0.001

The number of lesbians with strong emotional relationships with women is overwhelmingly greater than in the control group. It is interesting to note that a considerable number of controls had no strong emotional relationships at all.

TABLE 19 Number of Homosexual Partners

	Controls No.	Lesbians No.
None	100	6
1	12	17
2	2	10
3	1	21
4	–	18
5	–	16
6 or more	–	18
Not known	8	–

$$\chi^2 = 107.955 \text{ 6df } \chi^2 \text{ significant at } 0.1\% \text{ level. } P < 0.001$$

The result is, of course, taken for granted in that the number of homosexual partners in the lesbian group far outweighs that among the controls. It is interesting to note however that homosexual relationships occurred in the control group also.

TABLE 20 Number of Heterosexual Partners

	Controls No.	Lesbians No.
None	60	42
1	22	19
2	16	21
3	11	9
4	2	9
5	3	4
6 or more	8	2
Not known	1	–

$$\chi^2 = 11.93 \text{ 6df } \chi^2 \text{ not significant. } P > 0.05$$

It is most interesting to note that there is no significant difference between the two groups with regard to the number of heterosexual partners.

TABLE 21 Data on Married Subjects

	Controls No.	Lesbians No.
Number married	21	25
Husband alive	20	19
Happily married	15	5
Unhappily married	6	20
Separated	1	6
Divorced	3	10
Neither separated nor divorced	2	4
Number with children	14	16
Children loved	12	12
Children not loved	1	4
Not known	1	–

The data indicate the greater frequency of unhappy marriage and a greater separation and divorce rate in the lesbian than in the control group. However, love for their children was equal in both groups.

TABLE 22 Incidence of Psychosomatic Conditions

			Controls No.	Lesbians No.
*	Asthma	Yes	2	14
		No	121	92
**	Other allergies	Yes	26	19
		No	97	87

  * χ^2 significant at 0.1%. $P < 0.001$
  ** χ^2 not significant. $P > 0.05$

A much higher proportion of the lesbians had asthma compared with the proportion of the control group.

The proportion of sufferers from other allergies is similar for both groups.

TABLE 23 Personal History of Psychological or Mental Conditions

			Controls No.	Lesbians No.
*	Traumatic sexual experience			
	In childhood	Yes	11	35
		No	112	71
	In adolescence	Yes	4	30
		No	119	76
**	Psychological illness	Yes	14	56
		No	109	50
***	Hospitalisation in a mental hospital	Yes	2	18
		No	121	88
****	Alcoholism	Yes	–	16
		No	123	90

  * χ^2 significant at 0.1% level. $P < 0.001$
  ** χ^2 significant at 0.1% level. $P < 0.001$
  *** χ^2 significant at 0.1% level. $P < 0.001$
  **** χ^2 significant at 0.1% level. $P < 0.001$

The proportion of subjects who suffered sexual traumata in childhood and adolescence is much higher in the lesbian than in the control group. The same holds good for both psychological and mental illnesses. Alcoholism did not occur in the control group, but the incidence was high in the lesbian group.

TABLE 24 Family History of Mental Illness, Alcoholism and Homosexuality

			Controls No.	Lesbians No.
*	Mental illness	Yes	15	25
		No	106	80
		Not known	1	1
**	Alcoholism	Yes	9	24
		No	111	81
		Not known	3	1
***	Homosexuality	Yes	1	29
		No	120	76
		Not known	2	1

*	χ^2 significant at 5% level. $0.01 < P < 0.05$
**	χ^2 significant at 1% level. $0.001 < P < 0.01$
***	χ^2 significant at 0.1% level. $P < 0.001$

Starting with the last item first: homosexuality appears to have a genetic factor, as its occurrence is significantly higher in proportion with family history of the lesbian group than in that of the control group. A high degree of significance is found in the proportion of families with a history of alcoholism in the lesbian group compared with the control group. The proportion of families with a history of mental illness is significantly higher in the lesbian than in the control group.

TABLE 25 Characteristic Personality Traits

		Controls No.	Lesbians No.
Highly aggressive	Yes	14	42
	No	108	64
	Unknown	1	

χ^2 significant at 0.1% level. $P < 0.001$

Bad tempered	Yes	13	39
	No	7	22
	Neither	103	45

χ^2 not significant. $P > 0.05$

Abusive	Yes	1	32
	No	19	29
	Neither	103	45

χ^2 significant at 0.1% level. $P < 0.001$

Violent	Yes	–	44
	No	20	62
	Neither	103	

χ^2 significant at 1% level. $0.01 < P < 0.01$

TABLE 25 (continued)

		No.	No.
Strongly inhibited			
a) very tense	Yes	36	85
	No	86	21
	Unknown	1	

$\chi^2 = 58.494$ χ^2 significant at 0.1% level. $P < 0.001$

b) extremely shy	Yes	37	70
	No	86	36

χ^2 significant at 0.1% level. $P < 0.001$

Easily suggestible	Yes	33	44
	No	90	62

χ^2 significant at 5% level. $0.01 < P < 0.05$

'Joie de vivre'	Yes	115	75
	No	8	31

χ^2 significant at 0.1% level. $P < 0.001$

Enjoying leisure	Yes	119	85
	No	3	21
	Not known	1	

χ^2 significant at 0.1% level. $P < 0.001$

Adaptability in:			
a) Work relationships	Yes	115	81
	No	7	25
	Neither	1	

χ^2 significant at 0.1% level. $P < 0.001$

b) Social intercourse	Yes	81	66
	No	42	40

χ^2 not significant

c) Personal relationships	Yes	103	52
	No	19	54
	Not known	1	

χ^2 significant at 0.1% level. $P < 0.001$

The proportion of lesbians who were:
1. very aggressive, 2. abusive, 3. violent,
is much greater than the proportion in the control group.

The proportion of lesbians who were nervously tense and extremely shy is greater than the proportion in the control group. The proportion of lesbians who were 'easily suggestible' is greater than the proportion for the controls. A smaller proportion of lesbians enjoyed leisure than in the control group, and the same is true with regard to 'joie de vivre'. A much greater proportion of the control group were adaptable in their relationships at work and in private life, than was the case in the lesbian group. There is no statistical difference between the two groups with regard to adaptability in social intercourse.

TABLE 26 Guilt Feeling about Sex

			Controls No.	Lesbians No.
*	Outside marriage	Yes	64	19
		No	58	87
		Unknown	1	
**	Inside marriage	Yes	3	4
		No	118	102
		Unknown	2	

* χ^2 significant at 0.1% level. $P < 0.001$
** χ^2 not significant. $P > 0.05$

The lesbians investigated showed far less guilt feeling about sex outside marriage than the controls. There was no significant difference between the two groups with regard to guilt feelings about sex inside marriage.

TABLE 27 Reaction to Stress Situations

	Controls No.	Lesbians No.
Well	92	33
Badly	27	73
Unknown	4	–

$\chi^2 = 48.419$ χ^2 significant at 0.1% level. $P < 0.001$

The proportion of lesbians who reacted well to stress situations is very much lower than the proportion in the control group.

TABLE 28 Sexual Manifestations in 108 Lesbians (controls not asked)

UNDISGUISED SEX DREAMS

With a male	With a female	With either	Voyeur dreams	No sex dreams
10	29	33	25	11

ORGASMS IN ROLE OF

Male	Female	Either	No orgasm
22	27	46	13

SEEING HERSELF IN MASTURBATION FANTASIES AS

Male	Female	Either	No masturbation	No fantasy
28	10	45	22	3

Appendix 2:

New Developments in Homosexual Organisations

It is not surprising that minorities are in a state of permanent revolution, as they have to fight unceasingly for their place in society. Homosexuals suffer more than other minorities from a sense of insecurity, because their very existence represents a threat to the most intimate emotional life of so-called 'normal' people. Homosexuality is based on bisexuality, which is the heritage of all human beings. This fact is at the root of the peculiar fear, hostility and rejection of 'deviance' by 'ordinary' men and women who deny and suppress their own homosexual tendencies. Fear and aggression have led to the infliction of many kinds of persecution on homosexuals, who are well aware that they live on a razor's edge in our society; nevertheless they go on fighting for their right of recognition as people who are worth just as much as those of a 'normal' psychosexual orientation. During the last years, their efforts have multiplied, and have led to an increased solidarity and a stronger collective identity. The existing organisations have not only grown, but in many cases have changed their strategy, their policy and, in some cases, their character. A number of new organisations have been formed, thus broadening the front of fighting forces, and creating a new momentum for the movement. This may give homosexuals a better chance to break through the barriers of prejudice and injustice still existing in many strata of our society.

During the last few years, a new spirit of community has developed between lesbians and male homosexuals, which is reflected in a number of groups with mixed membership; but first I want to speak of organisations which cater exclusively for women.

LESBIAN ORGANISATIONS

The first of these was the Minorities Research Group, formed in 1963, and since 1968 called the Minorities Research Trust. It was instrumental in the creation of autonomous groups all over the country. These independent groups were and are very much alive, and they have increased in number. The magazine *Arena Three* contributed much towards bringing the groups and individual members together, through information about developments on the lesbian scene as a whole, and in the individual groups.

Arena Three underwent a decisive change in November 1971, when it came under new management. The London editor and co-ordinator, a trained social worker, gave it a new look. She included articles of social significance, not only for lesbians, but for all women. The magazine is leased on a yearly basis from its founder and former editor. All homosexual organisations subsist on voluntary contributions, and this causes serious problems in keeping them running. Because of financial difficulties, *Arena Three* will in future be published quarterly under the name *Gay Girl*.

Kenric has increased its membership during the last few years, but its policy and character remain unchanged.

In April 1972 a new venture altered the lesbian scene – the publication of the magazine *Sappho*. It is published by homosexual women for *all* women, most of the content being written by readers and subscribers. The magazine depends on reader feed-back to provide a forum for lesbian opinion, and discussion of the problems encountered by homosexual and bisexual women. *Sappho* is the only magazine organising monthly meetings as an integral part of its function. Prominent people give talks at these meetings, with lively discussions afterwards. The group has aired members' views on such topics as artficial insemination for lesbians, and adoption of children by them. The meetings have already become well-known, and attract not only English subscribers, but also lesbians from abroad. *Sappho* supports the Women's Liberation Movement in the belief that all women are subject to the same discrimination in a male-dominated society. Since many women need help in coming to terms with their homosexuality, *Sappho* has a qualified counselling and referral service for subscribers. Those needing help in legal matters are given the names of solicitiors sympathetic to the situation of homosexual women, whether they be single, couples, or married. *Sappho* exchanges information with homophile organisations and publications in Britain and abroad.

MIXED ORGANISATIONS

The *Albany Trust* was founded by men and, to start with, catered for male homosexuals only, but women soon joined in increasing numbers. Many of them sought the help and counsel of the Trust in their personal and social problems. In 1970 the organisation underwent a fundamental change. Antony Grey had left the Trust, and its case worker did not stay long under the new directorship. Counselling became a more and more difficult task, and the financial position also deteriorated. In spite of the Trust's great reputation, funds were inadequate for the employment of trained social workers, and it was thereforefore decided to give up counselling altogether. Demands for help from women and men all over the country did not, however, diminish – rather the opposite. The Albany Trust again acted as a referral agency, sending clients to other organisations – in the first place, the Samaritans. Although some activities were cut down and its accommodation was reduced, the Trust contined to pursue its most important projects – education and research in both the sociological and psychological fields. In 1971, Antony Grey agreed to become the Managing Trustee, and since then he has done much to make the efforts of the Trust more concentrated than before. He has broadened the basis for informing and educating the public in general, and professional bodies in particular, about the social and psychological needs of the homosexual. He gave many talks at universities, extended his contacts with social organisations, social workers and medical consultants, and was even invited to talk to the B.M.A. It is of considerable interest in this context to report on an inquiry about doctors' attitudes to homosexuality. Results from the questionnaire survey are given in the synopsis of a paper by Dr Philip A. Morris, to be published in the *British Journal of Psychiatry*. He asked 150 general practitioners and 150 psychiatrists about their opinion of, and attitude to, homosexuality. Most doctors (G.P.s as well as psychiatrists) did not consider homosexuality to be an illness, and would not give treatment for the condition *per se*. They would try, however, to help psychological disturbances of a secondary nature, for instance anxiety states and guilt feelings.

The Albany Trust is a registered charity, and so is the *Albany Society Ltd*. They are totally distinct from one another, except for the fact that all the Trustees of the Albany Trust are members of the Council of Management of the Albany Society. Other members of the Management Council have no affiliation with the Trust. They are chosen from a number of different homophile groups. The main objects of the Society, as stated in its Memorandum, are :

> To promote psychological health by collecting data and conducting research; to publish the results in writing, films, lectures and other media; to take suitable steps based thereon for the public benefit; to improve the social and general conditions necessary for such healthy psychological development.

It should be noted that the word 'homosexuality' is not mentioned, because the organisation is concerned with the whole field of sexuality, and not with one aspect only. Homosexuality is, however, its principal concern. The Albany Society was founded in 1968, but has lately come to the fore through reorganisation, and the launching of new programmes.

The name of the *Campaign for Homosexual Equality* (C.H.E.) implies the main objective of the organisation. It evolved from the North Western Law Reform Committee, which worked for the reform of the law on homosexuality. C.H.E. was founded in 1970, and can boast a rapid growth since its small beginnings in Manchester. It has, in 1973, 60 branches all over the country;

London is now the most important centre after Manchester, which remains its headquarters. The membership in mid-1972 was 3,000, 30 per cent being women. The programme of C.H.E. contains an interesting paragraph, which I quote:

Attitudes towards the woman's role in society are clearly related to prejudice against homosexuals. Many people mistakenly think that homosexual men are feminine or 'effeminate', and that to be feminine is inferior to being masculine. Thus the cause of homosexual equality has objectives in common with the cause of women's liberation – and faces similar obstacles. We see our action against prejudice in these wider forms and welcome women to join C.H.E.

Founded by men, the movement now includes many women, whose influence in the organisation has markedly increased in the last year.

The tenor and purpose of C.H.E. are aggressive. Its aims are in essence the same as those of most homophile societies; it is the tactics which may differ. It is therefore unnecessary to spell out their objectives in detail.

Scotland possesses well-equipped organisations designed to educate the public and to promote the well-being of the 'outsider'. Closely connected in spirit and collaboration with C.H.E. is the *Scottish Minorities Group* (S.M.G.). It caters for both sexes, but has a separate Women's Group situated in Edinburgh. Perhaps the best witness to Scottish concern for the problems of homosexuality is the *Ean Simpson Care and Counselling Unit,* designed to give help to homosexual men and women in social and emotional difficulties. It is sponsored by the Church of Scotland's Welfare Committee, and a professionally skilled staff deals with counselling. This group and the S.M.G. are supported by leading figures in Scottish universities and the Church.

The *Gay Liberation Front* (G.L.F.), founded in 1971, is the most radical of all the homophile movements. Their display of rebellion in public has given them notoriety, which is a stumbling-block preventing many people from taking them seriously, or even troubling to find out what lies behind the facade. Their manifesto is, in my view, an articulate document of progressive thinking. They do not believe that the homosexual has any chance of finding his proper place in our society, and they act, accordingly, by opposing the whole structure of bourgeois society. They claim that it is the family which teaches false images of what is male and female, and is therefore the arch-oppressor. They reject gender fixation in their drive for truth and emotional freedom. If one looks at these postulates in an objective spirit, one finds them in line with the thoughts of many progressive people, and compatible with modern bio-psychological ideas. Their argument that life in a commune is a more adequate form of bond-formation than the family is confirmed not only by sociologists and anthropologists, but also by many young people all over the world, whatever their psychosexual orientation. Both men and women of G.L.F. are courageous people, cocking a snook at public opinion, and going into action at a moment's notice when provoked by bigotry, hypocrisy or plain exploitation. The male members of G.L.F. reject absolutely the idea of any form of male superiority. They are thus natural adherents of the Women's Liberation movements, since they identify with women as human beings and as homosexuals.

The G.L.F. is antagonistic to psychiatry, and I have heard members make rather sweeping statements about psychiatrists – those enemies who believe in 'curing' homosexuality. These prejudices are the result of defensive over-reaction. On the other hand, they have considerable insight into their own psychological difficulties, as expressed in the G.L.F. Manifesto :

> The oppression . . . lies in the head of every one of us. This means freeing our heads from self-oppression and male chauvinism, and no longer organising our lives according to the pattern with which we are indoctrinated by straight society.

To my mind the G.L.F. goes courageously to the roots of society's malformations. They rightly point out that the idea of male sexual and social superiority has produced many of the evils from which we suffer.

Apart from these major organisations, a number of new smaller groups have been founded during the last few years. They make their own important contribution to the whole, but I must limit myself to a short account of three which I think are of special significance.

Friend was started by C.H.E. in 1971 as an organisation for befriending and counselling. Young homosexuals particularly were in dire need of mental and social support, and *Friend* seemed to fill this need. Befrienders and counsellors came forward and made themselves available at a centre in the northwest of London, five evenings weekly. Although *Friend* had initially been founded by C.H.E., it is now autonomous, with local groups outside London.

Integroup is a new group loosely connected with C.H.E., established in August 1972. It has a special place among all other homophile organisations, because it aims to bring together homosexual and heterosexual people. Personal contacts between 'gay' and 'straight' people should lead not only to better mutual understanding but also to the abolition of the ghetto existence of homosexual women and men. This group has been welcomed with enthusiasm by members of the different homophile organisations. Meetings and discussion groups are held once monthly in private homes.

Parent's Inquiry is an attempt to bring together parents of homosexual children to try to explain to them the true nature, indeed naturalness, of the psychosexual orientation of their offspring. The foundation of this enterprise was the work of one woman, Mrs Rose Robertson. She has created a new source of active help for the young homosexual, with possibilities of better understanding between parents and children. She overcame considerable resistance against her effort. As a rule parents blame themselves for the condition, which they cannot help considering an aberration and misfortune. One of the problems which prevents a relaxed acceptance is fear of what relatives and neighbours will say. The venture started only a short while ago, and up to March 1973, thirty parents have participated. Mrs Robertson rightly believes than an organisation of parents who come to terms with the homosexual orientation of their children has a positive influence on other parents in the same situation. It is obvious that this organisation touches on most sensitive spots in heterosexual adults. In attempting to break down family prejudice, the heart of resistance against the homosexual and the root of much neurotic illness in both children and parents, Mrs Robertson performs a considerable social service for both the homosexual and the heterosexual.

The *National Federation of Homophile Organisations* (N.F.H.O.) is an umbrella organisation which provides a forum for discussion of relevant problems, with a view to taking active steps to solve them, or at least lessen their impact. The organisation acts as a centre for communication between individual groups, ten of which had joined in 1971 when it was established. C.H.E. and the S.M.G. are among them. The N.F.H.O. rightly assumes that it is sensible to fight battles against a strong enemy with a well-trained army rather than with single companies. The organisation brings the member groups together at regular intervals, and arranges conferences with outside social bodies.

Perhaps the greatest difficulty facing the whole homophile movement is the care and professional help needed by many homosexuals who suffer from a sense of isolation, and are maladjusted to their milieu. A considerable number exhibit more serious disturbances. Many, though not all, homophile groups are profoundly concerned with the care of these cases. The N.F.H.O. has made it its special task to find an answer to the problem, either through befriending or counselling, or both.

The idea of *befriending* has found expression primarily in *Friend*. It is not, however, a simple task to decide who needs befriending and who needs professional help, be it through psychotherapy or counselling. Last year, the N.F.H.O. convened a three-day conference to discuss this. Individual social workers, psychiatrists and representatives of a Council for Social Services joined the delegates from homophile groups for discussion. Several speakers asserted that ignorance about the problems of homosexuals among social workers, and even psychiatrists, made referral for counselling a hit-or-miss task. Even if counsellors were informed and willing, their inhibited attitudes to homosexuals could make contact with clients difficult.

Counselling should obviously only be done by trained social workers with considerable experience and skill. The difficulty lies in finding them, for they are generally fully occupied. Befriending is an easier job. It needs, however, some training as well as empathy. Good will alone is not enough. The role of 'friend' to an insecure person should only be undertaken by someone who has a certain social and emotional stability. He must be a good listener, and not come forward with advice. Befrienders have to collaborate with counsellors and psychiatrists in case their protegés need more help than a layman can give.

The task of the N.F.H.O. can be summarised as follows :

(a) to give information to the medical profession (psychiatrists included) and social workers about homosexuality.

(b) to choose befrienders who fulfil the necessary conditions.

The task of befriending, if a task it is, is not without a pastoral flavour, and I want to end this review of developments by mentioning the influence exerted by churchmen in the homophile community.

A number of priests are active in almost all the groups. The London co-ordinator of *Friend*, for example, is a clergyman. The Samaritans, who undertake much counselling work for homosexuals, have two eminent 'pastors' actively dealing with it. But there is a more fundamental link between homosexuality and religion. Mother Church attracts those who are unwelcome in society, and offers them special comfort and a constructive way out. People in social isolation tend to seek the confessional as an alternative to the psychiatrist or a friend, neither of whom can be as reliable or trustworthy. The need for permanence, impossible to find in human relationships, can be fulfilled to some extent through religion. However, not every servant of the Church is without prejudice towards the homosexual; until recently the opposite was the rule. It is therefore not surprising that a need exists to worship in a service where 'gay' people are sure of approval and the company of the like-minded. America was, as far as I know, the first country to institute religious services for homosexuals. The Reverend Roy Perry started it all. He is a declared homosexual, and the author of *The Lord's My Shepherd and He Knows I'm Gay*. Needless to say, this book got him into trouble, but, undeterred by persecution, he started services in his own parlour. By now there are 36 'gay churches' – that is, derelict buildings converted for worship – in the United States. An interesting by-product of Roy Perry's enterprise is the appeal the 'gay' churches have for heterosexual people; for example, in a Los Angeles church, they represent 20 per cent of the congregation.

Roy Perry's enterprise became the model for the 'Fellowship in Christ the Liberator' in England, which was started in October 1972 in London. It holds regular services every week.

The F.C.L., as it is called, states in a leaflet that it provides the opportunity for those who feel they have been rejected or never fully accepted by other Christian communities to worship God freely and openly as they are. It makes clear at the same time that the Fellowship is not exclusively 'gay', because everyone, regardless of his or her sexual orientation, is welcome. This wise attitude is to be expected from any church. Perhaps some walls, erected by the Church centuries ago against the deviant, are coming down.

Or are they? In a recent T.V. broadcast on the permissive society, Bishop Trevor Huddlestone replied to a question about the attitude of the Church to homosexuality: 'The Church does not condemn homosexuality. The Church does condemn homosexual acts which lead to perversion.'

It is an intriguing fact that many priests have attitudes to homosexuality similar to those of such radical freedom fighters as the Women's Liberation Workshop, though the Church remains more cautious and reserved. Many lesbians have joined Women's Liberation, and there is no question of their being singled out by their heterosexual sisters. I learnt through a personal communication from the Women's Liberation Workshop that they consider sexual orientation a strictly private affair, and never judge any woman from this point of view. They have observed, however, that lesbians have a particularly strong solidarity with each other and with the movement.

The homophile community has sympathisers, if not allies, among groups with powerful voices. Their help could be decisive in the creation of a better climate for changing the still negative attitudes of society as a whole.

Bibliography

Abe, K. and Moran, P. A. P.	Parental age of homosexuals, *British Journal of Psychiatry*, Vol. 115 No. 520, London, 1969.
Albany Trust	*Winter Talks*, London, 1962-63.
Arena Three	A monthly lesbian journal, published in London.
Barney, Natalie	*Pensées d'une amazone*, Paris, 1962.
„ „	*Traits et portraits*, Paris, 1963.
de Beauvoir, Simone	*The Second Sex*, tr. and ed. H. M. Parshley, London and New York, 1969.
Bene, Eva	Female homosexuality, *British Journal of Psychiatry*, Vol. III No. 478, London, Sept. 1965.
„ „	Male homosexuality, *British Journal of Psychiatry*, Vol. III No. 478, London, Sept. 1965.

H

Benjamin, Harry	Transvestism and transsexualism in the male and female, *Journal of Sex Research*, Vol. 3 No. 2, May 1967, reprinted by the Albany Trust, London, 1969.
„ „	Newer aspects of the transsexual phenomenon, *Journal of Sex Research*, Vol 5 No. 2, May 1969, reprinted by the Albany Trust, London, 1969.
Blackham, H. J.	*Six Existentialist Thinkers*, London, 1957.
Bonaparte, Marie	*Female Sexuality*, London, 1953.
Bowlby, John	*Attachment and Loss*, International Psycho-analytical Library, No. 79, London, 1969.
„ „	*Personality and Mental Illness*, London, 1940.
Brecher, Ruth and Edward (ed.)	*An Analysis of Human Sexual Response*, London, 1967.
British Medical Journal	*Female Homosexuality*, Vol. I, London, 1969.
Brown, Norman O.	*Life against Death*, New York and London, 1959.
Brun, Rudolf	*General Theory of Neurosis*, New York, 1951.
Chapman, Diana	What is a Lesbian?, *Man and Society*, London, winter 1965.
Chedd, Graham	Struggling into Manhood, *New Scientist*, London, June 5th 1969.
Cory, Donald Webster	*The Lesbian in America*, New York, 1964.

Crisp, Quentin — *The Naked Civil Servant*, London, 1968.

Daniel, Marc — Sex, law and society in France today, *Man and Society*, London, winter 1966.

Dörner, Günter — Prophylaxe und Therapie angeborener Sexualdeviationen, *Deutsche Medizinische Wochenschrift-Sonderdruck*, 2 February 1969, Stuttgart.

Eliade, Mircea — *Myths, Dreams and Mysteries*, New York and London, 1968.

Ellis, H. — *Psychology of Sex*, London and New York, 1909.

Fairbairn, W. Ronald — *Psycho-analytic Studies of the Personality*, London, 1966.

Fenichel, O. — *The Psycho-analytic Theory of Neurosis*, London, 1945.

Ford, C. S. and Beach, F.A. — *Patterns of Sexual Behaviour*, London, 1952.

Fox, Beatrice and di Scipio, Wm. J. — An exploratory study in the treatment of homosexuality by combining principles from psycho-analytic theory and conditioning : theoretical and methodical considerations, *British Journal of Medical Psychology*, Vol. 41 No. 39, London, 1968.

Freeman, Thomas — Critique of behaviour therapy, *British Journal of Medical Psychology*, Vol. 41 No. 39, London, 1968.

Freud, Sigmund — *Collected Papers*, Vol. 1, London, 1949, My views on the part played by sexuality in the aetiology of the neuroses. (1905)

Freud, Sigmund

Ibid. Vol. II, 1949,
a) The psychogenesis of a case of homosexuality in a woman. (1920)
b) A child is being beaten. (1919)

,,   ,,

Ibid. Vol. III, 1949,
a) Fragment of an analysis of a case of
hysteria. (1905)
b) Analysis of a phobia in a five-year-
old boy. (1909)

,,   ,,

Ibid. Vol. IV, 1949,
a) On Narcissism. (1914)
b) Repression. (1915)
c) Instincts and their vicissitudes. (1915)
d) Contributions to the psychology of
love. The most prevalent form of degradation in erotic life. (1912)

,,   ,,

Ibid. Vol. V, 1969,
a) Some psychological consequences of
the anatomical distinction between
the sexes. (1925)
b) Female sexuality. (1931)

,,   ,,

*Three Essays on the Theory of Sex-
uality,* London, 1962.

,,   ,,

The Interpretation of Dreams, London,
1950.

Friedan, Betty

The Feminine Mystique, New York,
1964.

Furlong, Monica

Paradoxes of love, *Man and Society,*
London, winter 1966.

Geiwitz, P. James

Non-Freudian Personality Theories,
Basic Concepts in Psychology Series,
Belmont, California, 1969.

Gelder, M. G. Desensitization and psychotherapy research, *British Journal of Medical Psychology*, Vol. 41 No. 39, London, 1968.

Grant, V. W. *The Psychology of Sexual Emotion*, London, 1957.

Groddek, Georg *The Book of the It*, tr. V. M. Collins, London, 1950, first published, Vienna, 1923.

„   „ *The World of Man*, London, 1967.

Grundlach, E. and Riess, W.Birth order and sex of siblings in a sample of Lesbians and non-Lesbians, *Psychological Reports*, Vol. 20, London, 1967.

Harding, M. Esther *Psychic Energy – Its Source and Goal*, Bollingen Series, Washington, D.C., 1950.

Hauser, Richard The drug of self-pity, *Man and Society*, London, autumn 1963.

Henry, W. G. *Sex Variants*, London, 1950.

Hirschfeld, Magnus *Die Homosexualität des Mannes und Weibes*, Berlin, 1914.

„   „ *Geschlechtskunde*, Stuttgart, 1926.

Hopkins, June The lesbian personality, *British Journal of Psychiatry*, Vol. 115 No. 529, London, 1969.

Hunt, M. M. *The Natural History of Love*, London, 1960.

Jones, Ernest *Sigmund Freud, Life and Work*, (3 Vols.) London and New York, 1953.

Jung, C. G.   *Contributions to Analytical Psychology,*
                                London, 1928.

„   „   *Modern Man in Search of a Soul,*
                                London, 1933.

Kelly, Joanna   Some thoughts on Lesbianism, *Journal
                                of Medical Women's Federation,* Vol.
                                47 No. 4 London, October 1965.

Kenyon, Frank   Reports on female homosexuality, IV
                                and V, *British Journal of Psychiatry,*
                                Vol. 117 No. 516, London, Nov. 1968.

Kinsey, Alfred C., Pome-   *Sexual Behaviour in the Human*
roy, Wardell B., Martin,   *Female,* New York and London, 1966.
Clyde E., and Gebhard,
Paul H.

Klein, Melanie   *Contributions to Psycho-analysis, 1921-
                                1945,* London, 1968.

„   „   *Love, Hate and Reparation,* (with Joan
                                Riviere), London, 1967.

„   „   *Developments in Psycho-analysis,* (with
                                Paula Hermann, Susan Isaacs, and Joan
                                Riviere), London, 1952.

„   „   Envy and Gratitude, London, 1962,
                                (second edition).

Klimmer, Dr Rudolph   *Die Homosexualität,* third edition,
                                Hamburg, 1965.

Kline, Paul   The validity of the dynamic personality
                                inventory, *British Journal of Medical
                                Psychology,* Vol. 41 No. 307, London,
                                1968.

Kremer, Malvina W., and Rifkin, Alfred — The early development of homosexuality: a study of adolescent Lesbians, *American Journal of Psychiatry*, Vol. 126 No. 1, New York, 1969.

Ladder, The — Publications of Daughters of Bilitis, *Monthly Journal*, San Francisco, 1962-70.

Lancet, The — *An Extra Chromosome*, Leading Article, Vol. II No. 7577, London, 1968.

Lenz, W. — Neue Erkenntnisse aus der Chromosomenforschung beim Menschen, *Medizinische Klinik*, Vol. 56 No. 25, pp. 1073-1079, Munich, Berlin, Vienna, 1961.

Lévi-Strauss, Claude — *The Elementary Structure of Kinship*, London, 1969.

Lorenz, Konrad — *King Solomon's Ring*, London, 1952.

„   „ — *On Aggression*, London, 1966.

Magee, Bryan — *1 in 20 – a Study of Homosexuality in Men and Women*, London, 1966.

Malcolm, Norman — *Dreaming*, London, 1959.

Masters, W. H., and Johnson, V. E. — *Human Sexual Response*, London, 1966.

Meyerowitz, Eva — *The Divine Kingship in Ghana and Ancient Egypt*, London, 1960.

„   „ — *The Akan of Ghana, their Ancient Beliefs*, London, 1958.

Millar, T. P. — Who's afraid of Sigmund Freud? *British Journal of Psychiatry*, Vol. 115 No. 521, London, 1969.

Morris, Desmond   *The Naked Ape*, London, 1967.

Murdoch, Iris   *Sartre*, London and Yale, 1952.

Nagera, Humberto   *Basic Psycho-analytic Concepts on the Libido Theory*, London, 1969.

Newman, L. E., and Robert J. Stoller   Gender identity disturbances in inter-sexed patients, *American Journal of Psychiatry*, Vol. 124 No. 9, New York, 1968.

Orme, J. E.   Are obsessionals neurotic or are neurotics obsessional?, *British Journal of Medical Psychology*, Vol. 41 No. 415, London, 1968.

Ouspensky, P. D.   *In Search of the Miraculous*, London, 1950.

Reich, W.   *The Function of the Orgasm*, New York, 1942.

Rycroft, Charles   *Anxiety and Neurosis*, London, 1968.

Saklatvala, Beram   *Sappho of Lesbos, Her Works Restored*, London, 1968.

Sartre, Jean-Paul   *Sketch for a Theory of the Emotions*, tr. Philip Mairet, London, 1962.

„   „   *The Psychology of Imagination*, London, 1962.

Schlegel, Dr W. S.   Über die Ursachen des homosexuellen Verhaltens, in *Das Grosse Tabu*, pp. 147-162. Zeugnisse und Dokumente zum Problem der Homosexualität, ed. Schlegel, Munich, 1967.

Schofield, Michael — *The Sexual Behaviour of Young People*, London, 1965.

di Scipio, Wm. J. — Modified progressive desensitization and homosexuality, *British Journal of Medical Psychology*, Vol. 41 Part 3, London, 1968.

Simon, Robert J., — A case of female transsexualism, Jackson Memorial Hospital, Miami, *American Journal of Psychiatry*, Vol. 124 No. 9, New York, 1968.

Slater, Eliot — Parental age of homosexuals, and The Sibs and Children of homosexuals, *Symposium on Nuclear Sex*, London, 1958.

„ — Birth Order and maternal age of homosexuals, *Lancet* I pp. 69-71, London, 1962.

Socarides, Charles W., — The desire for sexual transformation – a psychiatric evaluation of transsexualism, *American Journal of Psychiatry*, Vol. 125, New York, 1969.

Sontag, Susan — *Against Interpretation*, New York and London, 1967.

Sprigge, Elizabeth — *Gertrude Stein, her Life and Work*, London, 1957.

Stekel, W. — *Onanie und Homosexualität*, Berlin, 1917.

Storr, Anthony — *Human Aggression*, London, 1968.
„   „ — *Sexual Deviation*, London, 1964.

Times, The — *Discovery claimed on homosexuality, Report from Bonn on Dr Dörner's investigation*, London, March 13th 1969.

Tinbergen, N.   *The Study of Instinct*, London, 1951.

West, D. J.   *Homosexuality*, London, 1968.

Winnicott, D. W.   *The Child, the Family and the Outside World*, London, 1969.

„   „   *The Maturational Processes and the Facilitating Environment*, London, 1965.

Wolff, Charlotte   *On the Way to Myself*, London, 1969.

Index

B. ORGANISATIONS and PLACES

C. PUBLICATIONS

INDEX OF TOPICS